I use colored markers to underline passages when I re _____ "pay attention!" Blue means "very poetic." Green means "super weird or hilarious." There is a lot of green in my Bible! Dan helps make sense of the bizarre and demonstrates why we can have confidence that the Bible is trustworthy and God inspired.

—DAVID CROWDER, Grammy-nominated artist, musician, and author

In our culture the Bible has, for many people, become an obstacle in the journey of faith. Biblical stories about sex, slavery, and divine violence are often too bizarre and disturbing for most modern readers. Dan Kimball understands this from personal and pastoral experience, and he's given us a thoughtful guide for reading these problematic parts of the Bible. If you're struggling to make moral sense of the Bible, or know someone who is, this book is for you!

—TIM MACKIE, The Bible Project

The Bible presents many problems to many readers, and they can be forceful and fearless in their questioning traditional beliefs in the Bible. It's because Dan's pastoral heart has heard people ask these questions and because he has worked through their issues that there is no one in the world better to write this book than Dan Kimball. A book full of theological wisdom and pastoral care for honest Bible readers who have genuine and difficult questions about the Bible.

—SCOT MCKNIGHT, professor of New Testament, Northern Seminary

We need this book. Dan Kimball has long been a guide for a generation trying to find their footing in a post-Christian world, for those of us who want to believe, yet struggle to make sense of the Bible in our age. Yet again, he steps in.to offer kind, intelligent, wise, and, as you'd expect from Dan, funny guidance.

—JOHN MARK COMER, pastor of vision and teaching,
Bridgetown Church; author, _The Ruthless Elimination of Hurry_

Dan Kimball answers tough questions with both clarity and a genuine sympathy for those who struggle with them. His compassion and sensitivity are a result of his own struggles with the strange book called the Bible. In this book, Kimball describes how to resolve those doubts. We need to read the Bible cautiously and carefully, with ancient eyes, not modern ones. This book is Kimball's winsome and insightful tutorial on how to accomplish that task.

—GREGORY KOUKL, president, Stand to Reason (str.org);
author, _Tactics_ and _The Story of Reality_

An essential resource for anyone whose questions about the difficult and often bizarre parts of the Bible lead them to doubt Christianity. It should be on the bookshelf of every pastor and parent who gets peppered with "gotcha!" questions about the Bible. It should be read with an open mind by skeptics and anyone on a spiritual deconstruction journey. Chances are, there's someone in your life who needs to read it right now.

—Brett McCracken, author, *The Wisdom Pyramid: Feeding Your Soul in a Post-Truth World*; senior editor, Gospel Coalition

The Bible is the most amazing and life-changing book ever. Yet today, many are confused by Bible verses that seem strange and disturbing. The good news is that when you learn how (not) to read the Bible, you will find there are answers and explanations that make sense. Dan shows ways of gaining confidence in how and why the Bible was written, and how to make sense of difficult Bible passages.

—Josh McDowell, apologist; author, *Evidence That Demands a Verdict* and *More Than a Carpenter*; josh.org

Dan Kimball asks a question that I and many of my fellow nonbelievers have been asking: "How do thinking people understand and believe the weird and disturbing things found in the Bible?" As Dan points out, many of them don't, and as a consequence they leave the faith. Although I made a similar transition myself, it must be admitted that most initial salvos from atheists against the many disturbing and morally problematic biblical passages we quote have explanations, or at least historical context for what they're trying to convey. While my skepticism remains undeterred, I will confess (if I may) that I learned a lot reading this book.

—Michael Shermer, atheist; publisher, *Skeptic* magazine; presidential fellow, Chapman University; author, *The Moral Arc*

What a brilliant and easy to understand guide to the Bible difficulties that perplex Christians and drive the mockery of skeptics. Dan writes with a humility and clarity that will draw you in and won't let you put this book down. I'll be recommending it for years to come—this is the most accessible resource I've seen on the topic.

—Natasha Crain, speaker; blogger; author, *Talking with Your Kids about Jesus*

Dan Kimball is a man after my own heart: part investigator, part pastor, and part storyteller. Dan deftly explains how to read the Bible the way it was meant to be read. Perplexed by difficult passages in Scripture? Struggling to respond to friends and family members who sometimes misread the text and assume the worst of God? This timely book will equip you to read more clearly and explain more concisely. It will change the way you consider and defend the truth.

—J. Warner Wallace, *Dateline* featured cold-case detective; author;
Cold-Case Christianity; senior fellow, Colson Center for Christian Worldview

Dan Kimball once again raises his voice to help us understand how this generation is learning about faith and the Bible. He shows ways to help understand the difficult parts of Scripture while being faithful to its historical and beautiful truths. Insightful, powerful, and practical—you'll love this book!

—Margaret Feinberg, author, *More Power to You*

Dan Kimball's book is a wise, honest guide to caricatures about the Bible as well as to challenging and difficult to understand passages. It is accessible, readable, and engaging. Kimball speaks with great pastoral concern and insight about the most troubling or perplexing questions raised by Scripture.

—Paul Copan, Pledger Family Chair of Philosophy and Ethics,
Palm Beach Atlantic University; author, *Is God a Moral Monster?*

Hand this book to a seeker who is struggling with Scripture or to a young person who is ready to give up on Christianity. Dan Kimball walks through the hardest passages of Scripture and the ways they are mocked on social media. On science, he shows how texts like Genesis 1 were not meant to answer our modern questions about evolution but to teach the ancient Israelites about the one true God and the goodness of creation.

—Deborah Haarsma, astronomer; president, BioLogos

Whether it's learning to master a sport, cooking, driving, or some other skill, there are times when learning how not to think or perform a task is crucial to success. Dan Kimball has rendered such a service with his provocative, humorous, but ultimately instructive book. Never has the need for reading Scripture accurately, within the contexts of its ancient writers, been so dire. This book reorients readers to make that task possible.

—Dr. Michael S. Heiser, bestselling author; executive director,
Awakening School of Theology and Ministry; host, *Naked Bible Podcast*

Dan Kimball takes us through the weird, the bad, and the ugly of the Bible with penetrating insight. Whether its misogyny, slavery, or violence, Kimball takes an honest approach and shows us how (not) to read the Bible and why we can still believe in a God who loves all people. A valuable resource for doubters, seekers, and anyone confused about whether the Bible is true and good for people.

—Rev. Dr. Michael F. Bird (PhD, University of Queensland), academic
dean and lecturer in theology, Ridley College, Melbourne

Many people, even Christians, write off the Bible without really reading it. Or perhaps they selectively read it and avoid the parts that embarrass them. Dan Kimball takes us right to these controversial passages and helps us set them in the broader context of Scripture. Thank you, Dan, for this insightful, well-written, profound, but readable book on an important topic. Reading it will transform your attitude toward the Bible and toward God himself.

—Tremper Longman III, PhD, distinguished scholar and
professor emeritus of biblical studies, Westmont College

Dan Kimball is an absolute genius at helping Christians see why many people reject God because they read the Bible! He goes deep into those strong negative reactions to help us feel their power before gently showing us a better way. Reading crazy passages in light of the whole story shows us the power of the redemption of God through Jesus.

—Gerry Breshears, PhD, professor of theology, Western Seminary, Portland

With his characteristic warmth, wit, and depth of thought, Dan Kimball takes us on an honest journey through some of the strangest and most challenging parts of Scripture. He helps us navigate the complexity and arrive on the far side of the Bible's most perplexing stories with a renewed confidence in God's love and grace. This book is a must-read for anyone struggling to make sense of the difficult and disturbing parts of the Bible.

—Jay Kim, pastor; author, *Analog Church*

HOW (NOT)
TO READ
THE BIBLE

OTHER BOOKS BY DAN KIMBALL

Adventures in Churchland
The Emerging Church
Emerging Worship
Listening to the Beliefs of Emerging Churches (contributor)
They Like Jesus but Not the Church

HOW (NOT) TO READ THE BIBLE

Making Sense of the Anti-women, Anti-science, Pro-violence, Pro-slavery, and Other Crazy Sounding Parts of Scripture

DAN KIMBALL

ZONDERVAN
REFLECTIVE

ZONDERVAN REFLECTIVE

How (Not) to Read the Bible
Copyright © 2020 by Dan Kimball

Requests for information should be addressed to:
Zondervan, 3900 Sparks Dr. SE, Grand Rapids, Michigan 49546

Zondervan titles may be purchased in bulk for educational, business, fundraising, or sales promotional use. For information, please email SpecialMarkets@Zondervan.com.

ISBN 978-0-310-25418-8 (softcover)
ISBN 978-0-310-11377-5 (audio)
ISBN 978-0-310-11376-8 (ebook)

Cover Design: Darren Welch Design
Cover Images: © *iStock*
Interior Design: Denise Froehlich

Printed in the United States of America

20 21 22 23 24 /LSC/ 10 9 8 7 6 5 4 3 2 1

C O N T E N T S

FOREWORD

I love this book. And it's not just because Dan is my friend. I love it because he tackles some of the toughest challenges of our day with biblical faithfulness. Even though I am an apologist, I took a ton of insights away from this book. And I know you will too.

As a college professor, speaker, and part-time high school teacher, I interact with young people regularly. The questions that Dan addresses in this book are exactly the ones that come up frequently in my conversations with both Christians and non-Christians. I'm guessing you have wrestled with these questions as well:

- Does the Bible demean women?
- Is the Bible anti-science?
- How could a loving God command such violence in the Old Testament?
- Does the Bible endorse slavery?

These are real questions that many people today wrestle with. While these questions are not necessarily new, because of technology, younger generations today are bombarded with them like never before. In order to be confident in our own faith, and to help seekers with genuine questions, we must have answers to these questions. (See 1 Peter 3:15.)

Specifically, there are a few reasons I love this book. First, it's practical. Some apologetics books, like *Evidence That Demands a Verdict*, offer answers and evidence for faith. Other books, like *Tactics: A Game Plan for Discussing Your Christian Convictions*, are designed to help believers navigate spiritual conversations. Yet this book offers both content and methodology—a rare trait for a book of its kind. This book not only will help you find answers to some difficult questions, it also will help you learn how to read your Bible well.

Second, it's interesting. This is not a dry apologetics book. Dan uses a ton of contemporary examples. For example, in chapter 3, he discusses the importance of reading a particular Bible verse in light of the broader storyline. How does he make this point sink in? He cites this famous line from the Star Wars movies: "Just for once let me look on you with my own eyes." This line makes no sense in isolation. But if you know who spoke it (Darth Vader) and why he spoke it (he removed his mask to see his son, Luke Skywalker, who had just learned that Vader is his father, shortly before Vader's death), then it makes more sense. The same is true for Bible verses.

Third, it's honest. When addressing difficult issues, the temptation is to overstate our case. Dan offers thoughtful and forceful responses to many tough questions. But he doesn't overstate his case. I was really struck by how, in the last chapter of the book, he says that there is no truly satisfactory *emotional* answer to why God commanded the killing of children and infants. There's no escaping it—these passages are jarring. Of course, Dan believes God is just. But the point is that this book is refreshingly honest about the emotional challenges of faith.

A ton more could be said about this book. I hope you will read it. *How (Not) to Read the Bible* is perfect for a small group. And it is ideal to give to a nonbelieving friend so you can discuss the content together.

—SEAN MCDOWELL

ACKNOWLEDGMENTS

I'd like to adapt an older phrase and add a twist to it: "Behind every church leader, pastor, Christian writer, teacher, there is a strong theologian." I say that after many years of being in church leadership with teaching as my primary role and after writing several books. Theologians and Bible scholars are rock stars. A pastor may have a Bible degree, but most of us who lead or write are dependent on *trusted* (very important word here) scholars who have dedicated their lives to the intense study, constant learning, and use of the biblical languages (long after those of us who have seminary degrees can barely remember the Hebrew or Greek alphabet). These individuals faithfully pour themselves into deep study so we can benefit from their work.

This book is a practical theology book built on the work of scholars and apologists—many of whom have now become good friends as I've pestered them with my questions. I want to thank Scot McKnight (my New Testament guru), Tim Mackie, Gerry Breshears, John Walton, Paul Copan, Sean McDowell, Josh McDowell, Lee Strobel, Greg Koukl, Michael Heiser, Dan Wallace, Stan Gundry, Tremper Longman, Darrell Bock, Craig Keener, Craig Blomberg, Chuck Conniry, and many others who have influenced me in different ways. They have helped me understand the depths of Scripture, which helps me to better understand God. While the Holy Spirit is our foremost guide and teacher, I am grateful the Spirit uses these scholars and biblical theologians through their dedication to truth and as they share their learnings and insights. These are reflected throughout this book. I couldn't have written this book without them.

I also acknowledge my appreciation for Michael Shermer, Richard Dawkins, Sam Harris, and the new atheists along with all those who challenge Christianity. I have tried to address many of these challenges in this book. We never want to be closed-minded or afraid to read critiques or mockery of historical Christianity. I appreciate their criticisms because they force me to pause, think, and reexamine the Scriptures to be able to "give reason for the hope that we have."

I also acknowledge and greatly thank John Raymond and Ryan Pazdur from Zondervan for their patience and most of all friendship while I was writing this book. Also, Brian Phipps from Zondervan for using his careful editing skills with this book. I want to thank Jay Kim and Isaac Serrano, my theologically thinking pastor friends and coleaders of the ReGeneration Project. I am grateful for Western Seminary, where I serve on the faculty, and for their belief in the importance of theology for new generations. I thank Vintage Faith Church for being a church that desires theological thinking and for the encouragement to write this book.

And last, I thank Becky, Katie, and Claire—the book is finally done.

PRELUDE

BECOMING ATHEIST BY
READING THE BIBLE

> Reading the Bible is the fast track to atheism.
>
> —PENN JILLETTE

Sitting on my desk is a printed email from a university student who, after growing up in a Christian family and being active in his church, is no longer a Christian. The email lists several reasons why he went from being a Christian, and even a leader in a campus ministry, to becoming an atheist.

It's not an angry email. The student isn't disillusioned by the church, and when we later met in person, he told me he had a positive church experience and is thankful for his former youth leader.

He didn't leave the faith because of boring preaching or irrelevant worship music.

He told me he left because he finally got around to reading the Bible.

Yes, reading the Bible led him to become an atheist.

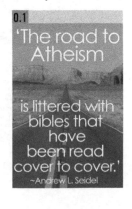

0.1 'The road to Atheism is littered with bibles that have been read cover to cover.' ~Andrew L. Seidel

Before going away to college, this student regularly attended church and listened to sermons every week. He attended church Bible studies for many years. He knows all the popular Bible stories—Daniel in the lions' den, David and Goliath, and many others. He loves Jesus' teaching in the Sermon on the Mount, where he talks about not judging others and giving to the needy and loving your enemies.

When he left to attend college, however, he began reading parts of the Bible that he had never read before, stories he couldn't recall ever being preached or taught in the youth group and church he grew up in. The more he read, the more questions and objections he had. I found him to be an extremely intelligent, friendly person, open to discussion, and kind and positive as he spoke about his church experience. He shared that after being active in his high school youth group, in college he joined a study group with an on-campus Christian ministry. They chose the Old Testament book of Exodus for their study, but as he read and studied it, he noticed things he hadn't seen before, things that horrified him. He encountered disturbing, crazy-sounding Bible verses, and it was his reading of these verses that shook the foundation of his faith.

Why Is It Okay for God to Kill Children like King Herod Did?

In an email to his campus-ministry leader, he listed verses from Exodus 4:21–23 as an example. They cover the story of the last of the ten plagues God visited on Egypt, the plague where God instructed Moses to tell Pharaoh, "[Because] you refused to let [my people] go . . . I will kill your first-born son." And in Exodus 12:29–30, God followed through on that threat: "At midnight the LORD struck down all the firstborn in Egypt. . . . Pharaoh and all his officials and all the Egyptians got up during the night, and there was loud wailing in Egypt, for there was not a house without someone dead."

After reading this, the student wrote in his email, "I was devastated to think a loving God could predetermine the death of so many of the innocent." When we met, he said it's ironic that Christians recoil in horror and anger when they read the New Testament story of King Herod's trying to kill the newborn Jesus by killing all the boys two years old and under who were living in Bethlehem and nearby at the time of Jesus' birth.* Christians rightly see that as a horrendous act of evil—a massacre of toddlers and infants—and they see King Herod as wicked and heartless. Yet he never hears Christians complain about the Exodus story. Why is it okay for God to do the same thing King Herod does, but with Egyptian infants and toddlers? Why is it wicked and evil when Herod does it, but acceptable when God does it?

Slavery and Magical Underwear

As he continued reading Exodus, the student found other disturbing verses. He mentioned Exodus 21:20–21, which reads, "Anyone who beats their male or female slave with a rod must be punished if the slave dies as a direct result, but they are not to be punished if the slave recovers after a day or two, since the slave is their property." And in Exodus 21:7, we read that a father can sell his daughter to someone else. It angered him to read that God seems to consider a human being someone's property and appears to be perfectly fine with this property being beaten and sold.

He mentioned finding other strange things, like the clothing in Exodus 28:42–43. In this passage, priests are commanded to wear what sounds like "magical underwear" when they approach the altar in the Holy Place to worship God. If a priest doesn't wear this magical underwear, he will die. Understandably, this student began to wonder, "Why haven't I ever been told that the Bible endorses slavery and instructs us to wear magical underwear when we come before God?"

Why Doesn't God Like Women?

As the questions kept coming, he began researching online. But he said that made things even worse. The deeper he dug for answers, the more

---

*   Matthew 2:16.

disturbing were the things he found about the Bible. He discovered websites dedicated to exposing all the crazy and unsettling verses in the Bible. And it wasn't just the Old Testament that upset him. There were several passages in the New Testament. He mentioned 1 Timothy 2:11–12, where it says "a woman should learn in quietness and full submission. I do not permit a woman to teach or to assume authority over a man; she must be quiet." Another verse, 1 Corinthians 14:34–35, reads, "Women should remain silent in the churches. They are not allowed to speak, but must be in submission, as the law says. If they want to inquire about something, they should ask their own husbands at home; for it is disgraceful for a woman to speak in the church." These verses—right there in his Bible—seemed to be God's endorsement of men's superiority and even dominance over women. Was God commanding gender inequality, chauvinism, discrimination, and the oppression of women? It certainly appeared so.

Connecting with the Deconverting and Deconstructing

Searching online, he not only found other people raising questions about these disturbing Bible verses, he also discovered others like him—former Christians who had left their faith. Many had been raised in a church, but after taking a closer look at their Bibles, they discovered things they had never been taught. For instance, one young woman on Twitter writes, "I read the Bible cover-to-cover twice in my youth. I remember encountering verses that made me uncomfortable, but I dismissed them. I started reading it again last year. I got to the sixth chapter in Genesis before dropping my head and crying. The god I believed in was a monster."[1]

Finding this community and hearing stories that reflected his own experience contributed to his growing loss of confidence in the Christian faith in which he had been brought up. He found he could no longer believe in salvation through Jesus because the Jesus he had been taught about was in a Bible he could no longer trust. Pastors and church leaders regularly encourage us to read our Bibles. Yet here is the great irony. It was reading the Bible that caused this student—and an increasing number of others like him today—to leave Christianity.

It's Not Only Christians Who Notice This

But the problem goes farther than Christians leaving the faith in which they were raised. The Bible is a stumbling block for many non-Christians as well. The strange and disturbing verses they read prevent them from taking the Bible seriously. One Sunday morning, after I had finished teaching at our church, I stopped by a room where people go when they need prayer. A young woman came up to me, and I could tell she was upset. This isn't all that unusual, since people going through tough times and dealing with difficult issues often come to this room for prayer. But as I listened to her, I realized hers wasn't the typical prayer need. She didn't have a loved one with cancer or a relational breakup. She wasn't losing her job. She wanted prayer to help her understand what she was reading in her Bible. She told me she was exploring Christianity and had been coming to the Sunday worship gatherings for a couple of months. A few weeks ago, she decided to read the Bible for herself, but as she began reading in Genesis, she grew discouraged and found her excitement about Christianity sinking.

What was it that disturbed her?

She shared how right there on page one, the Bible seems to suggest that the earth was made in only six days. She had been taught her whole life in science classes and by the media that the universe is billions of years old. Then, quite unexpectedly, she read on page three about a "talking snake." She was shocked, thinking this was a fictional story, something like *The Jungle Book.* Farther along she read about people living to be well over nine hundred years old. She also read how the animals of the world followed Noah into a boat, like he was a fantastical Dr. Doolittle, but much worse, because God then killed thousands and thousands of people in a destructive flood, including children. She read about Abraham's being told by his wife to have an affair so they could have a baby. She read about the woman turned into a pillar of salt by God. She read about God's telling Abraham to kill his young son as a sacrifice.* She was visibly upset as she described all of this and told me she'd had to stop reading the Bible at this point, fearful of what else she would find in its pages. After all, this was only the first half of the first book of the Bible!

She told me how she had initially been excited about exploring faith in Jesus. In the teachings at church, she had heard about grace and forgiveness and was drawn to Jesus because of what she had heard about him. But she'd had no idea, no warning at all, that these disturbing and crazy ideas were also in the Christian Bible. Apologetically, she admitted that she wondered whether Christianity was a cult because she could not understand how thinking people could believe what she was reading to be true. How could they take all of this seriously? This young woman's interest in exploring faith in Jesus came to an abrupt halt after she began reading the Bible.

A vast number of people aren't exploring Christianity and will never make it to reading a Bible like this young woman did. They see only clever online memes with Bible verses about slavery, women being told to be silent, and talking snakes, and won't likely ever take the Bible seriously or explore the Christian faith.

Bloody Big Toes, a Sneezing Dead Boy, and End-Times Battle Maps

I assume you're reading this book because you saw the title and, like the young people I mentioned, have questions about some of the crazy things you've heard about or read in the Bible. You might be a Christian and find you are growing more uncomfortable as you become aware of Bible verses and stories you never paid much attention to before. And you might be

---

*   Genesis 1; 3:1; 5; 7–8; 16:1–4; 19:26; 22:2.

wondering, "How do thinking people understand and believe the weird and disturbing things found in the Bible?"

You might be reading this because you have a friend or family member who is doubting and even deconstructing their faith. They may have similar questions and you're reading this hoping for insight or a way to respond.

Or you might be reading this because you're not a Christian but are beginning to explore Jesus' teachings and what the Bible says. You may be wondering whether the Bible is credible or whether the Christian faith is built on historical facts or mythology, and why the Bible contains so much of the violence of the primitive people who wrote it.

I can totally relate to anyone who thinks the Bible is strange. I agree that it contains some bizarre and even embarrassing things. When I first tried to read the Bible as a teenager, it seemed more like a work of fiction, a book filled with epic battles and angels, stories of demons, and even a red dragon.* My Bible had paper with this cool, shiny, gold edging, and I placed it on a bookshelf between Bram Stoker's *Dracula* and J. R. R. Tolkien's Lord of the Rings trilogy. It seemed like a good fit there with my fantasy and horror books.

During my college years, when I read and studied the Bible more seriously, I was still disturbed by some of the oddities I found, like the talking serpent and a talking donkey too.† At this point, I wasn't just reading the Bible out of curiosity; I was seriously considering the claims of the Christian faith. Finding these bizarre things in the Bible, including worship rituals that involved killing animals and putting a dab of the blood on your right earlobe and on the big toe of your right foot, caused me to seriously question whether Christianity was really for me. I wondered, "What is this? Do Christians really believe this?"‡ I read the instructions God gives for when your house has mold in it, how when the mold gets cleaned out, in order to celebrate your mold-free home, you are to kill a

---

*   1 Samuel 11:1–11; 2 Samuel 10:10–19; Isaiah 37:36; Revelation 16:12–16; 12:3.
†   Numbers 22:28.
‡   Leviticus 14:25.

bird and sprinkle the blood of the bird around the house seven times.* I thought, "That poor little bird didn't cause the mold, so why did God require his people to kill it?" It didn't make any sense. There is an incredibly bizarre story of a young boy who died and then a prophet climbed on top of his body, stretched out on it, and then the dead boy suddenly sneezed seven times and came back to life.† And like many people find when they are first reading the Bible, I was surprised there was so much violence. Even Jesus, whom I tended to think of as a peace-loving Gandhi figure, appeared at times like a warrior in end-times military battles.

I knew that if the Bible is the foundation of Christianity—a key, even holy, text for Christians—I had to make some sense of these passages. My friends were concerned when they learned I was reading the Bible. There was even an unplanned intervention for me, where they let me know they had concerns that I was abandoning my intelligence and common sense and choosing to believe fables and myths. Ironically, my friends wanted to protect me from reading the Bible because they feared that it would change me in negative ways. They certainly didn't see it as a positive helpful book to read.[2]

Yes, There Are Puzzling and Disturbing Bible Verses, but There Are Explanations!

If you wonder about the validity of what the Bible teaches, I want you to know that I can relate to how you think and feel. My friends were worried that the Bible could possibly corrupt me. What if they were right? Christians all around the world see the Bible as a sacred book, but there are other sacred religious books out there. How do we know the Bible is *the one,* a revelation from God? Good and sincere people believe things that aren't true all the time. Who is to say the Bible and its teachings make sense for us today?

---

*   Leviticus 14:48–51.
†   2 Kings 4:32–35.

We can't just sweep questions like these under the rug and ignore them. They forced me to look at the origins of the Bible and whether there are ways of understanding the bizarre and unusual things in it. Although you may not know me personally, I can say this very confidently to you: I would not be writing this book if there were no explanations for these Bible verses. If there weren't reasonable responses, I likely would have become an agnostic and not taken the Bible seriously as God's inspired words. When I was exploring the validity of Christianity and the Bible, I had to wrestle with questions like these and study to find the truth. I did not want to follow a cult, a wishful religion, or a mindless faith. I wanted to follow truth. I had no pressure from family or peers pushing me to ignore the difficult things or to believe that the Scriptures are true and good if they aren't.

I would never, ever mislead anyone into believing in a faith that is not trustworthy. I can say with confidence that we can intelligently, and with faith, believe that the Scriptures are from God. If you knew me, you would know that I am never closed to learning new information and am always looking at current criticisms of Christianity and the Bible. No Christian should be afraid of or ignore difficult questions.

The Key: Learning How (Not) to Read the Bible

The good news is that there are responses to these bizarre Bible verses and difficult questions. You can be a thinking intelligent Christian and one hundred percent believe in the trustworthiness and inspiration of the Bible. Yes, these verses certainly do seem difficult to comprehend. However, I've learned that when we apply certain study methods and examine verses in their contexts, it can change how we view and read the Bible. That's what I'll be addressing in this book.

The overwhelming majority of the disturbing Bible verses that we read or see on memes are being read incorrectly. Yes, these verses are actually in the Bible. They are strange and difficult to understand. Absolutely. But we aren't taking into consideration how to read the Bible to understand their meaning. Applying some basic principles for reading any verse in the Bible makes a drastic difference.

The key to making sense of crazy and disturbing passages is to understand how *not* to read the Bible.

Here's where we are heading.

First, we'll learn what to do when we come across a crazy-sounding Bible passage. We'll start with some critical principles to utilize when we open a Bible or read any verse, and how these can drastically change how we understand a passage in the Bible. These are principles most people who criticize or are confused about the Bible don't know how to use.

Second, we'll look at several of the Bible passages most commonly objected to. We will look at five areas of challenge to the Bible and ways to address them. There are more than just five, but these are the most commonly discussed topics:

1. **The Anti-science Bible.** We'll focus on the creation story in the early chapters of Genesis, which is one of the most commonly mocked sections of the Bible. Does the Bible teach that the earth is only ten thousand years old? Is the only option believing that God created everything in the universe in six twenty-four-hour days? Does the Bible teach that evolution is false, and that we have to either reject the theory of evolution or reject the Bible? Does the Bible really teach that there was a talking snake?

2. **The Pro-violence Bible.** How do we worship and love a God who kills thousands and thousands of people, even children, in the pages of the Bible? If God is loving, how can the Bible, with its stories of violence, really be true? Is the Old Testament God a different God than Jesus?

3. **The Anti-women Bible.** In both the Old Testament and the New Testament of the Bible there are verses that clearly tell women to submit to men and to be silent and not to speak or teach. We see stories of men having multiple wives and even exchanging

women as property. Isn't the Bible just promoting misogyny and male chauvinism?

4. **The Pro-slavery, Anti-shrimp, and Bizarre-Commands Bible.** There are passages in the Bible about shrimp, slavery, and bloody big toes. There are many Bible verses that seem to suggest that the evil of slavery is okay. There are many bizarre verses about commands not to wear clothing with two types of fabric, about not eating shrimp, and about rituals that include dabbing blood on big toes and thumbs as part of worship. Don't these suggest the Bible is a primitive book and not to be taken seriously today?

5. **The Intolerant Only-One-Way-to-God Bible.** The Bible claims there is only one way to God. The world has more than seven billion people, and there are more than four thousand religions, including five major ones. Yet we see verses in the Bible claiming that God is the only truth, implying that all other religions and sacred texts are wrong. Isn't this an arrogant, oppressive, and irrelevant claim today?

While there are *plenty* more very strange and confusing subjects and verses in the Bible that we could cover, we can look at these five to start. They are some of the more frequently pointed out ones. We will walk through not just responses to these topics but, more important, how we get to those responses. That way, whenever other difficult questions and crazy verses are brought to your attention (and they will be), you will have some basic methods for addressing them.

Study Helps for Churches and Groups

Finally, a word to pastors and church leaders. I've organized this book so it can be used to develop a five- or six-week teaching series for worship gatherings, classes, and as a curriculum for small groups. You can find videos and teaching helps as well as the small-group curriculum free at www.dankimball.com.

PART 1

Never Read a Bible Verse

(OR YOU WILL HAVE TO BELIEVE

IN MAGICAL UNICORNS)

CHAPTER 1

Yes, There Are Unicorns in the Bible

God brought them out of Egypt; he hath as it were the strength of an unicorn.

—NUMBERS 23:22 KJV

And the unicorns shall come down with them.

—ISAIAH 34:7 KJV

Daniel has been my barber for a couple of years, and we've had many great chats. He is thirty years old, very bright, and I love getting my hair cut, not just for the haircut but also for the chance to talk with him. One day I went in, sat down, and he asked me a question.

"So, you believe in unicorns?"

Daniel knows I'm a Christian, and he is very open with me about the reasons he isn't one. We chat about theology, and he asks really great questions. But we'd never addressed the topic of unicorns before.

1.1 UNICORNS ARE MENTIONED 9X IN THE BIBLE. CATS ARE MENTIONED ZERO TIMES.

AND THAT'S ALL YOU NEED TO KNOW ABOUT THE BIBLE.

He had seen some online memes quoting Bible verses suggesting that unicorns existed. He thought it was pretty bizarre that Christians believe in unicorns, and he wanted to know if I believe that. Unicorns are mythical horses with a horn and magical powers living in forests. I had never heard the claim that unicorns are in the Bible, but after the haircut, I did an online search and learned there is, in fact, a connection between unicorns and the Bible.

One of the memes read: "FACT: Unicorns existed in the Bible" and had an image of a unicorn with a quote from Isaiah 34:7, which read, "And the unicorns shall come down with them . . . ." There was another meme (1.3) with a yellow warning sign and a silhouette of a unicorn on it, indicating a place where unicorns might cross the road.

Underneath the sign, it read, "Because the Bible tells me so." Listed were several verses, including Numbers 23:22, Psalm 22:21, and Isaiah 34:7. Another meme (1.2) had an image of a unicorn with one of these Bible verses written out followed by the words "Know your Bible."

Digging further, I found online discussions with people joking about this and asking why we don't see unicorns today if they are mentioned in the Bible. I've seen shirts with cartoon images of Noah's Ark in the distance and a sad unicorn standing on the shoreline, suggesting the unicorns missed the boat and this is why we don't see them today. I've seen another shirt filled with small letters written from the unicorns to Noah, saying, "Dear Noah, we could have sworn you said the ark wasn't leaving till 5. Sincerely, The Unicorns."

Obviously, these visuals and T-shirts are making a humorous point—that if you really knew what is in the Bible, you couldn't possibly take it seriously. And if you do, you must be ignorant to trust a book that teaches that mythical creatures existed. My barber saw the Bible verses suggesting that unicorns existed at one point, and it raised serious questions for him. This wasn't just an attempt to mock Christianity or the Bible. He saw the Bible being quoted in a way that seemed ridiculous and rather unbelievable. How do we respond to challenges like this?

We Have More Than a Unicorn Problem: The Bible Is Being Used to Discredit the Bible

Bible verse memes similar to the ones I just mentioned are all over the internet. They are being used in arguments about the Bible in interviews on television and in discussions on YouTube channels. The intent is to discredit the Bible. Many Christians grew up in Christian families, went to church, heard sermons, read parts of the Bible, and even memorized some verses. Usually these were positive sections with encouraging messages. When these Christians encounter the disturbing Bible verses, it can be alarming, shocking, and even embarrassing.

Memes point out that many Christians don't really know their Bibles. They suggest that if Christians really knew what was in the Bible, they wouldn't be a Christian— they'd become an atheist or agnostic. Consider meme 1.5. It refers to David killing two hundred men and presenting their foreskins as a bridal price to the father-in-law. Notice the headline: "YES, THIS IS IN THE BIBLE!"

There are many other examples, including variations (such as image 1.4) of a disturbing graphic of a woman with her mouth taped closed and a Bible verse that says, "Let your women keep silence in the churches: for it is not permitted unto them to speak. . . . If they will learn any thing, let them ask their husbands at home."*

When you look at this picture combined with this quote from the Bible, it's self-condemning. These are words from the Bible—how can you argue with that? The Bible sounds extremely demeaning to women, and when someone reads this and sees the image, it's natural for them to believe the Bible is anti-women. Or consider the YouTube video called "Crazy #$&! the Bible Says: Selling Your Daughter into Slavery." The person in the video writes out Exodus 21:7–11 and goes on to claim that the Bible endorses slavery, including selling your daughter as a slave.

"The Good Book" Is Now Seen as "The Evil Book"

Memes like 1.6 use an actual Bible verse to show God giving instruction about buying slaves from Leviticus 25:44.

Notice how the comment in the meme is pointing out that allegedly "90% of so-called religious people don't read their Bible." The implication is that if Christians really read their Bibles, they would reject what the Bible teaches. If you want to better understand how to respond to what the Bible says about women and slavery, we

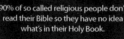

1.6

GOD SAYS IT'S OK TO BUY SLAVES!

"You may purchase male and female slaves..."
- Leviticus 25:44

90% of so called religious people don't read their Bible so they have no idea what's in their Holy Book.

---

* 1 Corinthians 14:34–35.

will look at the verses that seem anti-women and pro-slavery in parts 2 and 3 of this book.

But that's not all. In addition to being anti-woman and pro-slavery, it's not hard to find Bible verses that seem to endorse violence—even against babies and small children. There are memes and websites that quote verses like Psalm 137:9 where it reads, "Happy is the one who seizes your infants and dashes them against the rocks." Underneath the verse it says, with a hint of sarcasm, "Great God you have," suggesting that the Bible gives people advice on how to smash babies against rocks (1.7). If you are interested in how to respond to these questions, we will address the problem of violence in the Bible in part 6, "Rated NC-17: The Horror of God's Old Testament Violence."

I hear some version of this story over and over again. A person is struggling with their faith, and they find Bible passages that sound disturbing, so they go online to research them. From there, they find websites and YouTube videos dedicated to showing Bible verses that are pro-violent, pro-slavery, and anti-women. Or that highlight some of the bizarre Old Testament laws. One website called "Evil Bible" makes the claim that "God, according to the Bible, is directly responsible for mass murder, rape, pillage, plunder, slavery,

child abuse, and killing, not to mention the killing of unborn children."[1] Bible verses are being used to label the Bible as evil. What was once known as "The Good Book" is now considered "The Evil Book."

It's becoming more commonplace to see people quote Bible verses to illustrate how strange, crazy, and primitive sounding the Bible is.

Consider meme 1.8, which points out many of the strange restrictions God places upon people in the Bible.

Another commonly quoted Bible verse is Leviticus 11:7–8, which is used to mock Christians who play football. The visuals that accompany it attempt to show that it is hypocritical for a Christian to play football because the Bible clearly prohibits it (1.9).

In meme 1.9 you have a well-known Christian football player kneeling to pray, with the Leviticus 11:8 reference underneath the photograph. For those who aren't familiar with that verse, Leviticus 11:7–8 says, "And the pig, though it has a divided hoof, does not chew the cud; it is unclean for you. You must not eat their meat or touch their carcasses; they are unclean for you." The logic here is that a football player shouldn't touch the "pigskin"—the carcass of a pig—since the Bible says it is off-limits. This joke about biblical prohibitions on playing football became popular enough that it was mentioned in a Golden Globe award-winning national television show. In the show, the actor portraying the president of the United States challenged a Christian radio show host and asked the host a series of questions about the Bible: "Here's one that's really important 'cause we've got a lot of sports fans in this town: touching the skin of a dead pig makes one unclean. Leviticus 11:7. If they promise to wear gloves, can the Washington Redskins still play football? Can Notre Dame? Can West Point?"[2]

Millions of people who watched this popular television show heard the Bible quoted and were confronted with how ridiculous it sounds. Does the Bible really suggest that playing football should be prohibited? Some of those listening must have thought about how crazy Christians are for believing in an outdated and bizarre book like the Bible. We will address questions about Leviticus and if the Bible prohibits playing football in part 2 of this book.

I Would Run from the Bible Too If I Saw Only These Verses

In meme after meme, joke after joke, we see a Bible verse or verses quoted to make the same point—the Bible is bizarre and strange, even evil and harmful—and to discredit anyone who takes the Bible seriously. If I were reading these verses for the first time, seeing them in isolation like this, I would feel the same way. Bible portrayals like this make Christianity seem like a primitive, nonintelligent, and even sadistic religion. One blog commenter said, "The Bible contains sheer nonsense. Talking animals carrying on conversations (donkeys, snakes), worldwide floods, virgin births, sun stopping in the sky, etc."

These Verses Are Confusing Because We Have to Learn How (Not) to Read the Bible

Here is the good news. There are ways to better understand these crazy-sounding Bible verses. We must learn how to, and how *not* to, read the Bible. Most of the examples we've seen so far are a result of people who are *not* reading the Bible correctly. If you are willing to look beyond the visual image and explore beyond a literal, out-of-context reading of a verse, you'll discover the Bible is not "sheer nonsense." There are many strange things in it, but when we study what it really says, the Bible is an amazing, life-changing book written by people who were directed by God through God's Spirit. As we take a closer look at these and other Bible passages, my hope is that you will have your questions and concerns answered, and you will come to better know the author of the Bible.

Are Unicorns Really in the Bible?

Before we wrap up, let's return to the question of unicorns. Are they really mentioned in the Bible? When my barber asked about them, I was confused. I had read the Bible several times, and I don't recall ever reading the word "unicorn." So when I searched online and found the memes and discussions, I knew I had to look into this. Most of those mentioning unicorns were mocking the Bible. There was even a satirical website dedicated to unicorns that said, "Unicorns Are Real. The Bible says so."

Seeing all these references and quotes from the Bible seems convincing, but when you examine it further, you discover they are all based on faulty and misleading information. Almost any Christian who reads the Bible today never sees the word "unicorn." Contemporary translations don't use "unicorn," they use a more accurate term, "wild ox," in translation to English. However, you can still find the word "unicorn" in the King James Version of the Bible (KJV), a translation from the year 1611. That translation was authorized by King James I of England and utilized the best Greek and Hebrew texts (the languages in which the Bible was originally written) along with several other Bible translations they had access to at the time. When you read translations from that time period, you'll also encounter unfamiliar words like "thee" and "thou," which were common words at that time. Today we use "you" or "him" or "her" for "thee," and "my," "your," "his," or "hers" for "thy." Contemporary Bible translations use words that make sense to the readers they are translating for.

So where do you find references to unicorns? The word translated "unicorn" in the King James translation is the Hebrew word *re'em*. This word refers to an animal the original audience of the Bible would have been familiar with, and the best estimate of when that word was written is between 1400 and 700 BC. Scholars who study the Hebrew language and its usage at those times tell us it likely was referring to an animal of great strength that had a prominent horn.

In 1611, when the King James Bible was translated, the scholars translating this Hebrew didn't know the specific animal the Hebrew word *re'em* was referring to, so they looked at an older translation for help. When the Hebrew Bible was translated into Greek (an older translation called the Septuagint) sometime in the second or third century BC, those translators chose the Greek word *monokeros*, which, when translated to English literally means "one horn." When the King James translators encountered this unfamiliar word, they looked to the Greek translation for help and chose the English word "unicorn" (meaning one horn) to represent what they felt the original word meant, an animal with a prominent horn.

To be clear, they did not choose it to represent the mythical, magical, one-horned horse we think of today. If you were to think of a "one-horned animal" or "an animal with a prominent horn" today, you would likely think of the rhinoceros (interestingly, the scientific name for the Indian one-horned rhino is *rhinoceros unicornis*). And when the Old Testament was being written, there were various one-horned and multi-horned animals in existence. The original writers of the Bible would have been familiar with the now extinct but very large and powerful horned oxen the Assyrians called "rimu," also referred to as "aurochs." Today, we know there also once existed an animal that is now extinct, *Elasmotherium sibiricum*, an extremely large single-horned bull.

If you read and study the handful of verses that use the Hebrew word *re'em*, we know it refers to an animal of strength, similar to a bull with a prominent horn. This is why today's scholars translate the Hebrew word *re'em* with the English words "wild oxen." Cultural changes over time lead to shifts in the way words are used, and all of this makes a difference in translating ancient texts. Today, the English word "unicorn" refers to a mythical one-horned horse, but back when the Bible was written, no one would have put those two things together.

So were there unicorns in the Bible? The answer is yes, there were one-horned animals, a variety of oxen, an animal the people would have been familiar with. But were these animals the white magical, mythological horses with one horn that we think of today? No, of course not.

Here is why this matters. Today there are memes, graphics, and stories that make their way into online discussions—and even into conversations with barbers—that convince people that the Bible is filled with nonsense. These images and verses build a case that the Bible is crazy, and anyone who believes the Bible is crazy. All of this may look convincing, but after you research the original usage of the word in the

Bible, the context, and where the English translation first appeared, it's easy to see that the Bible does not teach that mythical unicorns existed.

Before We Get into the Strange and Bizarre Passages

This is why the study of the Bible is important today. There are fresh challenges to the Bible, crazy and unusual accusations being made, and most Christians have never had to think about these challenges before. It catches many people off-guard, especially if they haven't read or studied the Bible. In this book I want to show you how to read, interpret, and understand the Bible accurately. We'll look at the makeup of the Bible, because to understand what Bible verses mean we need to understand how these verses fit in the whole Bible. If we ignore this, we will all-too-easily believe that mythical, magical unicorns are in the Bible (along with talking snakes), that churches don't let women speak or ask questions, and many other crazy and very strange and weird-sounding things.

CHAPTER 2

The Bible Was Not
Written to Us

We believe the Bible was written for us, that it's for
everyone of all times and places because it's God's
Word. But it wasn't written to us. It wasn't written
in our language, it wasn't written with our culture in
mind or our culture in view.

—DR. JOHN WALTON, PROFESSOR, AUTHOR[1]

To make sense of some of the rather crazy-sounding Bible verses, we
need to first raise the question, "What is the Bible?" How we read and
study the Bible drastically changes depending on how we view it. At the
heart of all the confusion about these Bible verses is a misunderstanding
of *what* the Bible actually is and how it is unlike most any other book
you will read.

I'm writing this book with the assumption that not everyone who
reads the Bible is a Christian or follower of Jesus. So I won't be giving
short answers to complex topics, assuming that a Christian already knows
much of this and doesn't need the full story. Even if you already know
the answer, I hope this will show you *how* we come to the answers we

find. I want this book to make you think and stretch you, whether you're a Christian or not.

The truth is that some of the Bible passages in question are not all that easy to explain. There may be multiple opinions. There's not always a clear-cut, simple meaning to a text. I've read books and studied responses to some of the difficult parts of the Bible that are woefully simplistic, lacking real depth. So before we begin problem-solving individual verses, these next two chapters will look at the Bible as a whole. We will first examine four major facts about Bible study methods that we will use again and again throughout this book. I hope they will become a normal part of your own reading of the Bible. Here are the four facts about how to and how *not* to read the Bible:

1. The Bible is a library, not a book.
2. The Bible is written for us, but not to us.
3. Never read a Bible verse.
4. All of the Bible points to Jesus.

But before we dive into these four facts, let's take one step back. Why do we even call the Bible "the Bible"? You'll commonly find the words "Holy Bible" printed on the cover and spine, but that's just a name someone gave to the printed book. The book we call *the Bible* became known as *the Bible* sometime in the Middle Ages, and even more so with the advent of Bible printing and the spread of the King James translation. Calling it the Holy Bible makes sense, as the word "holy" means "set apart." Christians believe God has set apart and made distinct the writings collected in the Bible. They are sacred (a word similar to holy) writings. In the Bible itself you'll see it referring to the writings as "*Holy* Scriptures," which means these writings are sacred, distinct, and set apart by God because they are from him.*

What does the word "bible" mean? The word came from the Greek

---

*   Romans 1:2; 2 Timothy 3:15.

word *biblia*, which means "books." Note that it is plural—books, not book—and this is important. When I first got a Bible, I considered it a single book. It looked like a book with a front cover, a back cover, and pages in between. It had shiny gold-edged pages and a leather cover. It looked like a magical book, but it was still only a book. But if you really want to understand what the Bible is, don't think of it as a book. The Bible is a library.

1. The Bible Is a Library, Not a Book

Although the Bible often comes in print form as a single bound book, it is actually a collection of sixty-six books printed in one volume, a library of books. This library is diverse, containing writings of history, poetry, prophecy, and law. This library of diverse books was written in three different languages over a 1,500-year period by a whole bunch of different people from different cultures. Some books in this library were written more than a thousand years before the other books.

Every time I open the Bible, I try to visualize myself entering a library. I imagine walking in and pulling ancient scrolls and tablets (the formats much of the Bible was written in) off shelves from various sections, each dated and categorized by genre. Since we have now digitized the Bible for reading on our phones and tablets, it may be more difficult to visualize it this way. But that doesn't change the fact that the Bible is a library of books, not a single book. Knowing this really does impact how we study and make sense of it.

Imagine walking into a modern-day library and going to the poetry section. Poetry uses words with rhythm or rhyme to communicate in a way that stirs the imagination and emotions. Poetry often uses colorful words, sometimes exaggerated, to describe ideas or tell stories. Songs are often written as poetry. So when you go to the poetry section of a library and pull a book off the shelf, you would read it differently than a book in the history section. The way a history book is written means it is to be interpreted and understood quite differently than a poem.

Keep walking through the library and you'll come to a section containing writings from Europe in the medieval period (around 900 AD). The words and the style of writing from that time period, including how the writers understood the world and the struggles they faced, are different from the writing on a sports page in a contemporary newspaper. The terms and language and contexts are very different.

Walk over to the law section of the library. Here you find the thick law books lawyers use to research their cases, detailing the laws from different periods of history. As you read a law book, you pay attention to when it was written and where, as many of the laws change over time, and there may be different laws for different geographic areas (countries, states, cities, etc.). A law book from Germany in 1580 AD contains laws that applied at that time and in that culture, but they may not be applicable or even understandable for us today.

This is our Bible, a library of books written in many different genres and at many different times in history. All of this strongly impacts how we read and interpret individual Bible verses. Much depends on which book we are reading. Law books are read and interpreted quite differently from a poetry book. In the library of books that make up our Bible are books of poetry, history, law, wisdom, letters to specific churches or people, and prophecy written to certain people groups in a specific time period about their future.

The First and Second Testaments Are Combined into One Volume

The "library" most Christians refer to as the Bible contains sixty-six books, all published together in a single volume with two distinct parts. Which of the two major parts you are reading from makes a big difference in how you interpret a book or verse.

The first section, called the Old Testament, contains thirty-nine books. The second section, called the New Testament, contains twenty-seven books. The word "testament" simply means "covenant," and though it's not a word we use much today, it was very common at the time the Bible was written. A covenant means an "agreement" between two parties. The Old Covenant (or testament) is the agreement God made with the people of Israel (ethnically Jewish people) outlining in detail how they would relate to God and know him. The New Covenant (or testament) is the agreement God made with all people through Jesus, and in making this agreement, he did away with the Old Covenant (more on this later). The New Covenant outlines how all people today of every ethnic background (not just the Jewish people) can relate to God and worship him.

I don't like using the term "Old Testament" (which was just a name someone made up, as it wasn't part of an original title in the Bible). Saying this section is "old" can make it seem like it's not meaningful to people—which is far from true. The Old Testament is extremely important because it lays the foundation and tells the beginning of the story leading up to the New Testament and the coming of Jesus. I generally refer to the Old Testament as the *First Testament* or the *Hebrew Bible*, as most of it was written in Hebrew. The New Testament was written in Greek. "The Bible" is one volume of sixty-six books containing writings from two different covenants outlining the two major ways God provided for human beings to know him and relate to him.[2] Not understanding this can lead to much misuse and confusion.

A Library of Sixty-Six Books with Many Authors, Yet Only One

Like any library of many different books, the Bible has many human authors. Unlike most books we read today, the Bible isn't the product of one person. Our best understanding of the history of its writing is that it was written by more than forty authors from various walks of life, including shepherds, farmers, tent-makers, physicians, fishermen, priests, philosophers, and kings. These human authors lived in different time periods and had different life experiences, education, perspectives on the world, and different personalities and temperaments, which are all reflected in how and what they wrote. The Bible was also written in three different languages (Hebrew, Aramaic, and Greek).

This explains why you find different writing styles—these authors weren't all writing at the same time in history. The Bible was written beginning around 1400 BC (the time of Moses) through around 100 AD (the time following the death and resurrection of Jesus Christ and the birth of the early church). That's a time span of more than 1500 years! You would never read and interpret something written 3,400 years ago in the same way you would read a book written last week.

Even though it was written by many different authors, the Holy Bible, unlike other books, has something unique. Behind all those human authors is a single author. The library of books in the Bible was written by human authors who each had God's Spirit inspiring and guiding them.* The library of books in the Bible was and still is a primary way God communicates with us, giving us guidance. God wants us to know him, to know our origins and future, and to have guidance for life. So God intentionally and purposely oversaw the process of what was written, using the different personalities and life experiences and situations of each human author to communicate what he wished to say. Every word in the original writings of Scripture was the exact word that God wanted people to have.† So we say there were many authors of the Bible, but only one "Author."[3]

A Library of Books and Letters Written over 1,500 Years in Three Languages

In image 2.1 you can see what the Bible looks like if you divide the sixty-six books on different shelves of a library. This is overly simplistic, as many books within the Bible have more than one type of writing in them. But this is helpful as an overview of the entire Bible. Just like walking into a library, you will see sections of books in the library divided by genre. In the library of the Bible are sections on history, law, poetry, prophecy, wisdom, and apocalyptic literature.

The original manuscripts that make up the Bible were written on

---

*   2 Peter 1:21.
†   2 Timothy 3:16–17; 2 Peter 1:20.

various materials, including stone, parchment, and scrolls, so if you saw the originals, they wouldn't look like a shelf of books. And certainly not look like a single book, like we think of it now.

Notice that on the library shelves are the two main sections we mentioned, the Old Testament books and the New Testament books. Within the two main sections are the different types of books. Many of the New Testament books are actually letters written to specific churches or to specific people.

Just remember, whenever you open your Bible to a page, you are walking into an ancient historical library of sixty-six books written over a 1,500-year time period. The author was writing in a specific time period and addressing a specific culture. It may have been written in a specific

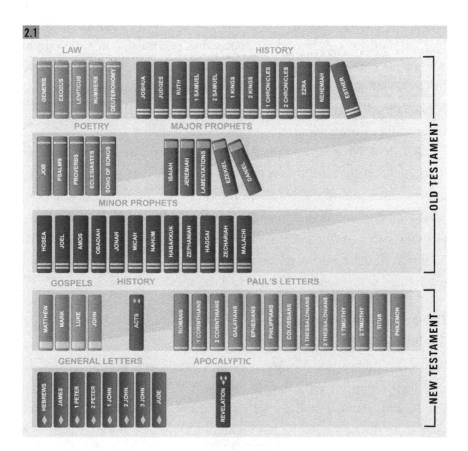

genre as well. When you open the book of Psalms, you are reaching into the poetry section of the Old Testament library. Many of the psalms were written between 500 and 1000 BC. The book of Acts in the New Testament is a history book likely written in the late 60s AD. Knowing when a book was written impacts how we read it and helps us to make sense of the parts we encounter that sound crazy.

2. The Bible Was Written for Us, but Not to Us

The second of the four facts you need to know to interpret the Bible correctly is that *the Bible was written for us, but not to us.* When the brilliant and highly respected Old Testament scholar John Walton spoke at my church, he repeated this phrase multiple times: "The Bible was written for us, but not to us." He explained that the Bible is 100 percent inspired by God, and we can have confidence that every word in the original documents of the Bible is exactly what God wanted it to say. We believe in God's full inspiration and the total trustworthiness of the Bible. The books in the library of the Bible are *for* all people at all times and places to read and gain wisdom from.

But the Bible wasn't originally written *to* us. It wasn't written in any modern language, and it wasn't written with our contemporary culture and its assumptions and values in mind. To get the most benefit from what God was communicating when he inspired the authors of the Bible to write, we need to enter their world to hear the words as the original audience would have heard them and as the author would have meant them to be understood. We must read the words on those terms.[4]

Though the Bible Wasn't Written to Us, We Get Instruction for Life from It

All of the Bible—*every* single page and word—has important insight and instruction for us today. Every word of the Old Testament and the New Testament is there for us to study and study from to know God more through what he has communicated. The Bible—taken as a whole—reveals the story of God, who God is and what he has done. It tells us about our salvation, our purpose, our origins, giving guidance for life, a vision for what is ahead, and most of all, telling us who Jesus is. When Paul the apostle wrote a letter to encourage a young leader, he stressed the importance of the Bible in this way: "From infancy you have known the Holy Scriptures, which are able to make you wise for salvation through faith in Christ Jesus. All Scripture is God-breathed and is useful for teaching, rebuking, correcting and training in righteousness, so that the servant of God may be thoroughly equipped for every good work."*

Paul was saying in his letter to Timothy that all of the Old Testament (the portion of the Bible they had at that time) is useful for making Timothy wise and equipping him for day-to-day life and purpose as a follower of Jesus. Today we also include the New Testament writings in the Holy Scriptures, and we believe all sixty-six books in the library of the Bible can equip us for practical living that honors God. However, in the same letter, Paul also gives a challenge to be someone "who correctly handles the word of truth."† This implies that some handle it incorrectly. There are even warnings in the Bible itself that some of the New Testament books "contain some things that are hard to understand, which ignorant and unstable people distort, as they do the other Scriptures, to their own destruction."‡

I actually find this encouraging. I love that the Bible itself says that some of the Bible will be hard to understand. So when we struggle with something in the Bible, we have to remember even Peter admitted that not all of it is easily understood. It also says that people will "distort" the Bible. This reaffirms what we've been learning, that it is critically important to invest time and effort into understanding how to and how *not to* properly read and study the Bible. Failure to do so is one of the primary reasons why people critique it and misunderstand what it says. Their interpretations are distortions of the original meaning.

---

*   2 Timothy 3:15–17.
†   2 Timothy 2:15.
‡   2 Peter 3:16.

We Have to Change Our Dangerous Way of Reading the Bible

Most people, when they start reading the Bible, want to immediately know "what does this mean to me and my life?" This assumes that when we read the Bible, we should read it as if what God was writing is specifically and directly written to us today. We may not even realize we do this, but we do it all the time. And sadly, even the preaching and teaching in some churches unintentionally does this, and it doesn't help people to understand the Bible. When we read the Bible in this way, we read into it our presuppositions—what we believe and understand based on our experience, worldview, culture, and knowledge. Our contemporary values and way of life are also part of the lens through which we read the Bible. And while there is much it can say to help us, if we view the Bible as mainly a "message for me," we will be in great trouble. We will end up picking and choosing the things we like reading and want to apply to our

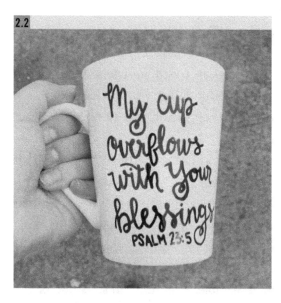
2.2

lives. We often focus on the "nice" and comforting Bible verses, like the one on the coffee mug in image 2.2.

This mug takes a verse from Psalm 23 and offers positive encouragement by restating God's blessings in our lives through the words David expressed in the psalm (a poetic song) he wrote. It's encouraging to relate to David in this

way because what he was experiencing of God's blessings was true, and we can experience that same blessing too. But not every promise or blessing is something we can directly apply to our lives today. We might take Bible verses and promises that are not meant for us and then be disappointed in God when they don't happen.

The Plans for Us to Wait Seventy Years for a Promise

An example of this is Jeremiah 29:11, a commonly misused verse: "'For I know the plans I have for you,' declares the LORD, 'plans to prosper you and not to harm you, plans to give you hope and a future.'"

Of course, it's wonderful to think God has plans for us to prosper. But we have to be careful we aren't taking Bible verses and applying a promise *to us* that God didn't make *to us*. It can lead to great disappointment and disillusionment. Jeremiah 29:11 wasn't written to us. That verse was written to the people of Israel to address their situation at the time. The people of Israel were in captivity, away from their promised homeland, living in Babylon. Their beautiful capital city of Jerusalem was destroyed, and they had been taken prisoner and then taken hundreds of miles away to Babylon. The irony of taking this verse as a promise, even in the original context, is that God is actually disappointing them with these words. He is telling them, "Yes, one day you will be free and prosper again, but the fact is it won't happen for *seventy years*."

The story behind the verse is that Israel is going to be stuck in Babylon for a while, and many of those hearing this promise won't be alive when the way back is open again. The people had disobeyed God, and God had allowed the Babylonians to destroy their city, kill many of them, and capture them. They are now prisoners, and God wants them to know he won't forget about them, but there will be suffering for some time to come. It was a full seventy years before they were freed and allowed to go back to Jerusalem, and most of the readers of that original promise were dead before it happened. I'm guessing that when you take a verse like this out of its original context and apply it to a situation in your life, you hope God doesn't wait seventy years to keep his promise.

All too often, we take a nice-sounding Bible verse and apply it directly to our life. For instance, Isaiah 12:2 says, "Surely God is my salvation; I will trust and not be afraid. The LORD, the LORD himself, is my strength and my defense." We like to claim that Bible verse and own it. We take comfort in it personally, which is a good thing to do, as God *is* our strength and defense. That verse is truth for all times because it reflects the unchanging character and nature of God. But we avoid claiming two verses later in the same book. Isaiah 34:2–3 says, "He will totally destroy them, he will give them over to slaughter. Their slain will be thrown out, their dead bodies will stink; the mountains will be soaked with their blood."

Can you picture that Bible promise as the theme verse for the annual women's retreat, with a coffee mug gift for each woman who

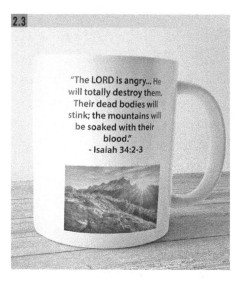

attends? Not all verses are written to us and apply to us. And we often pick and choose by taking the nice-sounding Bible verses and claiming they are true and applying them to our lives, while skipping past the negative crazy-sounding ones. We need to stop and ask: who was the Bible verse originally written to and why? As we will discover, many of the Bible verses that don't make sense to us today usually made sense to the original readers. If we don't step into that time and culture, there may be things we'll find confusing or odd. In the early 1980s, if someone had said, "I'm going to surf the web," those words would not have made sense. A person hearing that would have thought of someone surfing on a surfboard somewhere in the ocean. They might have guessed that the web was some kind of spider web. But it wouldn't have made sense because those words had different meanings at that time. That's true for locations as well. In my town in California we often say we are going "over the hill." All of us locals know it means we are taking a specific road over the mountain when we go from our town over to San Jose. But if you don't know the local context, hearing "going over the hill" could mean hiking over a hill in a state park near you or being so old you're "over the hill," neither of which has anything to do with the original context.[5]

There was a song that came out in 1963 called "Puff the Magic Dragon" by folk artists Peter, Paul, and Mary. The chorus contained these lyrics:

> Puff the magic dragon, lived by the sea
> And frolicked in the autumn mist in a land called Honali

The song was extremely popular and even reached number two on the music charts. Around that time, there were the beginnings of a countercultural revolution with a new generation starting to reject the social and ethical values of past generations. Drug experimentation was becoming more prevalent, and in the thinking of younger generations, the song "Puff the Magic Dragon" was rumored to be something more than a children's song about a mythical dragon. People began interpreting the lyrics based on their worldview and saw it as a song written about marijuana smoking. *Newsweek* magazine even had a cover story about covert drug messages being part of songs.

The rumor, based on the cultural views and assumptions of the time, was that "Puff" was an obvious metaphor for smoking pot. "Autumn mist" (another part of the lyrics) was understood to be a symbolic reference to clouds of marijuana smoke. And the land of "Honali" was interpreted as a reference to the Hawaiian village of Hanalei, which was known for its particularly potent marijuana plants.

Then one day the authors of the song made a statement to clarify what they meant when they wrote the song. They clearly and emphatically stated the song had no reference or hidden meaning whatsoever to drug culture. Cowriter of the song Peter Yarrow said, "When 'Puff' was written, I was too innocent to know about drugs. What kind of a mean-spirited SOB would write a children's song with a covert drug message?"

And the other cowriter, Leonard Lipton, said, "'Puff' is about loss of innocence, and having to face an adult world. It's surely not about drugs. I can tell you that at Cornell in 1959, no one smoked grass. I find the fact that people interpret it as a drug song annoying. It would be insidious to propagandize about drugs in a song for little kids."

I share this to show how easy it can be to take our worldview and then press it into something we read or hear, interpreting it through our lens. We can look at specific words and dissect them and use complicated contemporary analysis to do all this. Eventually, though, we need to step back and look at the more fundamental question: What was the author originally saying? We cannot simply read our own understandings into the meaning of a word or statement someone else wrote or said. And when we look at some of the bizarre-sounding parts of the Bible, we have to try to discover who the original audience was and view the text through their lens, not ours. If we don't, the possibilities for confusion are endless.

CHAPTER 3

Never Read a Bible Verse

If there was one bit of wisdom, one rule of thumb, one single skill I could impart, one useful tip I could leave that would serve you well the rest of your life, what would it be? What is the single most important practical skill I've ever learned as a Christian?

Here it is: Never read a Bible verse. That's right, never read a Bible verse. Instead, always read a paragraph at least.

—GREG KOUKL, AUTHOR AND APOLOGIST, STAND TO REASON[1]

When we are trying to make sense of disturbing or crazy-sounding Bible verses, one of the most helpful phrases we can keep in mind is found in the quote by Greg Koukl in the epigraph to this chapter: "Never read a Bible verse." Obviously, this is an exaggeration, but it's an exaggeration with a point. It's a memorable way of telling us that we should never read a Bible verse in isolation from the context.

Some of you might object that we do see Jesus and other New Testament authors quoting single verses. But back in that day, whenever you would quote a verse, it was understood that this was a shorthand way of referencing the larger section of Scripture from which that verse was taken. The Jewish people saturated their minds and hearts with the Scriptures in such a way that one verse was a trigger to help them remember the other passages surrounding it. They would know where a specific verse fit within the context of surrounding verses, the whole book, and the storyline of the current Bible they had. Quoting a Bible verse was different. They were quoting it with an awareness of the context. Today when people quote a Bible verse they often are *not* aware of the context.

Most people today, and even many Christians, don't know what comes before or after a specific verse from the Bible. So when we are reading a Bible verse on its own in isolation, it can be confusing. A Bible verse—taken on its own—can be misunderstood and misinterpreted and used in all kinds of ways that have nothing to do with the original meaning. This is one of the primary ways we see the Bible being used against itself by critics of the Bible. A verse is pulled out and placed on a visual or a meme, possibly even a rented billboard. Those who see the verse draw conclusions based on the current context in which the verse is seen and read, in isolation from the original context of the Bible.

Sadly, it's not just those who attack the Bible who do this. Bible-believing Christians do the same thing. We choose the nice happy types of verses for T-shirts and coffee mugs.

3. Never Read a Bible Verse

"Never read a Bible verse" is a reminder that *every* Bible verse is written in a context, in a specific time period and for a specific purpose. Every Bible verse fits within a larger story, and whenever we read any verse, we want to:

- Look at the specific Bible verse (many people stop here).
- Look at the paragraph the verse is in.
- Look at the chapter the Bible verse is in.
- Look at the book of the Bible that the chapter and verse are in.
- Look at where the book of the Bible the verse is in fits in the Bible's whole storyline.

This illustration might help you remember this principle. Have you ever seen a Star Wars movie? They begin with a rolling screen of words that set up what has happened in the Star Wars storyline leading up to the opening scene in the movie about to begin.

Without an understanding of the broader storyline, you would be confused by what follows. Even in a single movie of the Star Wars series, you need to reflect on earlier scenes, or some scenes in the movie won't make sense. Imagine taking a single line from a Star Wars movie without knowing which scene or which movie it is from and trying to make sense of what it means. You'd likely miss the full meaning of the line without the appropriate context.

Consider this line: "Just for once, let me look on you with my own eyes." We don't know who is saying it or what it refers to. Reading that one line on its own, we could come to all kinds of interesting theories about what it means. We could even develop sermons with different teachings based on what we think it is saying for living today. But when we look at the context, we see it is Anakin Skywalker (also Darth Vader) saying it while being held in Luke Skywalker's arms as he is about to die. It's right after Luke has learned that Anakin is his father. As he is dying, he asks to have his mask removed so he can see his son Luke with his own eyes, not through the mask covering his face. It's a pivotal scene in the larger Star Wars storyline. But without the full story, it wouldn't make much sense on its own.

Like Star Wars, the Bible is an epic story covering different time periods, different generations continuing the story, plots and twists within the storyline, and a variety of different characters. However, unlike Stars Wars, which is fiction, the Bible is a real story, grounded in history and a hundred percent inspired by God. It's a story telling us about the God who created everything and of his interactions with human beings and all he created. It is the most amazing, exciting story we can ever read and well worth becoming familiar with.

Sadly, we've lost our awareness of this epic story. Many people today can probably tell you the basic storyline of a Star Wars movie, but they

> 3.1
>
> The Gospel of John
> Chapter 1
>
> *In the beginning was the Word, and the Word was with God, and the Word was God. He was with God in the beginning. Through him all things were made; without him nothing was made that has been made. In him was life, and that life was the light of all mankind. The light shines in the darkness, and the darkness has not overcome it.*
>
> *There was a man sent from God whose name was John. He came as a witness to testify concerning that light, so that through him all might believe. He himself*

would struggle to tell you the storyline of the Bible. That's why there is so much confusion and misunderstanding when a Bible verse is read in isolation, especially when it sounds a little crazy.

Whenever we open up the Bible, we need a little Star Wars–like backstory. As you turn to a passage of the Bible, picture that opening scroll giving you the broader context of what you are about to read.

Every Bible Verse Is Part of a Bigger Story

As we learned earlier, the Bible is a library of sixty-six books written over a 1,500-year time period by more than forty authors from different cultures who wrote in three languages using all types of genres—yet it tells a unified story. That story has a beginning and an end, with all types of plot twists and characters entering and leaving the story.

With the success of the film versions several years ago, most people today are familiar with the basic storyline of The Lord of the Rings trilogy. Millions have seen the movies or read the books. If you were to open the third book in the trilogy, *Return of the King,* you might read about Gollum and his intense desire for the ring worn by Frodo. His desire was so intense he eventually bites off Frodo's finger to get it before falling into the fiery lava of Mount Doom. But if you are beginning your reading in the third book of the whole story, you are missing the backstory. You don't know Gollum's origins—where he came from and his relationship with the ring—and you won't understand why he is acting this way. You miss what is significant about the ring's power and why for most of the third book Frodo is wearing the ring around his neck and not on his finger. Many details of the plot and the actions of the characters would be confusing if you opened a novel or started watching a movie without starting at the beginning.

Jesus Has a Backstory Called the Old Testament

When you read about Jesus in the Bible, you need to understand that Jesus doesn't just appear one day out of nowhere. He has a backstory that begins long before his birth in Bethlehem. There are hints of him in the book of Genesis as far back as the garden of Eden* and in a promise made about him to Abraham.† The hints about Jesus become more clear in the writings of the prophet Isaiah,‡ leading right up to his birth in the New Testament. There is an entire story that precedes his birth, giving all that he says and does additional meaning.

We Need the Old Testament to Understand the New

The Old Testament was written to specific people groups in specific time periods for specific reasons. Many of the laws we read in the Old Testament no longer *directly* apply to us because they were made under the "old covenant," an agreement that outlined how certain people related to God at that time. Today, those who are Christians belong to the "new covenant" made possible through Jesus. This doesn't mean the Old Testament is useless or unimportant. As we've seen, we need to know the full story because it points us to the significance of Jesus and the New

---

*   Genesis 3:15.
†   Genesis 22:18.
‡   Isaiah 53.

Testament he established. Without knowledge of the Old Testament, we miss the breadth and depth of the New Testament, and, more importantly, we miss knowing the fullness of God through his work of creating and relating to people throughout the ages.

Much of the confusion over a single Bible verse comes from looking at that verse or story without knowing the *full* story. No single chart or graphic can capture the full complexity and beauty of the Bible's storyline, but I've found the one in image 3.2 helpful. We'll come back to it throughout the rest of this book, so take a moment to look it over and familiarize yourself with it.

The Storyline of the Bible Comes in Six Acts

We can't box God into time as we know it, but the events within the Bible do exist within a historical timeline, as real as our daily experience of life today. Image 3.2 is a timeline that starts on the left with the beginning of the Bible story and moves along in time to the right, to the end of the Bible story. Here are several things to note about this visual timeline:

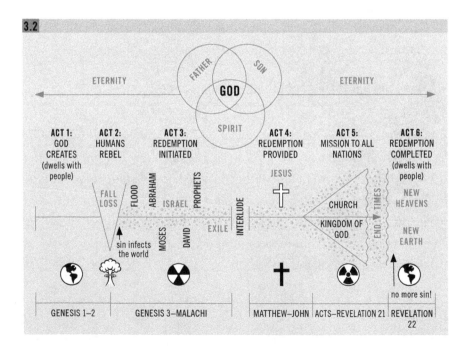

- The top of this diagram shows a line with arrows at each end. This reminds us that the Triune God (Father, Son, and Spirit) is eternal, even as God acts in time and history. God creates, which starts the storyline of the Bible, but God has always existed eternally before and after the events recorded and communicated to us in the Bible's storyline.

- The storyline shown here is broken into six acts of God working in history for the salvation of the world. This six-act breakdown of the Bible storyline, as well as some of the descriptions and titles I use, is an adaptation of several common ways various scholars have presented this material.[2]

- The dots scattered throughout the image represent the virus of sin in the world and the spread of sin after the fall and loss.[*]

- The symbols of globes, nuclear explosions, and radioactivity are metaphors indicating a shift or change in the creation. The first globe indicates the world created by God as good. We then see it followed by a symbol of a nuclear explosion representing the fall, the time when humans rebelled against God and sin entered the world. The radiation symbols indicate sin activity, its impact, and the resulting fallout. You might notice a decrease in sin's impact with the coming of Jesus and his kingdom breaking into this world, but sin is still there. The story ends with the world once again sin free in the new heaven and the new earth.

- At the bottom of the image are names of several books of the Bible and where they fit into the timeline of events. You can imagine this chart like an open Bible lying flat. If you open a Bible and find the division between the Old Testament (the First Testament) and the New Testament, you can lay it flat under the timeline with the left side covering the events from Genesis through Malachi. The right side of the open Bible is the section from Matthew through Revelation.

---

[*]   Genesis 3.

In the pages that follow, you'll see that I've split the Bible storyline into six acts. As you read, think of what you are reading as if it were a play-bill. When you attend a play, you are typically given a playbill with brief descriptions of the various scenes. Reading through the scenes can feel a bit confusing at first, especially if you aren't familiar with the story. But it can be very helpful in preparing you to understand the plot of the play you will be watching. As you read the Bible, you'll be able to place some of the crazy-sounding things you read in the right context to begin making sense of it all.

Act 1: God Creates and Dwells with People (Genesis 1–2)

God creates a wonderful, ordered universe, a world full of beauty and potential. You see God creating everything, including angelic beings (called "sons of God" in the Bible).[3] This also includes the creation of human beings in a way that is different from everything else—he makes them "in his image." Human beings were created to be in relationship with God as his children, and the garden of Eden was a sacred space where he could dwell with them. Humans were to manage and maintain his creation. You could see that God created a supernatural family (the angelic realm and his heavenly council) and a human family (beginning with Adam and Eve). He gives humans the task of overseeing this world and multiplying and creating new communities. Human beings exist in harmony with God and each other in the beginning. God dwelled among them. There is no inequality or discord between humans. God calls his creation "very good."

Act 2: Humans Rebel and the Fallout Happens (Genesis 3–11)

As the humans go about the tasks they've been given, they're faced with choices. They can do what is good or what is evil as determined by the God who created them. God established guidelines and boundaries for them, defining good and evil. The mysterious character of the Serpent (later identified as Satan, the enemy of God's people) enters the story to entice them not to trust God. Humans chose to doubt God's generosity and not to trust in God's guidance or the order he established. They wanted to define good and evil for themselves and to have God's order be centered on them instead of on God.

This first rebellion event is known as the fall, and it's like a nuclear explosion in the storyline of the Bible, altering the world that exists in several significant ways. Humanity's relationship with God is fractured, and their relationships with themselves, their families, and the earth break down. The fallout from the decision to disobey God is great and impacts everything. This is when "sin" (when humans act contrary to God's guidance) enters the world, and like a contamination or a virus, it alters the beauty of what was originally created. The greatest impact of all was the loss of access to God's presence.[4]

However, because God loves the people he created, he offers them hope, giving them a glimpse of future redemption and restoration. He tells them that one day someone (who we later learn is Jesus) will come to crush the Serpent's head, defeating the one who instigated the rebellion.*

Still, the bomb has been detonated and the resulting "fallout" now affects everything. This is shown by the radiation symbol. We see evil entering the world, spreading like a virus and contaminating everything with sin. Unlike the original creation, we now see:

* violence, murder, war
* male domination over women
* rape, abuse
* polygamy, harems, concubines, moving away from God's original marriage plan
* false gods being created and worshiped
* slavery
* ego and manipulations of all kinds to gain power, control, and wealth

Further rebellions against God occur by both human and divine beings.[5] We see a second rebellion of the angelic "sons of God" trying to

---

*   Genesis 3:15; Romans 16:20; Revelation 12:9; 20:2, 10.

imitate God and create their own family with humans. Evil continues to rise to such a level that God sends a flood (Genesis 6–9) to wipe the world clear and start over. He retains a seed of animal life and humanity, and people continue to multiply after the flood. Yet once again even after the post-flood restart, we see people rebelling against God at the Tower of Babel. It is here God disinherits them and disperses the nations across the earth. This ends the second act, leading up to where God is about to start over with one man, Abraham, through whom God will start a new family—the people of Israel.

Act 3: Redemption Initiated (Genesis 12–Malachi)

Despite the continued spread of sin and the resulting fallout, God has love for his creation, and he remembers his promise of someone who will come to defeat the evil that has been released. He reveals that he is going to enact this rescue plan through one family chosen from among the various people of the world—the people of Abraham, who later become the nation of Israel. Eventually, as the storyline of the Old Testament develops and the plot progresses, we meet Jesus, who is born through Abraham's lineage. He is the one promised, the one all of this is pointing to.

The radiation symbol here communicates the continued "fallout" due to the effects of the fall. The infection and contamination of sin is still present in all human beings, and it affects the world they live in. Much of the storyline of the Old Testament shows us that people consistently turn away from God's guidance and trust themselves over him. The third act of the Bible story—the portion from Genesis 12 through the book of Malachi at the end of the Old Testament—has three movements within this act.[6]

ACT 3, MOVEMENT 1: GOD CHOOSES ISRAEL TO BLESS THE NATIONS (GENESIS 12–DEUTERONOMY)

God makes a promise (a covenant) to a man named Abraham. God says he will bring Abraham into a land where his presence will be, and his family will become a nation that brings God's blessing to the world. The family grows, but they become enslaved in Egypt. As a nation, Egypt embodies all that's gone wrong with humanity: idolatry, worshiping false gods, injustice, slavery, and giving in to evil.

The story continues as God raises up a descendant of Abraham named Moses and defeats Egypt's evil, rescuing his people and bringing them to Mount Sinai. God uses Moses to lead Israel and enters into a covenant (a formal agreement, like a contract) with the Israelites. They are invited to obey the terms of the covenant, which start with the Ten Commandments and include several hundred other ways God sets in place for Israel to remain distinct from their neighbors who worship false gods. By being faithful to these commands, the people will become God's priestly representatives to the nations.

This is where we find many of the very crazy-sounding laws and practices that confuse people today. These laws were given to Israel, commands about not eating shrimp or not having tattoos. They seem odd and strange to us today, but to Israel at that time these laws made sense. And they were what was needed at this time in their history and their relationship to God.

Act 3, Movement 2: Israel's Royal Failure (Joshua, Judges, 1 and 2 Samuel, 1 and 2 Kings)

Israel enters the land God had promised to Abraham. They are to clear the land and drive out those who refuse to worship the one true God. But they blow it again and begin worshiping the gods of the nations around them, leading to further corruption and injustice. We see Israel committing acts of slavery, polygamy, and violence, and human beings putting themselves first instead of God. Even their best kings, David and Solomon, fail miserably.

Eventually, the leaders of Israel run the nation into the ground. God warns them over and over to turn back to him, but they repeatedly refuse. Then God allows the tribes of Israel to be conquered by the reigning superpower of the day, the Babylonians. Most of the Israelites are dragged into exile and captivity in Babylon. The irony of the story is that God's chosen people have shown they are no different than the surrounding nations, who in their rebellion are ruining God's good world.

ACT 3, MOVEMENT 3: ISRAEL'S EXILE AND THE PROPHETIC HOPE (ISAIAH, JEREMIAH, EZEKIEL, HOSEA–MALACHI)

Despite Israel's sin, all was not lost. Among the people of Israel was a vocal minority called the prophets. They had warned the people of Israel's coming downfall, but they also made it clear that this wasn't the end of the story for God's people. God had made a promise to them to restore divine blessing to the world through someone who was yet to be born, a descendant of Abraham and of King David. God's promise was still in force, that through a future leader, he would rescue the world. The stage is set for the coming of Jesus, the promised leader.

Intermission: the 400-Year Period between the Old and New Testaments

At this point in the story there is a 400-year period during which no new Scriptures are written. The Bible goes silent. Israel waits, hoping for the promise to be fulfilled, for a leader to be born who will rescue and redeem them. God is still active, and things are happening, but the events aren't considered inspired Scriptures, so they are not included in the Bible.

Act 4: Redemption Provided: Jesus (Matthew, Mark, Luke, John)

As act 4 begins, Jesus of Nazareth enters the stage. He is sometimes called Immanuel, meaning "God with us." The four gospels (Matthew, Mark, Luke, and John) in the New Testament present Jesus as the resolution to the conflict we witnessed throughout the Old Testament. We learn that Jesus was the one that God and the prophets spoke of, the one who comes to fulfill God's promise and return divine blessing to all nations. Jesus is of the lineage of Abraham and King David, and he is the fulfillment of all the promises made in the Old Testament, from the very beginning of Genesis to the prophets.

We learn that Jesus is the long-awaited "Messiah," or "anointed one," a reference to the practice of placing oil on the heads of God's appointed and chosen leaders. In Greek, this word is "Christ," and as the Christ, Jesus is the King who comes to redeem Israel and lead them to a new future with God. However, Jesus doesn't do this in the way they expected he would. Instead of coming as a military leader using force and power, he came as a servant who leads by serving others in their need. We begin to understand that Jesus is a human, but he is not ordinary. He is also divine, of the same nature as the Creator God, and we learn that God mysteriously but amazingly exists not as one solitary person, but eternally as three persons: Father, Son (Jesus), and Spirit. Eventually, Christians come to refer to this three-person community that exists in a single unity (God or the Godhead) as the "Trinity."

Jesus proclaimed that he was bringing God's kingdom back to the earth, and he would confront the tragic effects of evil and sin. But Jesus' plan to defeat humanity's evil and sin was unexpected. He would first let it defeat him. Jesus stirred up trouble by teaching things that upset the religious leaders of his day. He was arrested and killed by the common form of execution for criminals at that time, being crucified, or hung on a cross. We learn that this death was also not an ordinary death. Though Jesus suffered the physical pain of crucifixion like anyone else, he was also suffering the punishment for all human sin, dying for the sins of the world. His resurrection from death sealed his victory over human evil and the curse of death. All who put their faith in him and trust Jesus and his promises are now forgiven by God of their sin against him and belong to God again. The proof that they belong to God is that God's Spirit comes to dwell in them in a mysterious way, helping them to fight against their evil desires and to live a life of purpose and mission on the earth. The resurrection of Jesus from the dead confirms his identity and is God's stamp of approval on him as the appointed ruler of God's creation. Act 4 ends with the resurrection of Jesus and his ascension to heaven, where we are told he now rules the world from God's throne. He is the Promised One, the King whose death forgives the sins of all those who place their faith and trust in him.

Act 5: Mission to All Nations (Acts—Revelation 21)

After his resurrection, Jesus' followers experienced the power of the third person of God, the Holy Spirit, indwelling them. Here, near the temple in Jerusalem, the "church" was birthed, and as God's Spirit comes to "dwell" in people who put their faith in Jesus, there is no longer a need for a physical building or temple for people to meet God. The people of God are now spiritually God's temple, and all who follow Jesus are considered priests with equal access to God through Jesus.

After his resurrection and before he ascended to heaven, Jesus appeared in the flesh many times. He commanded his followers to go out as witnesses to share the incredible news of what he had done for the people of Israel and now, for all humanity. As the one promised to Abraham, it is through Jesus that the blessings of Israel are given to the other nations and people of the world. The free gift of salvation from the forever "fallout" of sin and evil, the forgiveness of sins and evils we have personally committed, and the promise of being with God for all eternity now are available to all those who believe what Jesus has done and put their faith in him. This Jesus movement became a multiethnic international movement.

The followers of Jesus started small communities with other believers in Jesus called "churches." People would gather weekly at local churches to celebrate their new way of life as redeemed humans enjoying an intimate covenant relationship with God. They would eat together and worship Jesus while challenging each other to follow his teachings. As the message of Jesus spread, new churches started, grew, and multiplied. Letters of instruction went to the churches, many of them written by a former persecutor of Jesus followers who himself became a follower of Jesus, a man named Paul (formerly called Saul). The church appointed leaders called "apostles." Many of the letters of instruction for the churches were inspired by God and became part of the Bible in the New Testament that was being collected and formed in these early years of the church. These writings were instructions providing guidance to all kinds of different churches facing a variety of challenges and problems as they learned to follow Jesus in the first-century world. A new world, sometimes called a "new creation," began with Jesus and the giving of God's Holy Spirit to his followers. Even today, the followers of Jesus continue to look ahead to the future, to a day when Jesus will return as he promised to finish what he started: conquer evil and fully establish his kingdom on earth, to live with us forever in a New Creation free from the fallout of sin and evil.

The radiation symbol at the bottom of the timeline chart is still present during act 5, but we begin to see it fade as God's Spirit is now present, empowering people in the church to live out the ongoing purposes of Jesus and change the world to conform more and more to the way God originally intended life to be. Sin and evil will not be gone in this act, as only the final act, the return of Jesus, can do that. The church has a mission to live out the teachings of Jesus, empowered by God's Spirit and trusting his promises so others will know the hope and forgiveness of Jesus and put their faith in him.

Act 6: Redemption Completed, God Dwells with People Again (Revelation 22)

The final act of the play tells us about a time yet to come. Jesus returns and a new creation is established. This is the grand ending to the story as well as the beginning of a new one. We see images of the garden of Eden here. It is a back-to-the-beginning story, a "re-creation" where God fixes what went wrong and makes all things new again, even better than they were before, by removing the potential for evil to ever infect God's creation or God's people again. People of all nations who put faith in Jesus are invited into this new creation where there is no more sin, and this means there is no more death or sickness or mourning or loss any longer. God has made all things good, and he dwells again with his people. In the timeline, you will notice the radiation symbol is now gone and the world is restored to the final fulfillment of God's purposes—the new heaven and the new earth planned from the beginning.

Although that was a long description and a lot to read, this "playbill" outline is a *very* quick overview of the Bible's storyline. The storyline gives you the outline of a Christian worldview, the lens through which a follower of Jesus views the past, the present, and the future. Once you have a basic understanding of the storyline, *everything* (that is not an overstatement) changes. You see how books of the Bible library fit into the whole. Whenever you open the Bible, you are opening it to a point in this storyline. So when you read a crazy-sounding Bible verse, know that it fits somewhere in the storyline. That is the key to understanding it.

The Bible Says We Should Be Vegetarians; Do You Eat Meat?

I hope you are beginning to see that it makes a difference knowing where a Bible verse fits into the larger storyline. I was on a walk in a town near where I live, and a group of people on the sidewalk were handing out pamphlets. They were promoting healthy living and the benefits of being a vegetarian. What caught my eye was a statement on one of the pamphlets that said the Bible teaches us to be vegetarians. They had printed a Bible verse on the pamphlet, Genesis 1:29, which says, "Then God said, 'I give you every seed-bearing plant on the face of the whole earth and every tree that has fruit with seed in it. They will be yours for food.'"

The verse is clearly a command to eat plants for food, not animals or fish. Based on reading this verse alone, taken straight from the Bible, you would think that God wants all human beings to be vegetarians. But what does this mean for those who follow Jesus and eat meat? Are they sinning, going against God's clear command here in Genesis 1:29? If this was all you knew about the Bible, you would certainly think so. It is clearly written in this verse that we are not to eat meat.

As you can guess, this is what we're trying to avoid—a Bible verse pulled out of context and used to prove a point that makes the Bible seem crazy or Christians appear hypocritical. But remember—"Never read a Bible verse!" Look at the context, and you learn in Genesis 9:3 that God says, "Everything that lives and moves about will be food for you. Just as I gave you the green plants, I now give you everything."

The pamphlet the vegetarian group passed out didn't include this verse, and to be fair, they may not have read the entire story. It's true that God did have a limitation on what people ate in Genesis 2, but by

Genesis 9, he had dropped that restriction. Later in the Bible, Jesus eats fish. In Luke 24:41–43, we read, "[Jesus] asked them, 'Do you have anything here to eat?' They gave him a piece of broiled fish, and he took it and ate it in their presence." It's clear Jesus was not vegetarian. We also see Jesus participating in the Passover meal (Luke 22:15–16), which, according to Exodus 12:3–8, requires eating lamb. So what does this mean for us today? The truth is that many Christians *are* vegetarians. It's a choice a person can freely make for many reasons, but you can't use one Bible verse to make a case for it.

This example helps us to see that we cannot pick one Bible verse and draw a conclusion from it in isolation. We must look where it fits in the Bible storyline. Not doing this can make a huge difference in what we understand about God and his relationship to us and can steer people into wrong thinking about what the Bible says.

4. All the Bible Points to Jesus (and Jesus Loved This Crazy Bible)

There is one final principle we need to understand. From the beginning in Genesis to the end in Revelation, all of the Bible points to Jesus. We don't see Jesus' name in the Old Testament, but as we have already pointed out, the storyline of the entire Bible revolves around him as the promised one sent by God to redeem God's people and rescue them from the fallout of evil and sin. When we understand that Jesus—the focal point of New Testament writings—is the one pointed to in the Old Testament, it leads to "aha!" moments as we read the Bible.

Jesus even said this about himself. After his resurrection, he spoke with two of his followers as he walked along the road beside them. They did not recognize that the man was Jesus. They were talking about his recent death, but were unable to make sense of why he had died.

"[Jesus] said to them, 'How foolish you are, and how slow to believe all that the prophets have spoken! Did not the Messiah have to suffer these things and then enter his glory?' And beginning with Moses and all the Prophets, he explained to them what was said in all the Scriptures concerning himself.'"*

When Jesus refers to Moses and all the Prophets and "all the Scriptures," he is speaking of what today we call the Old Testament. This was the "Bible" at that time. He is showing his followers how it all points to him. This does not mean we should be looking at every verse in the Old Testament to make allegorical connections to Jesus, trying to find Jesus in all the details. We just need to remember that the whole storyline points to him.

When we read the Old Testament, we need to keep this in mind. In speaking to the religious leaders of his own time, the people who were serious Bible students, Jesus warned them to not miss seeing him in the Scriptures.† The Bible points us to Jesus as the climax and main character of the story, and today, looking to the future, we anticipate his return and the creation of a new heaven and a new earth where he rules as king. Jesus is threaded throughout the entire Bible, and understanding this makes sense of some of the more confusing and difficult parts of the story.

With these four concepts in mind, let's look at some of the odd and strange rules and laws we find in the Old Testament. When a person picks up a Bible and begins reading, they often encounter odd regulations and wonder if Christians really believe these bizarre things. And why does no one actually follow these laws today if they are Christians? Or do Christians pick and choose laws they like and skip the ones they don't like?

---

*   Luke 24:25–27.
†   John 5:39–47.

Part 1 Summary Points

NEVER READ A BIBLE VERSE

As we end the first section of this book, let's review what we've learned.

- It is important to learn how (not) to study the Bible so when we see the many confusing and disturbing Bible verses, we won't be caught off-guard.
- Knowing the Bible storyline is so important to understanding the Bible. This storyline tells of God's creating the universe and human beings so he can dwell among us and be in relationship with us. The Bible begins and ends with the beautiful fact that God loves us as his children and wants us to be in his presence. (Note: it would be helpful to memorize the Bible storyline and be able to draw its six acts.)
- The majority of Bible verses that are pointed out today as disturbing or crazy are ones that are taken out of context and have reasonable explanations for them.
- Whenever we read the Bible, we should keep in mind these four key principles:
    1) The Bible is a library, not a book.
    2) The Bible was written for us, but not to us.
    3) Never read a Bible verse.
    4) All the Bible points to Jesus.

Knowing these four concepts provides a foundation for interpretation. In the remaining sections of this book, we'll look directly at several of the more crazy-sounding passages. And as we do this, we'll return to these four foundational principles.

PART 2

Stranger Things

SHRIMP, SLAVERY, AND THE

SKIN OF A DEAD PIG

CHAPTER 4

Strange and Stranger Things in the Old Testament

> Christians be like, God bless this pork that you commanded us not to eat.
>
> —ONLINE MEME

A popular national television show that won three Golden Globe Awards and twenty-six primetime Emmy Awards has an episode where a lead character, the president of the United States, confronts a Christian radio host.[1] The president, to demonstrate the irrelevance of the Bible, recites Bible verses, concluding with a confident speech to a room full of people. After quoting several Bible verses, he says, "I'm interested in selling my youngest daughter into slavery as sanctioned in Exodus 21:7. She's a Georgetown sophomore, speaks fluent Italian, always cleaned the table when it was her turn. What would a good price for her be?"

Does the Bible really condone selling your daughter into slavery? Exodus 21:7 says, "If a man sells his daughter as a servant, she is not to go free as male servants do." This is not the only passage like this. Several verses in the Old Testament and a few in the New Testament seem to endorse slavery. Is that true?

QUESTION: DOES THE BIBLE ALLOW YOU TO
SELL YOUR DAUGHTER INTO SLAVERY?

The actor portraying the president continues confidently quoting several Bible verses. Then he sarcastically asks questions to prove his point, that the Bible is out of date and makes all sorts of irrelevant and ridiculous statements.

We've looked at one of these references already, the question about playing football. Here he quotes Leviticus 11:7 and says, "Here's one that's really important, 'cause we've got a lot of sports fans in this town. Touching the skin of a dead pig makes one unclean, Leviticus 11:7. If they promise to wear gloves, can the Washington Redskins still play football? Can Notre Dame? Can West Point?"

When you look up Leviticus 11:7–8 it does say, "And the pig, though it has a divided hoof, does not chew the cud; it is unclean for you. You must not eat their meat or touch their carcasses; they are unclean for you." His point is to show that the Bible commands weird and unusual things that no one follows or obeys today. If they did, and the Bible clearly says not to touch a pig's skin, how can anyone play football, since a football is (he assumes) made from the skin of a pig?

4.2

QUESTION: DOES THE BIBLE SAY NOT TO
PLAY FOOTBALL? OR NOT TO EAT PORK?

The president continues his line of questioning, "Does the whole town really have to be together to stone my brother, John, for planting different crops side by side?"

"Can I burn my mother at a small family gathering for wearing garments made from two different threads?"

Both of these statements refer to Deuteronomy 22:9, 11, "Do not plant two kinds of seed in your vineyard; if you do, not only the crops you plant but also the fruit of the vineyard will be defiled. . . . Do not wear clothes of wool and linen woven together."

QUESTION: DOES THE BIBLE PROHIBIT PLANTING TWO DIFFERENT TYPES OF PLANTS TOGETHER IN THE SAME GARDEN AND EVEN HAVE THE DEATH PENALTY IF YOU DO?

QUESTION: DOES THE BIBLE PROHIBIT WEARING CLOTHING MADE OF TWO DIFFERENT FABRICS?

The scene ends with a clear message: the Bible is foolish, primitive, and disturbing. And anyone who believes it is a fool or a hypocrite. The Christian radio host doesn't know how to answer these questions, so she remains silent. Viewers are left with one conclusion—these bizarre and strange Bible verses have no explanation. Perhaps the Bible is crazy, outdated, and barbaric, and anyone who takes it seriously probably is crazy too.[2]

God Hates Shrimp, Yet Likes Slavery

Let's consider another strange Bible law, again from the book of Leviticus in the Old Testament. This one says we shouldn't eat shrimp. There are plenty of memes online quoting Leviticus 11:9–11: "'Of all the creatures living in the water of the seas and the streams you may eat any that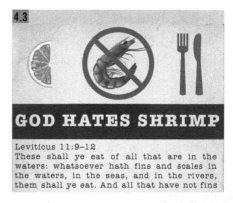

GOD HATES SHRIMP

Leviticus 11:9-12
These shall ye eat of all that are in the waters: whatsoever hath fins and scales in the waters, in the seas, and in the rivers, them shall ye eat. And all that have not fins

have fins and scales. But all creatures in the seas or streams that do not have fins and scales—whether among all the swarming things or among all the other living creatures in the water—you are to regard as unclean.

63

And since you are to regard them as unclean, you must not eat their meat; you must regard their carcasses as unclean."

Based on a plain reading of these Bible verses, a critic will argue that God doesn't want us to eat shrimp or lobster. God hates shrimp! When you say it this way, it sounds foolish and silly. This is one of many verses pulled from the Bible (often Old Testament laws) and used to degrade the credibility of the Bible in general. Verses like this are used to argue that Christians don't know their Bibles and the crazy things the Bible says (which often is true). Or they are used to illustrate how Christians pick and choose the Bible verses they like to back their political or ethical opinions while ignoring other Bible verses (like these). The goal is to demonstrate that the Bible is an archaic book filled with crazy sayings to discredit anything the Bible says.

Things the Bible bans

There are popular YouTube videos, blogs, and articles with titles like "Thirteen Weird Things the Bible Bans You May Not Know About" or "Eleven Things the Bible Bans but You Do Anyway" or "Seven Shocking Bible Verses You Won't Hear in Church." These often have similar lists of things that the Bible allegedly prohibits along with the Bible verse that says it. Here are some examples:

- Eating shrimp or lobster (Leviticus 11:10).
- Eating pork (Leviticus 11:7).
- Blending two types of fabric, such as a polyester blend (Leviticus 19:19).
- Getting a tattoo (Leviticus 19:28).
- Not getting rounded haircuts (Leviticus 19:27).

To the average person today, these all appear to be random things, and we naturally wonder why the Bible says these are off-limits. How do we make sense of these prohibitions?

QUESTION: DOES GOD SAY TATTOOS ARE WRONG? OR
GETTING A BOWL-CUT BEATLES-LIKE HAIRCUT?

Even if we are tempted to shrug aside the Bible's ban on things like tattoos, certain haircut styles, and eating shrimp, it's difficult to ignore something like slavery. Why does the Bible ban these things and then seem to advocate for an evil like slavery? Earlier, we read a verse that seems to give guidance on how a father can sell his daughter as property. And there are other verses, like Exodus 21:20–21, which says, "Anyone who beats their male or female slave with a rod must be punished if the slave dies as a direct result, but they are not to be punished if the slave recovers after a day or two, since the slave is their property."

This is clearly wrong, yet the Bible seems to indicate it is okay to beat a slave as long as the slave doesn't die. The allowance, and perhaps promotion, of slavery invites understandable anger. Atheist groups have rented billboards citing Bible verses from both the Old and New Testaments to suggest the Bible is pro-slavery. All of this makes the Bible seem crazy-sounding and evil. How do we make sense of any of this?

My Very Purple Bible

The underlying question behind the questions we've been asking is this: is the Bible credible and trustworthy? I would not want to be guided by a book that isn't true, nor would I spend time trying to convince others to follow a book filled with lies and false "truths." One of the reasons I've written this book is because I believe the Bible is true, and I believe there are reasonable answers and responses to each of these questions. It just takes some effort to read beyond the surface.

As I read, I love to mark up my Bible and write notes. I draw sketches and underline words. I use colored pencils, and I have developed a color code for how I underline. Anything that is positive, encouraging, or something to remember I underline in blue. A Bible verse that is more of a warning or something I should pay attention to, I underline in red. Something theological I underline in yellow. Something about prophecy I underline in green. The weird and strange stuff I underline in purple.

If you were to scan the pages of my Bible you'd see a heck of a lot of purple in it.

There are verses like the ones we've read that seem to approve of slavery, polygamy, killing birds to cure mold, bloody rituals, and extreme violence that involves the killing of both people and animals. Almost every other page has something purple, especially in the Old Testament.

Yet as much purple as there is, I still fully believe and trust in what the Bible teaches. When you dive in and look beneath the surface, even a strange or off-putting verse begins to make sense. Remember, "Never read a Bible verse." We have to do the hard work of understanding the full context, and that's what we'll do as we more closely examine questions about shrimp, the skin of a dead pig, and slavery.

CHAPTER 5

The Art of (Not) Cherry-Picking Bible Verses

Have you ever looked into some of the strange and unusual state laws in the United States? Several of these are still in the law books today and have never been repealed.

In Arizona: It is illegal for a donkey to sleep in a bathtub.

In Kentucky: It is illegal to carry ice cream in your back pocket.

In Connecticut: It is illegal

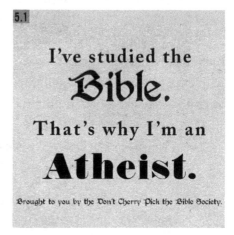

for any beautician or barber to whistle, hum, or sing while working on a customer.

Reading these nonsensical laws makes you wonder why they were ever passed in the first place. Who needs a law about carrying ice cream in your back pocket? Bizarre laws about donkeys sleeping in bathtubs seem pretty ridiculous to us. But when you look into the history behind them, there is always a backstory, and that backstory provides us with meaning. Knowing why they were originally put in place and when is the key to understanding.

For example, the law about not allowing a donkey to sleep in a bathtub was put into effect in 1924. The story is that a rancher had a donkey that frequently slept in an abandoned bathtub on the rancher's property. One day, a local dam broke, and the water from the reservoir washed the bathtub and the donkey into a basin. Local authorities were called to help rescue the donkey, but it was not easy to do. It required a lot of effort and manpower to finally rescue the animal. To prevent such a thing from ever happening again, they passed a law that prohibited donkeys from sleeping in bathtubs. At that time, for those involved, it made sense to have that law. It was likely never prosecuted, but it was put in place for a reason at a certain time for a certain purpose, a purpose most of us cannot relate to today, since few of us own a donkey.

The law against carrying ice cream in your pocket was originally passed to prevent horse theft. At the time it was passed, if you carried an ice cream cone in your pocket and walked by a horse, the horse would likely follow you because horses like sweet things. The horse would leave its owner and end up belonging to someone else. So a law was passed to ban ice cream cones in pockets as a way of preventing horse theft. It sounds crazy, but it made sense at that time. Apparently, having ice cream in your back pocket could make you a horse thief.

Strange Things from God That Are Confusing, Embarrassing, and Seem Anti-Jesus

For many people today, reading Bible verses with strange and even horrifying laws and commands can be confusing and even upsetting.

Some verses make no sense to us or even seem contrary to what we imagine God to be like. Since so many verses like this are from the early Old Testament books of the Bible, such as Exodus, Leviticus, and Deuteronomy, we need to look at what was happening in those books more specifically. To apply the principles from the first section, we need to never read a Bible verse and remember that the Bible was written for us, but not to us. Starting with these two principles, we'll take a look at few details that can make a major difference in making sense of verses about eating shrimp or wearing two types of fabric or touching a football.

Who Were These Bible Verses Written To?

In the examples of United States laws about donkeys and bathtubs and ice cream cones in back pockets, the first step in understanding them is looking at the backstory. So let's apply the same approach to the laws that prohibit shrimp, blends of fabric, and football.

Who were these Bible verses written to? The ancient Israelites.

Many of the verses we've mentioned come from the books of Exodus and Leviticus in the Old Testament. The original recipients of these books, the ancient Israelites, lived approximately 3,500 years ago. These weren't written to us, nor were they written to answer the kinds of questions we tend to ask today. Each book of the Bible was written to a specific group of people in a specific place, and by looking at our Bible timeline from part 1, we can place where these laws fit into the bigger story.

The books of Exodus and Leviticus were written to the Israelites after God rescued them from four hundred years of slavery in Egypt. While we don't know the specific dates these events took place, we know it happened roughly between 1550 and 1069 BC. For those four centuries, the people lived in a land where many different gods and goddesses were worshiped. God now was leading them from Egypt into the "promised land" where God would build his temple, where King David would rule, and through David's lineage the Savior of the world, Jesus, would eventually be born.

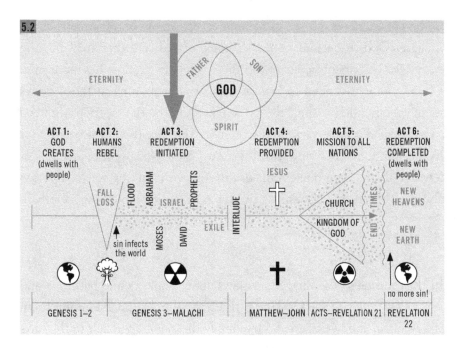

In God's long-term plans, there was an important future for the people of Israel, through whom the entire world would be blessed.

As God was leading Israel out of Egypt into the new land, they encountered the surrounding people groups who worshiped other gods and goddesses and practiced all kinds of evil things: degrading sexual rites, family members serving in prostitution, and offerings of child sacrifice. God did not want Israel to become like the other countries, so he had Moses write down loving guidelines and restrictions to keep them separate and distinct from the other nations. God didn't want the Israelites to pattern their lives after the people who worshiped and followed different gods.

In the first five books of the Bible, God instructed Moses to write down the history of the origin of the Israelite people to teach them it was God who created everything, not the gods of Egypt or other gods. He was making it clear that he is the one true God, and the other gods and goddesses of Egypt were not to be believed or worshiped. He was giving the Israelites instruction for how to relate to each other and how to worship and relate to him.

God wanted them to be holy, distinct from the people groups who lived around them. The word "holy" means set apart, separated, and kept away from the evil and false worship of the neighboring nations. God was concerned that they would be too easily influenced by the surrounding people groups and turn away from him to worship and follow other gods (which, sadly, they did at times despite God's warnings).

However, all these laws that God gave the Israelites were not intended to simply establish an ideal social system. It was God speaking into their ancient world and instructing them with codes of wisdom for them to know what living in the presence of God is like. So he used many things familiar to them in the ancient world, which are unfamiliar to us today.

This background provides some of the context for the crazy verses we find in Leviticus and Deuteronomy. Repeatedly, God warns the Israelites not to compromise and become like the people living around them:

- "Do not bow down before their gods or worship them or follow their practices."*
- "Do not let them live in your land or they will cause you to sin against me, because the worship of their gods will certainly be a snare to you."†
- "Be careful not to make a treaty with those who live in the land; for when they prostitute themselves to their gods and sacrifice to them, they will invite you and you will eat their sacrifices. And when you choose some of their daughters as wives for your sons and those daughters prostitute themselves to their gods, they will lead your sons to do the same."‡

This backstory provides a starting point for looking more closely at the Bible verses we've read from Exodus and Leviticus, the ones that

---

* Exodus 23:24.
† Exodus 23:33.
‡ Exodus 34:15–16.

sound so crazy to us. Let's try to understand them through the lens of who they were originally written to and why.

Why Couldn't They Plant Two Types of Crops Together or Wear Two Fabrics Back Then?

In the last chapter, we looked at a verse that gives some pretty extreme punishments for planting different crops side by side or for wearing garments made with two types of fabric. Here it is again from Deuteronomy 22:9–11: "Do not plant two kinds of seed in your vineyard; if you do, not only the crops you plant but also the fruit of the vineyard will be defiled. Do not plow with an ox and a donkey yoked together. Do not wear clothes of wool and linen woven together."

There is a similar verse in Leviticus 19:19. The book of Leviticus is where most of the strange verses appear, and it's important to understand that this book is more or less an instruction manual written for the priests and the people. Why is God repeatedly telling them not to mix two different kinds of things? God is wanting them to remain holy, set apart from the other people living around them so they don't practice horrible things. If you study the practices of the surrounding people groups, those who worship false gods, they would intentionally mix two things together as part of their worship. Some scholars believe that the Canaanites, who were living in the land at the time, had a magical practice of "wedding" different seeds together to have offspring in an attempt to conjure up fertile crops.[1] There is a strong likelihood that the prohibitions against mixing different kinds of seeds, animals, and materials together were designed to discourage and prevent the Israelites from imitating the fertility cult practices of the Canaanites. This wasn't gardening advice or a set of random, pointless rules. It was a very specific way for God to tell his people, the ones he rescued from slavery in Egypt, that they were not to be like the other people living around them. They were not to participate in fertility rites patterned after the worship rituals of false gods.

When you look at the restrictions about not mixing fabrics for clothing, you find that the priests' garments and the fabrics used in the tabernacle of that time (the tabernacle was the place of worship prior to the temple) were made of wool and linen—two different types of material. Only priests could wear this type of blended fabric for clothing. This may sound strange to us today, but think of someone who isn't a police officer making and wearing a police uniform, pretending to be a police officer. The restrictions regarding clothing weren't just fashion preferences or style choices. They were requirements distinguishing what a priest would wear when leading the people in worship of their holy God.

These restrictions about plants and clothing actually have a good rationale behind them. God wanted his people to have a distinct identity, to remain holy, and to not imitate the fertility rites of the neighboring countries. God was providing a foundation and a structure for the roles of worship leaders by making them distinct from the people. He wanted them to be reminded that this was a new era for them, and they were not to mimic or imitate the worship practices of those around them. It may still sound crazy to us, but we don't live in that time period, and we aren't bound by these laws. (Later we'll examine why these particular laws are no longer valid.) What matters is that the laws had a purpose and a meaning for the people at that time.

Why Not Eat Shrimp, Touch a Pigskin, and Cook a Goat in Its Mother's Milk?

Another set of Bible verses talk about not eating shellfish. Leviticus 11:9–11 says not to eat shellfish, which includes not eating shrimp. But why would this be a command in the Bible? What we have here are dietary laws and restrictions that lay out what are called clean and unclean foods. The dietary laws God gave to the Israelites did more than specify shellfish like shrimp; they also included prohibitions against eating pork and many other types of seafood, most insects, scavenger birds, and various other animals. All of this sounds strange to us, but why did God do this at that time?

One possible rationale for these foods being restricted is for general health reasons. This was a pre-scientific era, and God may have been protecting his people from potential sickness and harm. As we know today, shrimp are filter-feeders prone to containing live bacteria if eaten uncooked. The same is true for pork and several other meats—if you don't cook them well, you can get pretty sick. That's one possibility. But most likely, the restrictions were about more than just healthy living. Most scholars agree that God gave the dietary laws to reinforce the same concept we discussed before—keeping the people distinct and separate from the other people groups. One of the most practical ways to make this distinction is by making their diet—the food they could and could not eat—distinct. The reason is the same: God wants his people to remain loyal to him, the one true God. Every time we read about God giving a strange instruction about refraining from something, a command that sounds bizarre to us today, we need to remember that it wouldn't have sounded bizarre to the people at that time. These restrictions were common ways of identifying your ethnicity and religious affiliation. The restrictions may not make sense to us, but they were normal for the Israelites at that time in history.

5.3

AMAZING NONSENSE IN THE BIBLE

"Do not cook a young goat in its mother's milk!"
- Exodus 23:19

Still, even with this understanding, there are occasionally some extra-weird restrictions. A very odd verse in Exodus 23:19, repeated in Deuteronomy 14:21, says, "Do not cook a young goat in its mother's milk."

What a bizarre thing to have in the Bible. I found a series of online memes called "Amazing Nonsense in the Bible," and this was one of the verses cited. I found another meme where someone asked the question, "What is the most weird $$## up verse in the Bible you can find?" The answer: a drawing of a goat being boiled in milk—Exodus 23:19.

Although this verse seems extremely bizarre to us, back at the time when it was written, it would not have been all that strange to hear. The ancient Israelites would have known what that meant because it was specifically talking about their world and customs. There is one theory that this could be referring to a Canaanite custom of boiling a kid goat (a baby goat) in its mother's milk as a worship ritual. It was something like a lucky fertility charm.[2] The people believed that boiling the baby goat in its mother's milk would appease their gods and give them bountiful growth for their livestock.

So one possible reason why God gave this instruction is because he wanted the ancient Israelites to understand that what is holy must be kept separate from what is unclean or ordinary. The nation of Israel must be separate from other nations. To participate in a Canaanite fertility worship ritual would be to violate God's holiness and invoke other gods. Also, God may have wanted the Israelites to keep the opposites of life and death distinct. A mother's milk is a life-sustaining force that must not be used to flavor the younger animal after death.[3]

Further thoughts: although sacrificing animals was commonplace in that world, using a goat in this way was very different. A goat is the animal God chose for the Israelites to use in the sacred act of atonement, an annual ritual asking God to forgive their sin. The goat, especially, was not to be used to imitate what other people groups were doing as a religious offering to other gods. Some also believe that the practice itself was morally wrong, an affront to God's created purposes. It involved taking the milk God intended to give life to the animal and instead using it to kill the goat in a torturous way.

Whatever the reasons for the prohibition, this act, which sounds strange to us, had a deeper meaning for the ancient Israelites. What looks like a bizarre command to us actually would have been significant to an ancient Israelite. But we are now in post-Jesus times and we are no longer under the laws of the Israelites (more on this in the next chapter), and we also aren't dealing with neighbors who boil goats in their mothers' milk and we aren't interested in imitating their practice, so we do not have to worry about this instruction.

Touching the Skin of a Dead Pig and Playing Football

I hope that by this point you see a pattern emerging as we look at the context for one verse after another. We can keep doing this, verse after verse. Consider Leviticus 11:7–8, which instructs the Israelites to not touch the skin of a dead pig. During that time period, surrounding people groups consumed pigs for food. Pigs also were part of the rituals of these religions and closely tied to their gods of the netherworld. The likely reason God gave these restrictions to the Israelites was to remind them each day that they were distinct from other people groups who worshiped other gods. From our standpoint today, the laws don't make sense and we aren't being asked to obey them, but to the Israelites at that time, they would have. They would have known the practices of other people groups, and through repetition and the application of the laws to every area of life—food, clothing, relationships—God was instructing them to remain distinct and holy as they entered the promised land.

As we saw in the last chapter, this verse is often used in a mocking way to imply that Christians shouldn't play football if they want to obey the Bible. Yet footballs are not made of actual pigskin, despite the "pigskin" nickname. Pro and collegiate footballs are made with cowhide leather, while others are often made with synthetic material or vulcanized rubber. In fact, football exteriors were never made of pigskin. They got the nickname "pigskin" because in years past, the bladder of a pig or another animal was inflated to use as the inner part of the ball. The pig bladder was wrapped in some form of leather, often deer or cowhide. The football was nicknamed "pigskin" because of the pig bladder inside. The use of pig bladders in footballs was stopped in the late 1800s. Today we use only cowhide and various forms of rubber to make footballs.

We should not assume that those criticizing the Bible have done their homework to discover the why and the backstory. This particular error was missed in the writing and approval of the script for a Grammy award-winning television series viewed by millions of people. It gave incorrect facts about the pigskin in general.

An even bigger problem is the one we'll examine in the next chapter: these laws don't apply to us any longer. They never did. They were meant for a specific group of people, in a specific place, for a specific time period, which has long since ended. Even if footballs were made of pigskin, we could touch them as much as we want without offending God or breaking his laws.

When someone quotes Leviticus to say that Christians shouldn't eat shrimp, or when we see "God hates shrimp" memes, or someone questions why Christians wear polyester blends, what should be obvious is a lack of understanding of the Bible. Using these verses to mock the Bible's validity simply shows that the person doing the mocking doesn't understand what the Bible is saying.

The truth is that Christians today can enjoy shrimp all they want. They can wear all types of mixed fabrics. They can play football. Why? Because those Bible verses were written to a specific people group, in a specific place, for a specific time period, and for a specific purpose. When you study the entire Bible (rather than picking and choosing individual verses), you see that many of these verses don't apply to followers of Jesus today. Using them in the way these memes do or as an attempt to discredit the Bible simply shows us how *not* to read the Bible.

Crazy Bible Verses Are Often Crazy for a Non-crazy Reason

Television shows like the one I mentioned, along with the hundreds of memes filled with Bible quotes about not eating shrimp, are attempting to convince us the Bible is irrelevant for us today. Sadly, they do this by misusing and misunderstanding the Bible. When someone isn't familiar with the Bible, these claims can be very convincing. For Christians who aren't aware of these passages or don't think much about them, the criticism comes across as convincing or at least confusing. These attacks allege that Christians are hypocrites when they choose to follow some parts of the Bible but not others.

But as we have seen, when you know the Bible story and where these verses fit into that larger story, all these arguments evaporate. Yes, God gave some rather strange laws, by today's standards. But the ancient Israelites to whom the laws were written would have been fully aware of what God was doing. It wouldn't have sounded strange and bizarre to them.

If These Laws Were Only for Israel at the Time, Do They Apply to Us Today?

As we've learned, these verses were not written to us, but for us. Does this mean that all the instruction in the Law (Genesis, Exodus, Leviticus, Numbers, and Deuteronomy) is no longer valid for us today? What about verses like "You shall not murder" in Exodus 20:13 or "You shall not steal" in Exodus 20:15? Does this mean that because the ban on eating shrimp isn't valid for today, we can steal because the "You shall not steal" commandment is no longer valid either? We'll look at these questions, as well as the issue of slavery in the Bible, in the next chapter.

These verses are just a few samples. There are many other strange things (by our standards) in this section of the Bible. I didn't mention verses that talk about not cutting your hair on the sides of your head and not trimming your beard (Leviticus 19:27), or not eating fat (Leviticus 7:23), or not cursing your mother or father or you will die (Leviticus 20:9).[4] Or what about the story where Moses takes the blood of a ram and puts it on the right earlobe of a priest, on his right thumb, and on the big toe of his right foot (Leviticus 8:23–24)? As you might guess, each of these verses has a backstory and a clear reason. For this book, I simply want to lay out a few examples so you understand how to begin making sense of them.

I close with a popular verse that affects many people today: Don't get a tattoo (Leviticus 19:28). The full Bible verse reads, "Do not cut your bodies for the dead or put tattoo marks on yourselves. I am the LORD." The Bible isn't speaking about our practice of contemporary tattooing, which involves injecting ink under the skin to form permanent images.

Today's tattoos involve artwork and are typically done for personal creative expression.

Leviticus wasn't talking about tattoos like these. Instead—no surprise here—God was keeping his people from participating in the religious practices of the neighboring Canaanites. They would slash their bodies and mark them with branding or ink for ritualistic purposes related to the worship of their gods. Tattooing and the marking of the body was a rite for honoring their gods and the dead. God was prohibiting worship practices related to false deities. Today's tattoos are nothing like the practices being prohibited in Leviticus, so there is no restriction on getting a tattoo today. That said, the larger story of the Bible teaches us that we should not find our personal sense of worth from our appearance or achievements, so if this is why we are getting tattoos, it would go against Jesus and his teachings.

Why Cherry-Picking Is a Smart Thing to Do

In the next chapter, we'll look more closely at why these verses—which were specifically written to Israel—aren't verses we need to follow today. We'll address the accusation that Christians "cherry-pick" the Bible, choosing to follow and affirm the nice verses they agree with while ignoring verses that are odd or confusing. The meme in image 5.4 is an example of this common criticism. Under the headline "Cherry Picking," it reads, "If a Bible verse doesn't support how I feel I'll ignore it and find one that does."

5.4

CHERRY PICKING

IF A BIBLE VERSE DOESN'T SUPPORT HOW I FEEL
I'LL IGNORE IT AND FIND ONE THAT DOES

Cherry-picking from the Bible is not good if we are affirming only the things we like. However, we need to do some strategic cherry-picking. The truth is that there are good reasons—not just our personal preferences—why some Bible verses should be followed while others should not be. Proper cherry-picking is required when you follow good Bible-study methods.

If you had an actual cherry tree, you would want to learn how to be a good cherry picker. You would pay attention to the entire tree and the season of the year. When it's time for cherry-picking, you would pay attention to the color of the fruit. If the cherries aren't dark enough, they aren't ripe. If you pick them too soon, they won't have the sugar that sweetens them. Some might be old and have bugs, so you don't want to eat those. Knowing when to pick and what to look for is important when harvesting cherries. You "cherry-pick" some and leave others on the branches that aren't meant to be picked yet. There's nothing wrong with this since you want to get cherries that are good to eat.

Yes, there is bad Bible cherry-picking, ignoring verses because of a personal preference. Done right, you determine which "cherries" (verses) are for consumption today and which ones aren't.

CHAPTER 6

Making Sense of Shrimp, the Skin of a Dead Pig, and Slavery

Do your best to present yourself to God as one approved, a worker who does not need to be ashamed and who correctly handles the word of truth.

—2 TIMOTHY 2:15

We have seen how crazy-sounding Bible verses all have backstories that help us better understand what they meant to the people at the time they were given. God didn't want them to do certain things, practices that could have compromised their faith in God. But what about something that is not a prohibition, but more of an endorsement, such as the practice of slavery? Why did God allow some things and not others back in Old Testament times? What should we be doing today?

Why Do We Follow Some Commands but Not Others?

If we believe some laws were specific for Israel and they made sense back then, why do we not still follow them today? Many of the verses we studied in the last chapter are found in the same books where it says

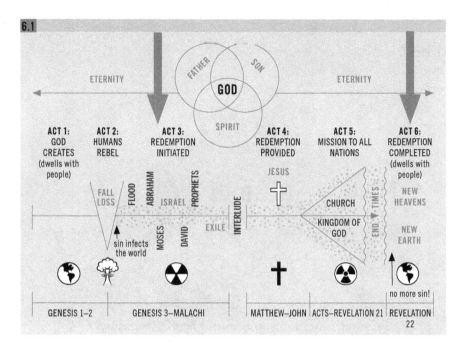

6.1

ETERNITY	ETERNITY
GOD	

ACT 1: GOD CREATES (dwells with people)
ACT 2: HUMANS REBEL
ACT 3: REDEMPTION INITIATED
ACT 4: REDEMPTION PROVIDED
ACT 5: MISSION TO ALL NATIONS
ACT 6: REDEMPTION COMPLETED (dwells with people)

FATHER — SON — SPIRIT

FALL LOSS · FLOOD · ABRAHAM · ISRAEL · PROPHETS · MOSES · DAVID · EXILE · INTERLUDE
sin infects the world

JESUS
CHURCH
KINGDOM OF GOD
END TIMES
NEW HEAVENS
NEW EARTH
no more sin!

GENESIS 1–2 | GENESIS 3–MALACHI | MATTHEW–JOHN | ACTS–REVELATION 21 | REVELATION 22

"You shall not murder" and "You shall not steal."* How do we know what is valid for today and what isn't? The answer to these questions takes us back to the Bible storyline.

In the Bible storyline (6.1), the arrow on the left points to "Moses." This is approximately the time when these Bible verses were first given to the ancient Israelites, around 1350 BC. God was instructing the Israelites on how to follow him and remain holy as they were entering a land inhabited by people groups who worshiped other gods. The larger arrow jumps to where we are today, almost 3,500 years later, to the place labeled "church." When Jesus came, everything changed, and from the time of Jesus onward, we have to look at everything in the Bible through a new lens of interpretation. In the Old Testament, we see God relating to people one way. In the New Testament we have a new covenant with God through Jesus, a new way for human beings to relate to God.

The New Testament writings tell us that the strange-sounding verses

---

* Exodus 20:13–15.

we've read—and all the rest of the 613 different Old Testament laws—were given to convict people everywhere of our inability to follow all that God requires for us to worship him and live in perfect harmony with him and one another. This inability is due to our imperfection and the fallout of sin, and it points us to our need for a Savior. We all fail trying to please God on our own, and this becomes clear as we look at his guidelines. We will never be able to be perfect or to remain constantly holy and set apart from the values of the world. Because of this, we ultimately need a way of being clean before God and forgiven for our shortcomings. This is why Jesus came.

The Old Testament and all the things written in this first section of the Bible point us to our full need for Jesus (Romans 7:7–9; Galatians 3:24). When Jesus came and died on the cross and rose again, it revealed a major shift in how we relate to God, and we see this change reflected in the teachings of the New Testament, which give us new guidelines.

A new covenant, or arrangement between God and people, began. This new covenant is not limited to a particular people group. Now all can have forgiveness and be seen as holy and set apart by God, not through what we do, but through what Jesus did. We are set apart by putting our faith in Jesus, and this changes how the laws of the Old Testament function for those who follow Jesus.

The Old Testament is still extremely important for us today. By reading it, we learn who God is and all he did in times past, as well as our origins and why and how Jesus came. It's necessary for followers of Jesus to know and study the Old Testament. But we need to also understand why we apply or don't apply specific worship practices and dietary and civil laws today. We are now in a "post-Jesus" time period in the storyline, and the way God related to people "pre-Jesus" is different than the way God relates to us "post-Jesus."

"Post-Jesus" there is no longer a need to sacrifice animals, like the Israelites did, to show our faith and devotion to God because Jesus was the final sacrifice for all people. There is no longer a need for the temple, as God's Spirit now dwells in those who put their faith in Jesus. Collectively and individually, followers of Jesus are the "temple." There is no longer a need to be bound to the "law" (the section that contains the Bible verses we've been looking at) because Jesus started a new covenant with God, and his followers follow the writings of this new covenant, the New Testament.

All of this reading about an old covenant and a new covenant as well as sacrifices and the law of Moses can be confusing. I don't want to oversimplify this, but perhaps image 6.2 will help.

All the crazy things we've looked at fall under "Old Testament law" and were needed for their time to help the people of God know who he is and how to live with each other. Some of the laws were to show the Israelites how to worship God, and they involved a sacrificial system with some strange-sounding worship rituals. Some of these were intended to keep the Israelites distinct from other people groups who lived around them. None of these Old Testament laws are still binding on Christians today. We live in a different time period now that Jesus has come.

When Jesus came, there was something of a reboot, a fulfillment and expansion of the Old Testament that introduced a new and better way

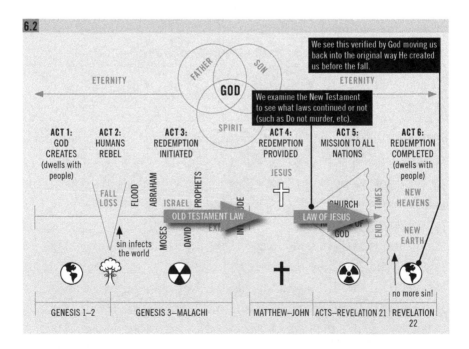

for us to relate to God. This was taught by Jesus and his followers, as we read in the New Testament. When Jesus died on the cross, he put an end to the Old Testament law and introduced a new law called the "law of Christ."* For those who want to dig deeper, you can read about this shift in Galatians 3:23–24; 6:2; and 1 Corinthians 9:21.

In image 6.2, you can see the Old Testament law arrow ending on the timeline. It stops with Jesus' death and resurrection, which means all the strange dietary laws and bizarre worship rituals and sacrifices and rules ended and are no longer required today. But then a new arrow starts with Jesus, signifying the beginning of the new law, the one we are to obey today, the law of Jesus.

What is the law of Jesus? Jesus taught that the greatest commands from the Old Testament were to "Love the Lord your God with all your heart and with all your soul and with all your mind. . . . And . . . Love your neighbor as yourself."† If we obey these two commands, we are fulfilling what God required of his people, the goal or ultimate reason why he gave them laws in the first place. As Jesus said, "All the Law and the Prophets hang on these two commandments."‡

Defining Love for God and Others through the New Testament

This means that if we want to follow Jesus, we should pour ourselves into looking into the New Testament to discover what this "love" looks like. Sometimes people will say, "I only want to focus on the greatest commandments, to love God and love others." Which is wonderful, but what does that mean? I've met people who will say this and then define what that "love" looks like according to their own personal feelings rather than a study of the New Testament teaching. There is a danger in defining love on our own terms or by our own cultural values, as we can be deceived into thinking that we are loving God and others as God would want us

---

*   Romans 10:4; Galatians 3:23–25; Ephesians 2:15.
†   Matthew 22:37–39.
‡   Matthew 22:40.

to, when we're really just doing what we want. The actions that define love differ from culture to culture. What makes our personal sense of "love" better than that of another culture or time? The solution to this problem is to study what God guided the New Testament writers to say about loving God with all our heart, mind, and strength and loving our neighbor as ourselves. How does God define love?

That's one of the primary reasons God gave us the New Testament, all twenty-seven books and letters, in its own section of our Bible library. We'll want to look at the words of Jesus in the first four books of the New Testament (the Gospels). But we will also need to study the rest of the New Testament to fully grasp what it means to love God and love others. Without the rest of the New Testament, we would miss a great deal of the how and why of what it means to love others. The entire New Testament more clearly defines the love God requires of us and what our lives should look like if we want to love God. The whole of the New Testament describes what it means to follow Jesus and the commands we should obey for moral and ethical living, including what it looks like to love other people.

Just as in Old Testament times, when it was tempting for Israel to adopt the worship practices, morals, and ethics of the neighboring people groups, we must resist that temptation as well. The people of God in Old Testament times broke their covenant with God by allowing cultural pressure to influence them in ways contrary to God's laws. Today, we no longer rely on the laws God established with Israel in the "pre-Jesus" time period to define our distinct identity as God's people. We look to what God established for the "post-Jesus" time period. The New Testament tells us what it means to love God with our whole lives and outlines the morals, ethics, and guidelines for life and worship that God wants us to follow today.

The New Testament Is a Fresh Start with God, but We Don't Dismiss the Old

When Jesus came as a descendant of Abraham, he taught that he was here to "fulfill" the requirements and the purpose of the law. This might sound like he was erasing the Old Testament laws, rituals, and dietary restrictions and starting over from scratch. But that's not what happened. There are some things God established in the Old Testament that continue with Jesus in the New Testament, and there are some things that came to an end. The simplest way to know what continues and what doesn't is to read the New Testament to see what was explicitly carried on from the Old Testament and what wasn't. Things like Old Testament dietary restrictions on eating shrimp and pork aren't continued in the New Testament. One reason is that Jesus declared that all foods are now "clean."*

Another example is from the apostle Paul, when he is writing to a young leader of the church discussing people putting restrictions on marriage or food. Paul writes, "For everything God created is good, and nothing is to be rejected if it is received with thanksgiving, because it is consecrated by the word of God and prayer."† Paul is saying that food is good. He affirms that the mark of being set apart is a heart grateful to God, not dietary restrictions. Those restrictions were necessary for a time to help the people understand they were different from the other peoples, but they were pointing to the ultimate mark of being different—gratitude and thanksgiving to God.

What about clothing and the restrictions against wearing two types of fabrics? If you look at the "post-Jesus" New Testament writings, you don't see anything that restricts the type of fabric used in our clothing, since clothing is no longer a marker of a special role or relationship with God (as it was with the priests of the Old Testament). Instead, the New Testament directs us to be modest in what we wear.‡ It doesn't specify types of materials since we aren't dealing with the context of ancient Israel. We also don't have to worry about not cooking a goat in its mother's milk (although I am sure that would get you arrested for animal cruelty if you tried it). These were laws regarding the specific practices of competing faiths, and we don't see the New Testament continuing these prohibitions.

---

*   See Mark 7:17–23.
†   1 Timothy 4:4–5.
‡   1 Peter 3:2–5; 1 Timothy 2:9–10.

The New Testament Reveals Which Old Testament Guidelines Continue

However, not everything is dismissed from the laws of the Old Testament. Many of the moral, or nonceremonial, laws continue and are reinforced in the New Testament. For instance, the Old Testament says, "You shall not murder," and that doesn't come to an end in the New Testament. Many moral commands like these are repeated or affirmed in the New Testament. Jesus expands on many of the moral laws to clarify and strengthen their importance. He affirms what the Old Testament says about not murdering, but he draws attention to the underlying hatred that motivates murder, saying that "murdering" or hating someone in your heart is on par with physical murder in God's eyes. Jesus is concerned with our hearts, so he teaches the importance of looking behind the actions themselves to examine the motive or desire behind the action. Dietary laws and ritual instructions on how to worship God have changed, but most of the moral instructions on relationships and how to properly love others remain, even intensifying in their demands on us.

Here is a helpful summary from author Tim Keller of the change that occurred with Jesus and how we can know which Old Testament laws have continued in the teaching of the New Testament (and apply to us today):

> In short, *the coming of Christ changed how we worship, but not how we live*. The moral law outlines God's own character—his integrity, love, and faithfulness. And so everything the Old Testament says about loving our neighbor, caring for the poor, generosity with our possessions, social relationships, and commitment to our family is still in force. The New Testament continues to forbid killing or committing adultery, and all the sex ethic of the Old Testament is re-stated throughout the New Testament (Matt. 5:27–30; 1 Cor. 6:9–20; 1 Tim. 1:8–11). If the New Testament has reaffirmed a commandment, then it is still in force for us today.[1]

So while many of the Old Testament laws are no longer valid for today, some remain valid, in particular those regarding moral behavior detailing how we treat others, including what God says about murder and sexual ethics. When he spoke about murder, Jesus didn't say he was throwing out the old. He pushes us to consider God's intent in the law, to look at how murder begins with hatred in the heart prior to the action. When Jesus is asked about divorce and marriage, he does not adopt contemporary Roman and Greek ethics of the time but looks back to God's intention in the original creation in Genesis chapters 1 and 2. When asked about dietary laws or how to obey the Sabbath, we see Jesus giving new teaching. Jesus says that the purpose of the Sabbath goes beyond the ritual observance of the day. He teaches that dietary restrictions are no longer needed, since all foods are now declared clean, and the distinctions between ethnic groups belonging to God's people are coming to an end.

To know which laws still apply to us and which ones don't, we need to look at what Jesus and the writers of the New Testament say continued and understand why they said it. Only then are we prepared to decide which laws do not need to be continued. In general, laws regarding the ordering of the Israelite nation (civil laws), laws regarding temple sacrifice and worship (ceremonial laws), and dietary restrictions (some holiness laws) are no longer needed now that Jesus has come. In our Bible study, we have the amazing privilege of seeing how God has revealed himself through time to different people in different places, and we can use what God has revealed in the past to better follow Jesus today. The New Testament and Jesus' teaching help us to know what it looks like to love and worship God and love our neighbors as ourselves.

Wear Polyester Blends, Eat Shrimp, Enjoy Ham, and Play Football

So when you hear or read a reference to verses telling Christians not to eat shrimp or pork or wear clothing made of two different fabrics, like polyester blends, you know why those rules are no longer valid. When people mock or seek to discredit the Bible by pointing this out, all they show is their lack of understanding. It is easy to grab bizarre verses from the Old Testament and claim Christians are breaking the rules by not following them. But what it really shows is a lack of understanding the Bible storyline and the difference between the original covenant God made and the new covenant.

What About the Slavery Verses in Both Testaments?

Let's tackle the topic of slavery. There are Bible verses in the Old Testament that seem to indicate that God did not oppose slavery. Even more puzzling are sections of the New Testament that also speak about slavery without explicitly condemning it. We never find an "end all slavery immediately" verse in the Bible. This is a major and understandable criticism of the Bible, and whenever you hear or see verses from the Bible referring to slavery on memes or billboards, take the question very seriously. You may see verses like these:

In the Old Testament:

- "When you buy a Hebrew servant [slave] . . ." (Exodus 21:2).
- "If a man sells his daughter as a servant [slave] . . ." (Exodus 21:7).

And in the New Testament, verses like:

- "Slaves, obey your earthly masters with respect and fear" (Ephesians 6:5).
- "Teach slaves to be subject to their masters in everything, to try to please them, not to talk back to them" (Titus 2:9).

In our modern context, just reading these verses makes us cringe in horror and confusion, seeing that they are in the Bible. We can't help but wonder if God approves of slavery. You may even feel that the Bible is evil for endorsing slavery, and sadly, we know from history that the Bible was used to defend the practice of slavery in early America. So there are good reasons to question if the Bible advocates slavery.

Slavery is a serious topic. Our purpose is to better understand how to read the odd and strange parts of the Bible, so here are a few initial thoughts to help us make sense of these passages on slavery:

Slavery Is Evil

Taking a person against their will and forcing them to become the property of another is evil. We know from the Bible storyline that as a result of the fall, the infection of sin causes human beings to gravitate toward ego, power, and corruption. Slavery is one of many ways human beings have strayed from God's perfect creation.

God Gave Regulations to an Existing Condition *People* Created

According to both the Old Testament and the New Testament, slavery is wrong. This is very important to pay attention to. We see in Exodus 21:16 a clear condemnation of anyone who steals someone to make them a slave: "Anyone who kidnaps someone is to be put to death, whether the victim has been sold or is still in the kidnapper's possession."

And in the New Testament, in 1 Timothy 1:9–10, it says, "The law is made not for the righteous but for lawbreakers . . . for slave traders and liars and perjurers—and for whatever else is contrary to the sound doctrine."

The assumption in both Old and New Testaments is that slave trading is evil and is condemned in the Bible itself. So why are there verses about slavery that seem to suggest God allows it? To understand this, we need to return to the culture and context of the ancient world and remember that God didn't create the institution of slavery, nor did he ever command or direct people to have slaves. What we see in the Bible is God giving instructions to regulate a preexisting way of life that was pervasive at that time. Slavery was everywhere in the ancient world, embedded in the economic and social institutions of those times. God did not affirm or endorse slavery, but worked within the cultural framework of that time to begin a longer process of transformation that would lead to moving people out of slavery in any and every form.

It's important to remember that after the fall (see the timetable chart in chapter 3), human beings began developing all kinds of practices that God did not intend in his original creation. Human beings, not God, developed slavery. To see God's original design for human beings, before humans messed it up, we need only look at the beginning, the creation in the garden of Eden. Jesus modeled this for us when he was asked about marriage and divorce. He sent those asking questions back to the beginning to remind them of how God had originally created people before human beings rebelled against God and altered God's original setup.* The same is true with slavery. God did not create slavery, and what we find in the Bible is a process in which God is slowly moving people back toward a standard of greater respect and dignity for all people, not less. I'll give you some examples of what I mean by this, but keep this key idea in mind: God is not the originator of slavery.

Slavery in Our Culture Is Not the Same as in the Bible

Here is the key point on slavery for our purposes. In general, when we think of slavery, we think of the evils of the New World race-based chattel slavery and the Atlantic slave trade with the American colonies in the seventeenth and eighteenth centuries, which led to the Civil War. This form of slavery involved kidnapping and forced labor. It was evil.

This type of slavery, however, while it did exist in ancient times, was not the common and predominant form of slavery. Knowing this makes a significant difference in how we read the Bible verses about slavery. Here are some of the differences:

---

*   Matthew 19:1–9.

Slaves Who Lived at the Time of Moses Were
More like Servants or Bondservants

In modern translations of the Bible, the English word "slave" is not always used. Many translations use the word "servant." The two situations were very different.

In Ancient Israel, It Was Common to Sell Yourself
to Pay a Debt or Escape Poverty

It is difficult for us to comprehend this way of thinking, but it was quite common back then for the poor to sell themselves to escape poverty or pay a debt. When you sold yourself to someone as a servant, it meant your basic needs would be covered. And while there was an owner-servant relationship, it was not identical with the race-based slavery that began with kidnapping.

With verses like Exodus 21:7, "If a man sells his daughter as a servant [slave]," our framework has to shift from what we initially think of today to what it was like back at that time. Selling your daughter would be incredibly wicked to us today, and I'm not justifying it or endorsing it. But this was how things commonly functioned in that world, and God gives these instructions to reinforce and protect people in that context, as hard as that is for us to grasp today.

In this situation, it is highly likely the father is selling his daughter because he does not want her to starve or to be abandoned. In that day, options were limited, and it was often a choice between life and death. So when the Bible gives guidance to a father about selling his daughter into servitude, the Bible is not saying this is a good thing to do. It is recognizing that *if* a father were to find himself in a place where this was necessary (for reasons all too common at that time), he should do it in a way that protects her and preserves her dignity. Reading the entire chapter where this verse is found, we see an attempt to flesh out ways of protecting those who were in bondservant arrangements. For a father, if he had to sell his daughter as a slave to protect her or provide for her, he could not sell her to be given as a prostitute for physical pleasure. She could not be disposed of as a piece of property the new owner no longer desired. He must treat her like a family member, and if marriage is not a possibility in the future, she must eventually be set free.

I understand that all of this sounds extremely whacky and horribly primitive to our way of thinking in our culture today. Arranged marriages strike us as inherently wicked and unfair. But this was the norm in the ancient world. And in the context of this verse, the Bible's command is a move toward reinforcing protections for the daughter in that system, and not a blanket endorsement of the system. This was also a different form of slavery, often temporarily done for the sake of survival or even to advance oneself out of poverty. We must reframe what we read through that lens, taking into consideration the world they lived in, where people were selling themselves to serve others and arranging marriages all the time. This wasn't bizarre then. If anything, it was a way of protecting people caught up in the effects of fallout from human sin.

Keep in mind that God commanded the death penalty for those who kidnapped people and made them slaves (read Exodus 21:16 and 1 Timothy 1:10). Although this type of slavery did happen at times, we never see God endorsing it or teaching people to do this. Instead, we see God condemning it. And when we do find slavery being addressed in the Bible, it is generally speaking about the type of slavery that existed to help the poor survive in the ancient world, forms of slavery that were established for people to work off debt (Leviticus 25:39), for example. When we look at slavery in the context of the ancient world, we need to deprogram our normal definition and redefine it according to what it meant in that world.

New Testament Slavery Was Common: Even 30 Percent of the Population Were Slaves

I understand that slavery in New Testament times is a world we cannot imagine and have trouble understanding. But these slaves could serve as doctors and lawyers, they could go to school and be educated. This was a different cultural context, with more than 30 percent of the population in the New Testament Roman and Greek world living as slaves, or what today we might call servants. When we read Bible verses about slaves or servants in the New Testament, we have to look at what is being said through the lens of the culture at that time—which is not identical with the slavery we think of today.

Slavery Was Not Race Based the Way We Think of It Today

Today, when we think of the slave trade, it brings to mind the unjust enslavement of African people. That type of slavery was race based. However, in ancient Israel or at the time of the New Testament, you would not typically notice a racial difference between those serving as slaves and those who weren't slaves. When you look at the Old Testament, you find Israelites who had fellow Israelites as slaves (for a limited time). In New Testament times you would find Romans and Greeks of the same race and ethnicity having Roman and Greek slaves. Back then, slavery was not race based as slavery was in the United States.

Though It Might Not Sound Like It, the Bible Brought Positive Changes to Ancient Slavery

We likely aren't living in a culture where it is normal for people to sell themselves or sell their family members to others to pay off a debt or avoid the ravages of poverty. That's one reason why this is difficult for us to imagine or accept. As we have seen, the Bible explains how human beings, in their rebellion, changed God's original creation plans. It's clear that humans established slavery, not God. He was not establishing slavery or endorsing it. He was giving regulations to limit the evil that would spread from what humans had done. God was seeking better treatment for slaves in Israel than they would have received in the surrounding cultures outside of Israel. Leviticus 25:43 says, "Do not rule over them ruthlessly, but fear your God." When we read Bible verses about slavery, they are offering guidance, but this guidance was always intended to improve what already existed. Here are two quick examples:

1. Killing a slave merited punishment (Exodus 21:20).
2. Permanently injured slaves had to be set free (Exodus 21:26–27).

These biblical directions deviated significantly from the normal treatment of slaves at that time, part of God's process of gradually moving people toward a more dignified relationship between a slave and the household the slave served.

In the New Testament, We See God Moving the People Away from Slavery

We see the seeds of a movement (the church) that would equalize the worth of both slave and free people. Paul the apostle writes a letter to a slave owner named Philemon concerning a slave named Onesimus, who had run away from Philemon. Onesimus met Paul while Paul was in prison and had become a Christian during this time. Paul was sending Onesimus back to Philemon, and in the letter we read some amazing, radically countercultural things. Paul asks Philemon to not just take Onesimus back (after running away and stealing money from his master), but to receive him "no longer as a slave, but better than a slave, as a dear brother. He is very dear to me but even dearer to you, both as a fellow man and as a brother in the Lord."* What makes this so unusual for that time is that Paul does *not* want Philemon to punish Onesimus; even more, he is telling him that Onesimus is now his brother in the Lord. Paul promises to personally pay for any of the damages Onesimus's escape and absence may have cost Philemon. Paul stops short of explicitly ordering Philemon to free Onesimus, but in every other way he implies it. He makes it clear that Onesimus should be treated as a brother in Christ and expresses a wish that Onesimus would have the freedom available to him to help in Paul's ministry.

In other places in the New Testament we see a clear leveling of the divide between slave and nonslave, treating them as equals. Galatians

---

* Philemon 16.

3:28 says, "There is neither Jew nor Gentile, neither slave nor free, nor is there male and female, for you are all one in Christ Jesus."

In a world where at least 30 percent of the population were slaves, this was extremely forward thinking. It was nothing less than revolutionary! God is consistently seeking to move people away from the effects of the fall and reaffirming the original truth of our creation, that all human beings are created in his image and are equal. There was to be no male patriarchy or misogyny (see the next chapter for more on this). No ethnic hierarchies or racism. No difference of worth between slaves and nonslaves. God is laying the groundwork to change how human beings see each other. He is helping people blinded by the virus of sin and selfishness to see other people again, to look beyond financial status, wealth or poverty, skin color or education—to see that everyone is equal. When this shift of thinking begins to penetrate the hearts and minds of the followers of Jesus, it leads to tectonic shifts in cultures around the world. And it begins here, with God wanting his people to experience how God actually sees them, as his image bearers.

It Was Wrong to Use the Bible to Justify Slavery in America

Those who used the Bible to support race-based slavery in the United States were seeking to justify an evil and wicked practice. They did not use correct or intelligent Bible study methods. They didn't ask questions about the original audience or study the culture of the original readers. Not all Christians agreed with these readings of the Bible at that time. Many Christians fought against slavery and condemned the incorrect usage of the Bible in this way. Christians such as Wilbur Wilberforce and many others fought against slavery. Today many Christian organizations and churches are fighting against modern trafficking. Yes, there were Christians who used the Bible to back slavery—that was clearly wrong and evil. Bible study methods are important. Looking at Bible verses through the lens of the entire storyline of the Bible, you cannot conclude that God endorses slavery.

Why Don't Jesus and the Bible Writers Just Say, "End All Slavery"?

We can't know why Jesus didn't just say, "No more slavery!" We don't know why he didn't address this practice or the hundreds of other evils in the world. Some have surmised that because more than 30 percent of the population were slaves, it could have led to economic upheaval and likely more poverty and starvation. In general, Jesus did not focus on specific civil laws or governments, but addressed the desires and motives of the human heart. I'll admit, it would have made things a lot easier if Jesus or Paul had just said, "All slaves go free!" But they didn't, and there must have been reasons, but we don't see those given in the Bible. What we do find in the Bible is the *progression of instruction*. The Old Testament gave guidance to protect slaves and give them more dignity. This made Israel distinct from other nations. The New Testament moves one step farther, declaring that regardless of whether one is the slave or the one the slave serves, they are equals, brothers and sisters in Jesus.

Two foundational ideas guide this progression. The first is that God originally created us in his image and all human beings have value and worth because of this. The second is that in the New Covenant, all those who follow Jesus are now part of the same family, brothers and sisters, and this takes priority over all social, economic, racial, and gender distinctions. The Bible lays the foundation that frees people from the evil practice of slavery, but this change occurs slowly over time, through the heart, instead of from social change through governmental power and laws. However, whenever the heart changes, social change inevitably follows. When isolated verses are used to claim God and the Bible are evil, those saying this aren't looking beyond the surface.

A Summary of Shrimp, Pigkins, and Slavery

This is a complex and sensitive topic. Whenever you see a meme or a verse quoted from Leviticus criticizing Christians for eating shrimp, wearing two types of fabric, or playing football, you can confidently point out that the person hasn't done their homework. The Bible does teach us how to correctly pick verses by understanding the difference between the "pre-Jesus" and "post-Jesus" time periods. So eat some shrimp, cook up some bacon,[2] play football, wear polyester blends, and plant two different seeds side by side in your garden.

God did not create slavery nor endorse it anywhere in the Bible. Humans created slavery. God gave regulations and guidance to improve the conditions of people trapped as slaves in this evil system. When we read Bible verses about slavery, we have to understand that slavery in the Bible is different from the race-based chattel slavery that was common in the trans-Atlantic slave trade. The form of slavery during the time of the Bible was a necessity for some people to survive in the socioeconomic conditions of that time. Picking and highlighting Bible verses from the Old and New Testaments that include the word "slavery" is a misuse of the Bible. We can thank God that all slavery today is universally viewed as an evil, and Christians are uniformly united in the fight against it.

Our next topic is the Bible passages that seem to suggest women should remain silent and submit to men. There are many things here for us to figure out, but as we've already seen, when we look deeper there are new things to discover.

Part 2 Summary Points

STRANGER THINGS

- The strange-sounding laws and rituals, including not eating shrimp and not wearing two types of fabrics, were specifically for the people of Israel during the pre-Jesus time period. They may not make sense to us today, but they would have had meaning for the people back in that time period.

- The law was not given as a code for Israel to simply have an ideal social system. It was to show the Israelites what it means to live in the presence of God. These guiding laws used many things familiar to them from their culture and world that helped them understand what it means to love God more and, as a result, to love people more.

- Christians today no longer have to follow those strange Old Testament laws. We need to examine the New Testament to see which laws in the New Testament apply today and which ones don't. While most of the civil and worship laws are no longer valid, most of the moral laws continue.

- Slavery is evil. God did not create it or endorse it. God specified the death penalty for slave traders in the Old Testament, and in the New Testament he clearly said it is sin. The Bible verses on slavery guide us in how to bring better treatment to people caught in a system that was established by humans.

- Most of ancient slavery in the time of the Old Testament and New Testament was different from the slavery we are familiar with in modern times. Back then people were bought as servants, the money going to pay a person's debt. Poverty forced others into servanthood just to stay alive. This slavery, or servanthood, was not race based.

- The New Testament laid the groundwork for the eventual demise of slavery, as it taught that all humans are of equal worth, all brothers and sisters, and all are children of God.

PART 3

Boys' Club Christianity

Is the Bible Anti-women and Does It Promote Misogyny?

CHAPTER 7

The Boys' Club Bible

I continue to be amazed when I see Christian women defending a Bible that denigrates women.

—SETH ANDREWS, FORMER CHRISTIAN,
FOUNDER OF THE THINKING ATHEIST

When I became a Christian, the first church I became a regular part of was a small church in London, England. I was living there for a year playing in a punk band, and I experienced an amazing small church community of around twenty mainly elderly people. They took me into their community and didn't judge me because I was playing punk music or dressed differently. And they began teaching me about Jesus.[1] The pastor and his wife were in their eighties, and although the pastor was the leader of the church, when I asked questions, his wife was always incredibly helpful. She knew the Bible really well and taught me a lot. Many of the elderly women in that church had a lot of Bible knowledge and welcomed questions. I had many Sunday lunchtime theology discussions with them in the basement of this church, eating sandwiches they brought to feed me. As I became ingrained in the life of this small church, I saw both men and women leading, teaching, and serving together, and I didn't think much about it.

When I moved back to the United States, I knew I needed to belong to a local church to continue following Jesus. One of the first churches I attended was large and very different from the small church I was part of in London. There were uber-happy greeters at the doors, with high-fiving and vigorous shaking of everyone's hands. As an introvert, I felt a rush of panic having to high-five someone I didn't know. I found a door that avoided the happy greeters and took a seat. Because I was by myself, I sat and read the bulletin as I waited for the service to start, wanting to look occupied and not alone.

As I scanned the bulletin, I couldn't help but notice that the pastors and elders of this church were all men. I knew that a pastor teaches the Bible and is there to care for the people of the church, but I had no idea what an "elder" was.[2] It was a new world for me. I assumed that an "elder" was someone elderly and retired, and they were listed there for some reason. I also noticed that on the list of leaders called pastors and elders it was only men's names listed. No women. Only men. And it was the same when I looked at the teachers of adult classes. All the classes were taught by men. There was a woman listed as the church secretary and a woman listed for the women's ministry. But she was called a "director," not a "pastor."

With this in mind, after reading the church bulletin, I was especially conscious of the gender differences during the worship service. There was a man leading the band and singing when the gathering started. There were two females as backup singers, but they were definitely in the background, smiling and lightly clapping as they sang. The preacher was male as well.

I would guess that half the people in this church were female, but from an outside perspective, there was no doubt this was a male-led church. If you are part of a church like this, you probably get used to it and might not even notice these things. But as a first-time visitor without much church experience, it was very noticeable to me. As I got involved in the life of that specific church, I saw that behind the scenes in the church office women were leading areas of ministry, and most of the time seemed to have the same function as men. There were "pastor" and "elder," titles which only the men had, but women were highly respected. So, I didn't think too much about the topic. That is, until the day I had a very awkward and uncomfortable Bible study session that I will never forget.

After I was part of that church for a while, I began leading a ministry and was at a home meeting with some young adults. During the meeting, the topic of women in leadership in the church came up. We had a hand-out from the church that instructed us to look up what it said about the church's stances on female pastors and elders. Beneath this were several Bible verse references—not the verses written out, just the references. We decided to look up them up to see what they were and read them out loud together. One of the women began with this verse: "A woman should learn in quietness and full submission. I do not permit a woman to teach or to assume authority over a man; she must be quiet."*

I still remember the uncomfortable feeling that began spreading around the room. There was an awkward pause and the female college student asked a question and made direct eye contact with me, looking puzzled. She asked, "A woman must be silent? She can't teach a man?" Before I had a chance to respond, someone else read another verse that said, "Women should remain silent in the churches. They are not allowed to speak, but must be in submission, as the law says. If they want to inquire about something, they should ask their own husbands at home; for it is disgraceful for a woman to speak in the church."†

The questions kept coming. "Women should remain silent in the church? It is disgraceful for a woman to speak in the church? They need to wait till they get home to ask their husbands questions?" "A woman is supposed to submit to her husband?" It felt quite surreal and jarring to hear these Bible verses being read out loud and then having all eyes fixed on me. In the room with me were several female college students

---

*   1 Timothy 2:11–12.
†   1 Corinthians 14:34–35.

studying economics and computer science, and another getting a PhD in microbiology.

I know I must have read these verses before while reading through the Bible. And I'm sure other Christians in that room had as well. But to be honest, at least I know I had kind of skipped over them since they sounded so strange. In my recollection of our church meetings and teachings, these verses were never directly discussed. Were we just ignoring them? And what would I tell these educated, smart college students sitting in my living room staring at me right now?

I sat there thinking, "Oh God, oh God, oh God, what do I say?" Then I responded with a sheepish, noncommittal answer. "I don't know. I am going to have to ask the pastors of the church about these verses," and we left it at that. I could tell it was not a satisfying answer, but in that moment, I didn't know what else to say. In truth, I wanted to hide behind the couch and wait until they all left, but I couldn't. I was embarrassed that I didn't know how to answer. And at that moment, I was embarrassed that these verses were in the Bible.

This began my investigation into these Bible verses, and as I looked, I found these were just the tip of the iceberg. When you start scanning the entirety of the Bible, including the New Testament, you'll read other verses that at surface reading can sound very demeaning to females: "Wives, submit yourselves to your own husbands as you do to the Lord. For the husband is the head of the wife."*

And the Old Testament has even more crazy-sounding Bible verses about:

- Fathers having the ability to sell their daughters as property to men (Exodus 21:7–11).
- If a woman is raped, she must marry her rapist (Deuteronomy 22:28–29).
- Many examples of polygamy, where men have multiple wives and

---

* Ephesians 5:22–23.

concubines (women servants whom they can have for physical pleasure), even Bible heroes like David, Abraham, and others (Genesis 16:1–3; Judges 8:30; 2 Samuel 5:13; 1 Chronicles 14:3).

If you are a thinking Christian in today's world or someone who is considering Christianity, I don't believe you have a choice—you must explore these verses. If you are a Christian and reading this, I'd like you to think about my earlier situation and what you would have said to those women. Perhaps you are like me and never really thought much about those verses, but that is no longer an option. Verses like these are now shared across the internet, and if you don't have a response when asked about them, you need to get one.

Women Be Silent and Ask Your Husbands Questions at Home

The meme in image 7.1, and many similar ones, includes Bible verses from 1 Corinthians 14:34–35 that clearly state, "Let your women keep silence in the churches: for it is not permitted unto them to speak; but they are commanded to be under obedience as also saith the law. And if they will learn any thing, let them ask their husbands at home: for it is a shame for women to speak in the church." The image shows a woman with her mouth taped over in silence and the words "shouldn't you be home in the kitchen?" above the verses and "Know Your Bible" below.

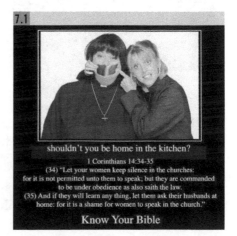

The assumption is that people seeing this probably don't realize this verse is in the Bible. And it's a verse from the New Testament, not the Old.

Image 7.2 shows a sign being held up in a protest supporting women's rights. It points out what the Bible says about women.

This list says that women should be silent, keepers at home (doing dishes, laundry, ironing, etc.), submissive to their husbands, silent in church, care-takers of children, and modestly dressed. It then lists several Bible verses (1 Timothy 2, Titus 2, 1 Peter 3) with a challenge to read the Bible to see for yourself that this is really in there. These verses can be quite uncomfortable to address. And this sign is challenging people to actually read what the Bible says regarding women. Granted, the part about doing the dishes and laundry is not in any Bible verse, but it's

a common assumption that the Bible teaches these are jobs for women.

CBS News once carried a story of someone who painted the rear of their pickup truck to say: "1 Cor. 14:34: Women shall be silent and submissive," along with "Read Your Bible" (7.3). The slogans caused a stir and were viewed as anti-women. At first it was assumed the person who owned the truck was also anti-women and wanting to support all of this. But it turned out the man was pro-women and was doing this to challenge people to see what is actually written in the Bible. He felt that most people ignored these verses or didn't read them. He said, "I want people to read the Bible. I want them to see the message and say, 'Is that true? . . . It's a hateful, hateful piece of work. . . .' Hopefully people will read it and learn for themselves."

Bible verses like these are coming up more and more today. We live in a culture that is fighting against inequality for women and seeking to affirm their right to equal respect, pay, value, and worth. There is still a great deal of misogyny in our society, and whenever it is pointed out and

confronted, we should add our support. But it can be awkward to talk about Bible verses that—at face value—seem to demean and devalue women. These verses have always been in the Bible. They aren't new. But people are now calling attention to them and asking if Christians really believe them. Have you ever stopped to think, "Do women really have to be silent in church?" That's what the Scriptures say, and passages like this are being noticed today.

If you are a thinking Christian or someone who is considering Christianity, you don't have a choice—you must explore these verses. If you are a Christian and reading this, I'd like you to think about the Bible study meeting I mentioned earlier. What would you say to those women? Perhaps you are like me, and you've never really thought much about this. But that is no longer an option. In our world today, these verses demand an explanation. As a non-Christian friend of mine put it, the Bible seems to teach that the church is a "boys' club for adults"—and I can understand why she said this. However, as we will soon learn, if we look at how these verses fit into the larger context of the whole Bible story, it significantly changes how we understand them.

CHAPTER 8

Can't Keep a Good
Woman Down

> Women should remain silent in the churches. They
> are not allowed to speak, but must be in submission,
> as the law says. If they want to inquire about
> something, they should ask their own husbands at
> home; for it is disgraceful for a woman to speak in the
> church.
>
> —1 CORINTHIANS 14:34–35

To understand misogynistic-sounding Bible verses such as, "I do not permit a woman to teach or to assume authority over a man; she must be quiet," or, "They are not allowed to speak, but must be in submission," we return to our guideline: Never read a Bible verse. Let's begin by going back and looking at where these verses fit in the whole Bible storyline. We'll begin to see how the Bible isn't anti-women at all; in fact, it's quite the opposite.

In the Beginning, There Were No Bible Verses That Sounded Anti-Women

When we return to the storyline of the Bible, we remember that in the very beginning, God created man and woman. Image 8.1 shows them created distinct but equal, and they existed in perfect harmony and relationship

8.1

In the beginning (Genesis 1–2)

harmony with God and each other

with God and with each other. In Genesis 1:27, it says, "So God created mankind in his own image, in the image of God he created them; male and female he created them."

There is no indication that one gender is superior or has greater value than the other. The story continues in Genesis 1:28: "God blessed them and said to them, 'Be fruitful and increase in number; fill the earth and subdue it. Rule over the fish of the sea and the birds in the sky and over every living creature that moves on the ground."

Here we see Adam and Eve given shared responsibility and a shared mission to take care of what God created. There is no indication of hierarchy or superiority in any way. This was an incredible time of man and woman living mutually in perfect community with each other and serving God together as equal image-bearers. God's original design is for man and woman to co-rule and co-reign in community with one another to advance God's purposes on earth.

There are some questions that come up when you read this phrase in Genesis 2:18: "It is not good for the man to be alone. I will make a helper suitable for him." It has been incorrectly taught that this verse indicates the woman is in some way less than the man when it says she was created as a "helper" for the man. In our contemporary English language, when we think of a "helper" we may think of an assistant to a more skilled person or a subordinate. However, the meaning of the word to the original audience of Genesis is more nuanced. The Hebrew word *ezer*, translated as "helper," appears not just here but more than twenty times in the Old Testament. And nearly every time it appears, it refers to God. We read in Psalm 33:20, "We wait in hope for the Lᴏʀᴅ; he is our *help* and our shield." And since this word frequently refers to God, who is clearly not inferior to those he helps, when it refers to the woman here, it is not saying she is inferior or of less importance. The point isn't about worth or value, but that God created both the man and woman so they would not be alone. God gives the man and the woman a partner, one who equally, but differently, reflects the image of God.

Another amazing thing we see in Genesis chapter 2 is the creative process of making man and woman. There is a strange part where God causes the man to fall into a deep sleep and removes one of his ribs, creating Eve from it. Keep in mind this is figurative language. It wasn't an actual "rib" (we will discuss if Eve is a "rib-woman" in chapter 12). The English word "rib" is translated from the Hebrew word *tselsa*, and in other places in the Hebrew Bible it is translated as "side." In architecture, the word is used to describe the opposing sides of a structure. For example, in the book of Exodus the words *tselo* (variant) and *tselot* (plural) are used to refer to the "sides" of the ark of the covenant or the "sides" of the altar. God was communicating that in the beginning he created Adam and Eve to be a beautiful image of two equal parts, side by side with no subordination or inequality. They weren't identical, but they were equal. They are mutually together, serving God in community together with no hierarchy, chauvinism, or polygamy. There are no "female in the kitchen" or "barefoot and pregnant" jokes. In the beginning, they were designed to serve God together as equals, and God even says they are "one flesh."[1]

Equality Is Broken and Everything Changes

But then . . . it happened. Man and woman didn't trust God. They went against his guidance and everything changed. In the Bible storyline, you'll recall the nuclear explosion that represents this colossal change (8.2).

The sad story unfolds in Genesis chapter 3. God shows how sin

8.2

**In the beginning
(Genesis 1–2)**

harmony with God and each other

sin alters God's original design

entered the world after Adam and Eve ate of the fruit of the tree and disrupted the beautiful way they related to God and to each other. They were instructed not to eat from this tree, but they did. And everything changed.

Eve chose to eat of the fruit first. It is implied that Adam was there with her. Genesis 3:6 makes it clear Adam "was with her." Her action was not a solo act—the woman against God—*both* man and woman participated in this act of disobedience. The harmony of their relationship changes immediately. Unity is broken and the virus of "sin" is turned loose on the world, beginning in the human heart. The creation they were tasked with ordering and caring for, including human beings, was affected by this "nuclear explosion" and the fallout that resulted. What happens next is sad but almost comical, as God confronts them. There is no longer peace and harmony. We see the first evidence of human selfishness and blame shifting. The man says to God in Genesis 3:12, "The woman you put here with me—she gave me some fruit from the tree, and I ate it." When God confronts the woman, she admits she was deceived and blames the serpent. "The serpent deceived me, and I ate" (v. 13).

Before God, Adam and Eve are both guilty, and both end up suffering the consequences of their actions. Romans 5:12 says that Adam is responsible since he was created first, and Paul is writing here to the Roman church to indicate that Adam is the representative head of the human race. We also see a mention of this in the New Testament letter 1 Timothy 2, where Paul writes that it was Eve who was deceived, not Adam. Paul clearly believed both are to blame. They were equal before God and share equal responsibility for their actions. We now live in the fallout of the explosion that disrupted God's original, perfect design.

114

Everything Changed and Inequality Began

What happens next is profoundly tragic. It's difficult to even begin to capture the long-term effects. In our timeline image (8.3) we see the symbol of a nuclear explosion and a shift between man and woman. A selfish hierarchy between man and woman replaces the harmony of the original creation.

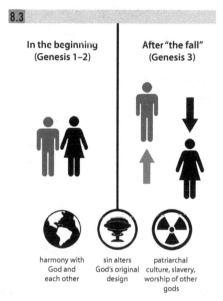

In the beginning (Genesis 1–2)

After "the fall" (Genesis 3)

harmony with God and each other

sin alters God's original design

patriarchal culture, slavery, worship of other gods

In Genesis 3:16–19, God describes to each one, man and woman, what they would now experience because of their actions. Their original purpose was to "be fruitful and multiply," but now the woman's childbearing would be accompanied with great pain. God had commanded them to "subdue the earth," but now man's work would be accompanied by painful toil, thorns, and thistles. Everyday survival for both the man and the woman would require sweat, struggle, and suffering.

We see a shift in their equality here too. We read that the corruption now changes the man and woman's relationship. God tells the woman, "Your desire will be for your husband, and he will rule over you,"* thus beginning the messy struggle for power and control. We see the drift from mutuality and equality to a patriarchal culture from here onward. Things change from the original harmony of creation. Humans are now infected with sin, which warps our thinking and our actions. We see the development of a hierarchy of men over women, just as God said would happen. We see a world of pain and mess due to human pride, ego, power, and control—everything that was so beautiful in the original creation is reversed.

---

*   Genesis 3:16.

In this aftermath of sin corrupting human beings, we see polygamy becoming prevalent. This is true even among those who play a major role in God's story leading up to Jesus. Jacob, who is the father of the twelve tribes of Israel, has twelve sons by four different women, two of whom are his wives and two of whom are servants of his wives. Solomon takes the "many wives" thing to an extreme with seven hundred wives and three hundred concubines. This is not God's desire from the beginning. It is wicked the way women were viewed as property. This time period is filled with great sadness and oppression—none of which was part of the original design.

The Old Testament has many Bible verses where women are identified as property.* We see rape laws requiring fathers to be paid for damages and the female victim forced to marry her rapist.† Women are considered spoils of war to be taken by the winning army.‡ As we saw before, these verses need to be viewed in light of the larger timeline and story to understand why we see this tragedy, injustice, and inequality happening. We will be looking at some of these passages in the next chapter and how to respond to the understandable criticism. But here is our guiding principle: even as we acknowledge the sad and horrific results of the fall and how it impacted the relationship of man and woman, we also see that God did not abandon women by endorsing the cultural patriarchy. It was never God's intention, and as with slavery, he was working through time, changing hearts to overturn the effects of human sin.

Glimpses of Equality and Hope in a Patriarchal Fallout Culture

Yes, the fallout affected humanity, and a thick cloud of radiation exists over the world. But what is the trajectory the Bible is pointing us toward? The Bible shows us times when women were treated as God originally designed. Even in the midst of the fallout and the patriarchal world that

---

*   Exodus 20:17; Deuteronomy 5:21; Judges 5:30.
†   Deuteronomy 22:28–29.
‡   Numbers 31:32–35; Deuteronomy 20:14; 21:10–15; Judges 5:30; 21:11–23.

developed, God raised up women to be prophets, teachers, leaders, and examples to both men and women. Here are a few examples we find in the Bible:

Miriam

Miriam, along with her brothers Moses and Aaron, led Israel out of Egypt. God sent them on a task to do this. This wasn't a self-led feminist rebellion; it was God himself charging Miriam with a major role in bringing his people Israel back into the land he promised them. Micah 6:4 affirms her role when God says:

> I brought you up out of Egypt
>> and redeemed you from the land of slavery.
> I sent Moses to lead you,
>> also Aaron and Miriam.

And Miriam wasn't just a leader, she was also a prophet. Here we have a female leader who is also a prophet and you never see any qualification that Miriam was allowed to prophesy only to women. She was prophesying as a spokesperson for God to both men and women, and her words are now part of Scripture for us to learn from today.

Deborah

In Judges, chapter 4, we meet a woman named Deborah who was a prophet, a judge, and a military leader for Israel. She led them as a woman and a prophet of God, and she is spoken of with respect and honor in the Scriptures. There is nothing mentioned about her stepping into roles that she wasn't supposed to be in.

Huldah

In 2 Kings 22 we meet a female prophet named Huldah. The backstory is that King Josiah had commissioned the rebuilding of the temple, and as they went into the building project, they discovered the Book of the

Law. When they read the Scriptures, the king and the people were upset because they realized how far they had fallen away from the ways of God. King Josiah needed someone to tell them what the Scriptures meant, so the high priest and the king's advisors turned to the prophet Huldah.

My good friend and Bible scholar Scot McKnight writes about Huldah and says, "Huldah is not chosen because no men were available. She is chosen because she is truly exceptional among the prophets."[2] There were other prophets that could have been chosen, such as Jeremiah, Zephaniah, Nahum, and Habakkuk. But Josiah did not ask for help from any of those men. Instead he chose Huldah. We see that Huldah took the Scriptures and taught what they meant and prophesied. Her prophecy was fulfilled thirty-five years later.* Huldah spoke on God's behalf and was an instructor, teacher, and prophet. Prophets were seen as mouthpieces for God, so this shows that God was not placing women in subservient roles. In Isaiah 8:3, we also see Isaiah's wife listed as a prophet.

Proverbs 31

Proverbs is a book of collected wisdom, and wisdom is personified as a woman in the opening chapters. Proverbs ends with a portrait of a woman who is described as hardworking, who runs a business, and provides for her family. She has employees and is highly respected and valued.

Joel's Prophecy

The prophet Joel, writing near the end of the Old Testament period, provides a future picture of how God's Spirit will clearly work through both men and women. We read in Joel 2:28–29:

> And afterward,
>   I will pour out my Spirit on all people.
> Your sons and daughters will prophesy,
>   your old men will dream dreams,

---

*   2 Kings 22.

your young men will see visions.

Even on my servants, both men and women,

I will pour out my Spirit in those days.

Other Examples of Influential Women

We read the story of Esther, who was forced to be in a king's harem and then marry the king, but was someone of strong character who rose up with great bravery in a time of crisis to stop the planned slaughter of the Jewish people. We see Ruth, a woman of integrity and honor. There are many examples throughout the Old Testament of women who loved God and were examples to us.

I include these brief observations from the Old Testament to remind us that when we see the negative, horrible-sounding Bible verses, we should remember there is more happening during this time period than what we read, often taken out of context. Yes, most of the leaders and voices were men due to the world being patriarchal. The Bible is telling us the story of what was happening in this world with the progression of fallout from human disobedience and God's plan to fix that. So there will be stories about men leading and men as central figures. But the amazing thing is that in the midst of this male-dominated world we see God bringing in women to represent him with authority as prophets, teachers, and leaders. We will look at some more of these Bible verses from the Old Testament in the next chapter. But let's not forget that as the Old Testament ends, we enter a whole new era of change that directly confronts this female-oppressed world. And it all begins when Jesus appears on the scene.

Understand the Way Women Were Treated during the Time of Jesus

In our timeline (8.4), Jesus is born, and he lived his life as an example and as a teacher. He died on the cross and rose again, and soon after the church was born. A new era begins with Jesus. He changes everything.

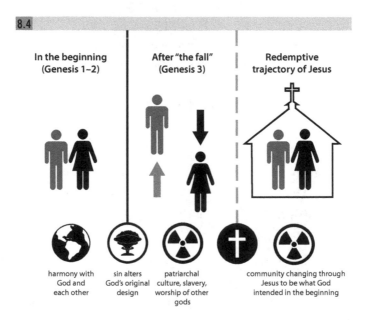

8.4

In the beginning (Genesis 1–2)

After "the fall" (Genesis 3)

Redemptive trajectory of Jesus

harmony with God and each other

sin alters God's original design

patriarchal culture, slavery, worship of other gods

community changing through Jesus to be what God intended in the beginning

As the church is born, we see God's Spirit working through the followers of Jesus. No longer is God's Spirit limited to a few people or the temple in Jerusalem, but the Spirit now dwells in those who put their faith in Jesus. Although there is still plenty of fallout in the world and in people, we see a trajectory of Jesus followers beginning to change the world. We see Jesus and then his disciples and the church continuing the trajectory of restoring God's original creation intentions. It's hard for us to grasp the significance of this since we didn't live in that world at that time. But the world we live in today, with our cultural values of equality for both men and women, are the product of Jesus and his followers.

The prevalent attitude toward women among most Jewish people at that time was not super positive. Jesus lived in a culture where women were generally not treated with the same respect, worth, and value as men. We know this from prayers from this time. For example, here's an actual prayer the rabbinical leaders would recite daily: "Praise be to God that he has not created me a Gentile [a non-Jew]! Praise be to God that he has not created me a woman! Praise be to God that he has not created me an ignoramus!"[3]

Another version of this prayer included thanks to God that the men praying weren't created to be a dog . . . or a woman. Jewish culture was patriarchal and often kept women in subordinate roles to men. In marriage, the male had the advantage. If a wife displeased her husband, he could divorce her—a wife was not granted the same right. We see this prejudice and negativity toward women throughout the Jewish religious writings going back to the time of Jesus. Josephus, the first-century Jewish historian, wrote, "The woman . . . is in all things inferior to the man." Other rabbinical writings at the time of Jesus say, "Four equalities are ascribed to women: they are gluttonous, eavesdroppers, lazy and jealous."[4]

But these feelings about the roles of men and women weren't limited to the Jewish culture during the time of Jesus. They were just as common in Greek and Roman culture. The Greek poets wrote how women are the source of evil in the world.[5] Roman law placed a wife under the absolute control of her husband, who had ownership of her and all her possessions. He could divorce her if she went out in public without a veil. A husband had the power of life and death over his wife, just as he did over his children. With the Greeks, women were not allowed to speak in public.[6] There were, of course, exceptions to this. But the exceptions seemed to be women who were born into a wealthy home or had achieved higher social status. Because of their wealth, they avoided some of the discrimination.

Overall, the world that Jesus lived in and the world the church was born into did not have equal respect, value, and rights for men and women. So when we read what Jesus did with regard to women, it should be recognized as countercultural, highly shocking, and extremely challenging to the religious leaders of his day. We see Jesus striving to change the culture he lived in through the way he treated women—with respect, dignity, and equality.

Jesus, the Rabbi Who Hangs Out with Women

Jesus is called a "rabbi" several times in the New Testament,* a word that means "teacher." In our culture today, "rabbi" refers to someone trained professionally for religious leadership in a synagogue, but at the time of Jesus, the term was one of dignity given by the Jews to their spiritual teachers. Jewish rabbis at the time of Jesus were encouraged not to teach or even speak with women. Jewish wisdom literature says that "he that talks much with womankind brings evil upon himself and neglects the study of the Law and at the last will inherit Gehenna [hell]."[7] With this as the general feeling about who a male rabbi should and shouldn't be hanging out with, what does Jesus do? He does the exact opposite of what was expected.

Jesus Spoke with Women, Even Scandalous Women

One instance recorded in the New Testament is when Jesus was passing through the city of Samaria.† This story shows Jesus breaking several customs. First, it was countercultural for a religious Jew, and especially someone seen as a rabbi, to even be in the city of Samaria. The city was about forty-two miles north of Jerusalem, and its inhabitants were despised by the Jews. Normally, a religious Jew or a rabbi would travel around Samaria to avoid going into it. Samaritans claimed the temple should be in Samaria, and the Jews claimed it should be in Jerusalem. Between that dispute and several others, they had an ongoing feud that fed their hatred for one another, and this had been going on for centuries. By being in that city, Jesus was rejecting the religious squabbles and politics of his day.

Jesus then goes to what was known as "Jacob's well," where a Samaritan woman came by herself. Because she was alone in the middle of the day, it may indicate that the rest of the women of that town did

---

*   Matthew 26:49; Mark 9:5; 10:51; 11:21; 14:45; John 1:49; 3:26; 9:2, etc.
†   John 4:1–42.

not like her. Jesus goes against the cultural norms by talking to a *woman* who was also a *Samaritan*. For a Jewish man, talking to a Samaritan woman was something to doubly avoid as they were seen as unclean from birth. Then, Jesus takes it even further because we learn from him that the woman had had five husbands and was with a man who was not her husband.* Jesus not only talked with her, he spoke openly about theology and discussed God with her—a woman!

Knowing the cultural background, you can imagine the shock of Jesus' disciples when they return and find him at the well talking with this woman. The Bible says it in an understated way, but the shock is there when we read in John 4:27, "His disciples returned and were surprised to find him talking with a woman. But no one asked, 'What do you want?' or 'Why are you talking with her?'" They probably couldn't believe that Jesus was doing this—speaking with a woman, which was taboo, and a Samaritan. This would have been unthinkable. They probably were so confused they didn't know what to say. And this incident is not the only one we find in the Bible. There are several accounts of Jesus speaking with and caring for various women, people a religious leader of his time would not associate with.†

Jesus Chose a Woman as the First Person to Whom He Revealed He Was the Christ

When you read the biblical account, you also find that the Samaritan woman is the one to whom Jesus first reveals that he is the Christ.‡ Jesus chose to first reveal the core of his mission and identity to a woman. He ended up staying with the Samaritan people for several days. For Jesus to lodge there, eat Samaritan food, and teach Samaritans is roughly equivalent to defying segregation in the United States during the 1950s or apartheid in South Africa in the 1980s—shocking, extremely difficult, and somewhat dangerous.[8] But Jesus is more concerned with what the

---

*   John 4:18.
†   John 7:53–8:11; 12:3.
‡   John 4:26.

truth of Scripture teaches about people than human opinions and cultural prejudice.

Jesus Traveled with Women

This may not sound like an important point, but we see Jesus breaking from norm in the way he traveled as well. He was not only accompanied by male followers but also several female followers.* Normally, to have these women traveling with the group would have been viewed as scandalous.[9] Ironically, the women in this traveling group are the ones supplying the financial means for them to be traveling together.†

Jesus Used Feminine Imagery for God as an Illustration

In Luke chapter 15, Jesus teaches a sequence of three parables about how valuable people are to God. In one parable, he uses a woman searching for a lost coin, comparing God to the woman who is on her hands and knees searching for the coin. On another occasion, Jesus describes himself metaphorically with feminine characteristics when he says he longs to gather his people under his wings like a mother hen does with her chicks.‡

Jesus Appeared to Women First After His Resurrection

Jesus could have appeared to anyone after his resurrection, but he chose to reveal himself first to women.§ Having women as the first ones to discover that his body was missing and to report it is highly unusual. The Scriptures tell how the resurrected Jesus commissioned them (women) to be the ones to tell the other disciples he was alive. According to Jewish law, women were not allowed to bear legal witness. Yet Jesus gave them the honorable task of being the very first to see him resurrected and the very first to tell others about it.

---

*   Luke 8:1–3.
†   Luke 8:3.
‡   Luke 13:34.
§   Luke 24:1–11.

The Church Extends What Jesus Started, through Both Men and Women

After Jesus was resurrected and then ascended to heaven, the church was born as the Holy Spirit came with power to those who put their faith in Jesus. The early church period was marked by men and women working in redemptive partnership to advance the gospel. The first public event in the new church is a sermon by Peter reminding the people of Israel of the words of the prophet Joel. In Acts 2:17–18 Peter quotes Joel to explain what is happening at that time with men and woman who receive the Holy Spirit, and notice that *both* men and women are said to begin prophesying: "'In the last days, God says, I will pour out my Spirit on all people. Your sons and daughters will prophesy, your young men will see visions, your old men will dream dreams. Even on my servants, both men and women, I will pour out my Spirit in those days, and they will prophesy."

At the very start of the church, the people were reminded that something was coming that would change the discriminatory and patriarchal culture around them. Here are a few examples of how this happened.

Paul Honored Women

Paul was the author of at least thirteen of the New Testament books, and in Romans 16, Paul mentions the names of people who worked in partnership to advance the work of the mission of the church in spreading the good news about Jesus. Many of the names mentioned are women. As you read these names, notice that Paul includes comments about some of the women such as, "She has been the benefactor of many people, including me." Paul also mentions that Priscilla and her husband risked their lives for him. Clearly, he's not saying the women just helped out in the kitchen and served coffee and snacks to the men. The women were at the core of helping launch and lead this new movement. These included:

Phoebe

Paul describes Phoebe as a deacon in Romans 16:1 2: "I commend to you our sister Phoebe, a deacon of the church in Cenchreae. I ask you to receive her in the Lord in a way worthy of his people and to give her any help she may need from you, for she has been the benefactor of many people, including me."

The way in which Paul commends Phoebe is consistent with the manner in which the writer of a letter would commend the person charged with the assignment of delivering the letter. Cultural practices of that time would have the one who delivered the letter read it and then answer the recipients' questions. Anyone who has ever read the letter Paul wrote to the Romans can only imagine the questions that would have arisen during that initial session. This significant responsibility was entrusted by Paul to a woman. Think about that: in all likelihood, the first ever exposition of Paul's letter to the Romans was done by a woman.

Priscilla and Her Husband, Aquila

Paul initially met this amazing married couple in Corinth. They then traveled with him to Ephesus, where he left them to continue the work he had begun. Now, apparently, they are ministering together in Rome. In Acts 18:26, we read that while still in Ephesus, they invited Apollos to their home, where they "explained to him the way of God more adequately." We see Paul listing Priscilla first, before her husband, Aquila, when describing their teaching relationship with Apollos. It would not have been common for a wife to be named before her husband. Nearly always, husbands were named before their wives, and when they were not, the author had a reason for reversing the order. It seems likely that Priscilla was a leader and teacher for Paul to address them like that.

Junia

In Romans 16:6–7, there is a fascinating passage that says, "Greet Mary, who worked very hard for you. Greet Andronicus and Junia, my fellow

Jews who have been in prison with me. They are outstanding among the apostles, and they were in Christ before I was."

Paul uses a title when he describes Andronicus and Junia as "apostles." Andronicus is likely a man, but most scholars believe Junia is a woman. Some translations list "Junias" rather than "Junia," and Junias would be a masculine name while Junia is feminine. But there is no record of anyone with the name Junias in first-century Greek writings. Junia, however, was a common woman's name, and the writings of the early church refer to Junia as a woman. The best and most reliable manuscripts, as well as the writings of the early church leaders, indicate that the person Paul is commending as an apostle is a woman named "Junia" and not a man named "Junias." So we very likely have a woman listed as an apostle here.

The Holy Spirit Gifted Both Men and Women to Serve on Mission

Every time we see a list of gifts that God's Spirit gave to enable the church to function on mission, we see no distinction made between men and women. We never see in these lists of what we call "spiritual gifts" in the New Testament that only certain gifts were for men and some were only for women. Read those lists and you will not see any such labeling. You can look at the examples in Romans 12:3–8, 1 Corinthians 12:7–11, 27–31, Ephesians 4:11–12, and 1 Peter 4:10–12. The Holy Spirit dwells within both men and women and empowers both to serve in the mission of the church.

Now, saying that, we do see differences in the contemporary church's beliefs about whether men and women both can serve in what are called the "offices" of the church. These are specific and formally titled roles of "pastor" and "elder." It is widely agreed that in the New Testament, the words "pastor" and "elder," along with the word "overseer," are interchangeable terms for those who are assigned to shepherd, care for, guide, and teach a local church. Different churches have different ways to structure their churches, and some believe that females can serve as pastors and elders, while others believe those are roles only for men. This is another whole other discussion about church leadership and more than we can discuss in this book. Please talk to your local church leaders about what they believe and why.

I can say that I know churches that have differing opinions and they both highly esteem and honor women and have them serving in leadership roles to influence the whole church. I plead with you—no matter what you believe on this issue—not to fight about it, not to think that those who hold a differing opinion do not take the Bible seriously. Now, of course some may hold strong opinions but have never truly studied the issue, and I hope this book challenges you to always study anything in the Bible beyond a surface reading. And if you are in a church that blatantly demeans females, makes chauvinistic jokes, and uses the Bible to advocate misogyny, get the heck out of there and find a church that honors women as equal in God's sight.

One Day We Will Be Back to the Way God Planned

Taking the images we've seen to this point and putting them together gives us a timeline proceeding from left to the right (8.5). This timeline shows that in the beginning God created men and women in his image to be distinct, but equal. There was no hierarchy or misogyny in the beginning. But human beings went against God's guidance, and this set off the nuclear explosion of sin and led to a great fallout that affected everything relationally and spiritually. We then see the rise of misogyny, patriarchy, and nonequality, and it surfaces in many ways in the Bible. Just because it is recorded in the Bible does not mean God agrees with it, nor did he create it. Instead, we see God working within the culture with the institutions and social patterns humans established (more on this in the next chapter), transforming them, but not approving of them.

When Jesus came, died, and rose again, and the Spirit of God gave birth to the church, we see changes beginning. The New Testament makes it clearer that God does not see women as subordinate or of lesser value than men. Women can serve both men and women with the gifts God gives, and one day, as the timeline shows on the far right, the time

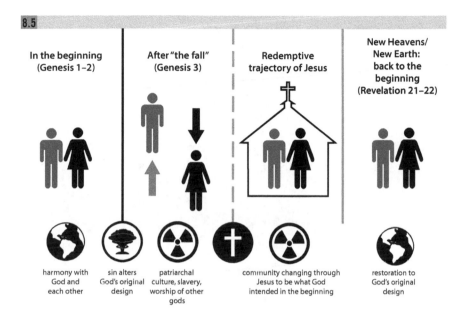

8.5

| In the beginning (Genesis 1–2) | After "the fall" (Genesis 3) | Redemptive trajectory of Jesus | New Heavens/ New Earth: back to the beginning (Revelation 21–22) |

| harmony with God and each other | sin alters God's original design | patriarchal culture, slavery, worship of other gods | community changing through Jesus to be what God intended in the beginning | restoration to God's original design |

period of the church will end Jesus will return and God will unfold the creation of the new heavens and a new earth. In many ways, what we see in the future brings us back to the beginning, to the original harmony of the garden where humans live as equals. There will be no more sin or even the potential for sin. And there will be no more power struggles between men and women or fights over equality.

This is the biblical explanation for why we see inequality and misogyny in this world. This corruption began with human beings, and we see it reflected in parts of the Bible. But this doesn't mean God approves of what humans did or the way they lived. Rather, we see God making changes, beginning to move things back to the way they were in the beginning.[10]

CHAPTER 9

Making Sense of
Inequality in the Bible

> There is neither Jew nor Gentile, neither slave nor
> free, nor is there male and female; for you are all one
> in Christ Jesus.
>
> —GALATIANS 3:28

We just walked through the Bible storyline to understand the origins of gender inequality and misogyny and how they developed over time. We saw how one day God will restore the harmony that was lost in the fall and return us to a state like the garden of Eden. What we see in that full Bible storyline is that God didn't create or endorse misogyny and female oppression. Human beings chose to go against God's original design, where man and woman were created equal. Human beings twisted God's original design, and men used their power to establish an unequal hierarchy over women. However, God sought to steer things back to his original design, away from the patriarchal cultures human beings had created. As we've seen several times already, we need to understand this backstory before we can interpret individual Bible verses that are extracted from the larger story. Remember, never read a Bible verse.[1]

We'll start with a sampling of Bible verses from the Old Testament and then look at the New Testament. Although we can't cover every verse on this topic, the same basic principles apply for any of the others we might see in the Bible.

If a Woman Is Raped, Does She Have to Marry Her Rapist?

In meme 9.1, the headline reads "Rape in the Bible." It quotes Deuteronomy 22:28–29, which says, "If a man happens to meet a virgin who is not pledged to be married and rapes her and they are discovered, he shall pay her father fifty shekels of silver. He must marry the young woman, for he has violated her. He can never divorce her as long as he

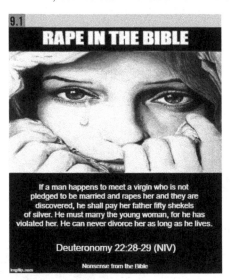

lives." And at the bottom it says, "Nonsense from the Bible."

Deuteronomy 22:28–29 is another wicked-sounding Bible verse that is increasingly being used to suggest that the Bible commands evil things and teaches that women are property. These verses were being spoken into a specific culture more than three thousand years ago, a world we are unfamiliar with today, so it's very difficult for us to fully grasp the significance and rationale for what is being taught. This was a single verse amidst hundreds of other specific guidelines, given to an ancient people group in response to a very despicable and desperate situation. And it was given in order to *protect* the woman.

First, we are looking at a time period when male patriarchy did, unfortunately, exist. A woman who was not married and had been sexually involved with a man was seen as lesser in value. This was a wrong belief, yes, but not one God had taught—it was human beings who developed this. At that time, a woman couldn't own property, and if she had no father, husband, or son, she would have no one to care for her and no legal protection. A woman's options were limited to selling herself into slavery or prostitution. God did not create this patriarchy; it was human beings and their sinful selfishness that created it.

Here we see God instructing the Israelites at that time to give dignity and respect to women in an existing patriarchal culture. Rape was seen as evil in that culture, and God elsewhere states that rape is a serious crime deserving capital punishment. In Deuteronomy 22:25–27, we read, "But if out in the country a man happens to meet a young woman pledged to be married and rapes her, only the man who has done this shall die. Do nothing to the woman; she has committed no sin deserving death. This case is like that of someone who attacks and murders a neighbor, for the man found the young woman out in the country, and though the betrothed woman screamed, there was no one to rescue her."

Here God equates rape with murder, and anytime you see stories of rape in the Bible, it is always shown as an evil act of violence. However, when rape did happen, there was an important difference in determining the best way to respond in that culture at that time. Put yourself, as best you can, in that time and culture. If a woman was raped, she was seen as no longer desirable for marriage. And if she remained unmarried, her life was virtually over. There were few options available to a woman at that time, and without a husband and family of her own, she had little hope for a future. In some cases, being married was a matter of survival. Without marriage she would likely end up neglected and impoverished, an all too common hardship for women in that culture.

We see a heartbreaking and gut-wrenching example of this in the Old Testament when a woman named Tamar was raped by her half brother. Not only did she suffer the pain of the rape but there was the even greater danger that if others knew of it, they would not want to marry her. So in this case, she asks her half brother, the one who raped her, to marry her. This is all evil and wrong, but it was a cultural norm back then. Essentially, she was calling her half brother to account for his wrong done to her, making her unmarriable and cutting off her future, by asking him to now provide for her through marriage. It was likely her only option.

None of this is good. Rape is evil, violent, wicked, and we should be glad that we live in a time and culture where women have opportunities and are not at the mercy of men for survival. But God was working from within these cultures, and we see God implementing laws that address a horrible situation and prevent it from getting worse. God was giving instruction in these laws to ensure a woman would be cared for and not put out on the street or discarded as a result of a crime she didn't commit. This law provided for a raped woman; her rapist would now have to financially provide for and support her. In our world today, this sounds unbelievable because women are not as dependent and have more options. It seems horribly cruel to even consider that whoever raped a woman would stay in relationship with her. But in that world, it was the equivalent of being sued by the victim and having to financially support the woman you had harmed. If the woman became his wife and part of his family, it meant he could never divorce her. This was God's way of creating accountability to prevent and deter crime.

With all of this in mind, it is important to note that the law requiring a rapist to marry his victim was not forced on the woman. It was the woman's legal right, if she chose, to pursue the law and request marriage or to reject it. What we read here is the command given to the rapist (not the woman), that he must pay fifty shekels, which was the normal bridal dowry for a wedding at that time, demonstrating that her value hadn't decreased due to the rape. These commands are given to the man, not the woman. This is what he must do; it does not say it is what she must do. We read in other parts of these early books of the Bible[*] that the woman could communicate through her father, who was the one responsible for her care, and choose not to marry her violator.

This is all complicated and very hard for us to culturally understand. None of this would be allowed in today's world. But it was such a different

---

[*]   Exodus 22:16–17.

world back then. If we examine it through the lens of that time and place, we see God intervening to make sure a woman was not left on her own when a crime was committed against her. Using this verse without a fuller look at the Bible and the ancient Israelite world is misleading. Yes, it makes a great meme or billboard and is an easy shot at the Bible, but when we examine it, we see it for what it really is: a law put in place to protect the innocent in a horrible situation in a patriarchal world.

Is It "Biblical Marriage" to Marry Many Wives?

Another set of crazy verses we consistently see pointed out are the examples of polygamy in the Bible. This is often brought up when Christians use the term "biblical marriage." After all, if you believe in "biblical marriage," then how do you explain polygamy? It seems to be common with many of the characters and heroes of the Old Testament, so is that "biblical marriage"? A popular infographic shows a series of marriage combinations, including polygamy. It argues that the Bible has many types of "marriages" in it, so saying there is only one cor- rect form is foolish and naïve. It means you don't know your Bible. The infographic shows polygamy, men having concubines (female

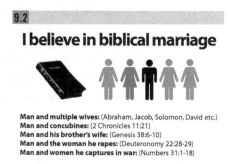

9.2

I believe in biblical marriage

Man and multiple wives: (Abraham, Jacob, Solomon, David etc.)
Man and concubines: (2 Chronicles 11:21)
Man and his brother's wife: (Genesis 38:6-10)
Man and the woman he rapes: (Deuteronomy 22:28-29)
Man and women he captures in war: (Numbers 31:1-18)

servants who did not have equal status as a wife), men marrying their rape victim, men marrying women captured in battle, and several others.

It's easy to see why Bible verses about polygamy, concubines, and forced marriages get shared online and mocked. Polygamy and having concubines is a consistent pattern for several major Bible characters who are viewed as heroes of faith. King David, Abraham, Gideon, and others had multiple wives and concubines.* Most people have likely heard of

---

*   1 Chronicles 14:3; 2 Samuel 5:13; Genesis 16:1–3; Judges 8:30.

the king of all polygamists, Solomon, who had 700 wives and 300 concubines.* All of this raises an honest question: does God allow men to
marry multiple wives, take on concubines for their pleasure, and treat
women as property?

Jesus Takes Us Back to the Original Marriage Design

Where did the practice of polygamy and concubines originate, and why
is it included in the Bible's timeline? When you look at the Bible story,
you need to see what God's original plan was from the beginning and
then the fallout from human beings going against God's original plan. So
we start at the beginning. When Jesus was asked about marriage, this
is exactly what he did. Jesus went back to the creation story in Genesis
chapters 1 and 2, and affirmed that God's plan for marriage was two
people, not many. He spoke about Adam and Eve becoming "one flesh."†
In speaking about the reality of divorce, Jesus said that divorce began
because of the hardening of human hearts, but then reminded everyone
that this was not God's original plan. Following the fallout, we immediately see the downward spiral of human beings rejecting God's original
design. In Genesis 4, Cain's son Lamech takes two wives, not one.

On and on it goes, with men taking not only multiple wives but
having concubines, women treated as property for a man's pleasure.
Polygamy becomes the norm in the ancient world of the Near East.
Even the Israelites stray from God's original design and adopt these cultural norms. At times, we see God working within these fallen cultural
practices (like polygamy and concubines), but we never see God endorsing them as good. The practices of polygamy and concubines became
ingrained in the culture. Some have suggested that because these practices were so widespread, if God had ordered a complete ban, it would
have led to many women being abandoned into poverty and starvation.

---

*   1 Kings 11:3.
†   Matthew 19:1–9.

In the ancient world, the options available to women were limited, and many were dependent on men for their safety and well-being. There was no social security or welfare system, and if dismissed from a polygamous marriage or from being a concubine, a woman would simply become homeless, abandoned by the people. Certainly evil and unfair, it was the norm.

The Bible offers a subtle commentary on these practices. Note that every time you see polygamy mentioned or a man who takes concubines, these things do not play out in their lives in good ways. Often, the characters who had multiple wives also had conflict, discord, competition, heartbreak, and messy relationships. God speaks to Solomon and tells him that his many wives have turned him against God and led him to worship other gods as a result.* King David caused great grief for his family—even causing the murder of an innocent man—after embracing several polygamous relationships. Having more than one wife was never seen as a good thing.† There is some irony in the beautiful depiction of courtship and marriage in the Old Testament book "Song of Songs." The book portrays the high point of human love as the marriage of two people, not a polygamous relationship. But most scholars believe this was written by Solomon, who had many wives and concubines. You also see God using the metaphor of marriage to depict the relationship between himself and Israel, and it is always God and *one* nation, not many nations.‡ In the last book of the Old Testament, Malachi,§ God gives an example of monogamous marriage as representative of his intent in designing marriage, referring to marriage between two people as a sacred covenant.

The New Testament removes any lingering doubts that polygamous marriage is not what God endorses or instructs. As we saw earlier, Jesus goes back to the beginning and emphasizes marriage as a man and woman, not multiple people, becoming "one flesh." We see in the New

---

*   1 Kings 11:4–10.
†   1 Samuel 18:27; 2 Samuel 11.
‡   Isaiah 54:5; Jeremiah 3:14.
§   Malachi 2:13–16.

Testament the model and instruction for church leaders in marriage to be "faithful to his wife."* Every example and marriage metaphor used clearly gives the standard for marriage being two people, not polygamous.†

Yes, there are several variations on marriage shown in the Bible, as the meme is pointing out. But the Bible story shows us that the original design was for two people, equals of value and worth, coming together as "one flesh" in a covenant of marriage before God. We see the New Testament reaffirm this when Jesus himself restates it. We see the trajectory of equality of men and women moving us toward a restoration of God's intended design, going back to the garden and his original creation purposes. We live in a fallen world, and in that fallout is inequality between the sexes resulting in human-designed institutions like polygamy and men having concubines. Yet God, in his love and grace, worked within these fallen systems to care for women in those systems.

The next time you read these Bible passages showing polygamy or you see this type of meme or hear jokes about "biblical marriage," I hope you will know that God did not endorse or advocate those types of marriages. These are not what Jesus pointed to as God's design and intention when asked about marriage. He went back to the original Genesis 1 and 2 design, when God's original creation and design was equality between a man and a woman in marriage, not for a man to marry multiple women or for men to have women as property for pleasure. God is working in the Old and New Testaments to move everything back to that design.

Does the Bible Say That Women Need to Submit and Be Silent?

Women should remain silent in the churches. They are not allowed to speak, but must be in submission, as the law says. If they want to

---

*   1 Timothy 3:2,12; Titus 1:6.
†   Ephesians 5:25–30; Revelation 19:7–8.

inquire about something, they should ask their own husbands at home; for it is disgraceful for a woman to speak in the church.

—1 CORINTHIANS 14:34–35

A woman should learn in quietness and full submission. I do not permit a woman to teach or to assume authority over a man; she must be quiet.

—1 TIMOTHY 2:11–12

How do we address the constant barrage of criticism against the Bible that it is sexist and misogynist? And the mother-of-all (pun intended) crazy-sounding Bible verses: women must be silent and submit. The Bible seems to say that women can't speak in church or it's a disgrace. That women can't teach men and are under the authority of men.

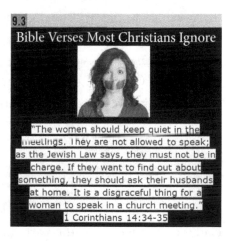

9.3
Bible Verses Most Christians Ignore

"The women should keep quiet in the meetings. They are not allowed to speak; as the Jewish Law says, they must not be in charge. If they want to find out about something, they should ask their husbands at home. It is a disgraceful thing for a woman to speak in a church meeting."
1 Corinthians 14:34-35

To understand these verses, I want to remind you to "never read a Bible verse," but instead ask the questions we have been asking and modeling for you in this book. Let's start by looking at who wrote the books (letters) that contain these Bible verses.

Who were these verses written by, to whom, and why?

Both of the Bible verses above were written by the apostle Paul in the post-resurrection time period when the church was being established. In our Bible timeline, this is when the new church is being instructed on how to worship God, how to live with each other, how to share Jesus with others, and how to live with morals and ethics that represent the followers of Jesus. Remember, at this time there was no New Testament. These letters (later part of the New Testament) were written because the early church was being developed. The new churches were facing many challenges because this was all new to them. They were still learning about who Jesus was. Making it even harder, they came from different cultures and backgrounds.

Some of the people following Jesus were from Jewish synagogues, and they may have understood the Old Testament law but were now being taught a new way of relating to God through Jesus. They might find some of the teaching confusing since they were used to the older ways of worshiping God in the temple and synagogues. People were coming into these churches from pagan backgrounds, having been immersed in the worship of other gods and goddesses. Paul wrote several letters to these churches during this dynamic, chaotic time period, a time filled with change and confusion about how churches should best function and operate. He wrote to instruct them in what to do as they met for worship and how to live their lives as followers of Jesus.

Crazy Things Happening in Their World Caused Crazy Bible Verses

Taking all of this into consideration, let's look at the verses closely, especially what is meant by the parts in these letters that say "women be silent" and "submit."

1 Corinthians 14:34–35

The letter to the Corinthian church was written by Paul around the year 55 AD. Four years prior to writing this letter, Paul spent a year and a half in the city of Corinth. He knew the church and he knew the people, and in the letter he indicates he had received a disturbing report of fighting and quarreling within the Corinthian church. From his letter we learn that all types of disruptive things were happening in their worship gatherings.* Before he tells women to "be silent" in this letter, Paul instructs the church about these sad divisions. Some were taking the Lord's Supper

---

* 1 Corinthians 11:1–14:39.

(sometimes called communion), while others weren't allowed to take it. Some were coming to the church meetings hungry because they were not included in the meal being served. Some were getting drunk on the wine used in the Lord's Supper. Some were going to the meetings while participating in ongoing open sin, with no evidence of sorrow or repentance. Paul tells them they are taking the Lord's Supper—a sacred and holy remembrance of the death and resurrection of Jesus—"in an unworthy manner." In other words, there were some pretty crazy things going on in the Corinthian church meetings. Paul was writing to correct these abuses and guide the people to unity.

1 Timothy 2:11–12

The second set of verses comes from a letter Paul wrote to the young church leader Timothy. Paul met Timothy around ten years earlier, and he had recruited him as a partner in ministry, traveling with him extensively.* The letter called "First Timothy" was the first of two letters we have that Paul wrote to Timothy in approximately 63 AD while Paul was in prison. Paul had been arrested for spreading the news about Jesus, and he was writing Timothy this letter to instruct him on structuring church leadership and appropriate conduct in a church's worship gatherings.

Timothy was living in Ephesus when this letter was written, and much like the letter to the Corinthian church, the church in Ephesus had significant problems. Remember, there was no "New Testament" and these churches were all new. Much was being figured out, and many of the people in these churches were coming from pagan backgrounds that included the worship of other gods. In Ephesus, the main religion was the worship of the goddess Artemis, and this posed a serious challenge to the new church, even leading to riots against those who were telling others about Jesus.† Many women in Ephesus were leaving the worship of Artemis and learning an entirely new way of relating to God through

---

* Acts 16:1–4.
† Acts 19:23–41.

Jesus. The Temple of Artemis (whom the Romans called Diana) was an all-female religion with castrated men serving as priests. Artemis was a fertility cult where worship involved sexual rites, including prostitution, practices that would shock people today. But the people of Ephesus, and many others at that time, believed these practices were what it meant to worship a god. All of this forms the backstory to the letter Paul is writing to Timothy. Some women in Ephesus were now part of the new faith, part of the worship gatherings of this new church, following Jesus, a man who died and returned from the dead.

In other parts of Paul's letter to Timothy, he addresses the issue of sensuality among younger widows. Why? Because this was the world they were living in and the culture of Ephesus.* We also read that these young widows, because they have nothing to do, become "busybodies" who talk "nonsense" (Paul's word). Paul was concerned for these women and wrote what he counsels them to do. In his letter to the Corinthians he mentions dress codes. All of this gives us the context to better understand what was happening in Corinth and Ephesus as we try to understand the verses that tell women to submit and be silent.

Paul Wanted Women to Speak

When we read these verses telling women to be "silent," we should read them in the context of other things Paul has said. Paul cannot literally mean that women should be totally silent, because just a few chapters earlier in the same letter, he acknowledges (with no sense of disapproval) that women prophesied and prayed aloud in the church.† We also see Paul talking about both men and women (with no distinctions made) singing, praying, and sharing with each other in the church meetings. So unless Paul is contradicting himself in the same letter, he doesn't intend for women to never speak a word. It must mean something else.

---

*   1 Timothy 5:11–12.
†   1 Corinthians 11:13.

In the same letter, Paul also writes about how God's Spirit gives out spiritual gifts that are special skills the Holy Spirit provides, enabling people to serve the church and others. Yet we see no instruction that men and women should be using these gifts differently.* Many of the gifts he mentions would involve speaking in church worship meetings. Unless Paul is contradicting himself, the verse cannot mean for women to be totally silent. As mentioned in the last chapter, Paul worked alongside women who had leadership roles of influence in churches. He also refers to a woman who is very likely an apostle. This passage cannot be saying women must be "silent" in church, as these tasks involved some speaking. It must mean something else.

Specific Instruction about a Temporary Silencing Was Normal in That Culture

Since the context does not mean total silence, we still need to try to understand what Paul might have meant in that culture at that time. When you look back at the lifestyle and world of the Romans and Greeks (the cultural world this letter was written in) it suggests a few options for making sense of these verses. Most likely, Paul's commands refer to specific cultural practices we don't know about in our contemporary world. Because we're looking back into a different culture and it is hard to understand exactly what was happening, there are several options scholars suggest for us to consider.

Option 1: A Common Custom

A common custom during that time period was that when you had not been educated on a topic, it was disrespectful to interrupt the teacher and ask questions. Question asking or commenting during a teaching wasn't accepted etiquette and the norm. Isocrates, a popular Greek orator and teacher, required his students to remain silent when he taught. Rabbi

---

* 1 Corinthians 12:7–30.

Akiba, a contemporary of Paul, and Philo, who was a first-century Jewish leader, also commended silence during teaching.[2]

The "silence" mentioned here doesn't mean an absolute tape-over-your-mouth not speaking. Instead, it likely means to adopt a "quiet demeanor" appropriate for students of that time period who wished to learn.[3] Also, when you see the words saying a woman "must be in submission," in this context it is talking about a posture of learning, not being in a lower or lesser position.

There may have been a problem in Ephesus if women who were worshipers of Artemis, a deity with an extremely different approach to worship and learning, were not seeking to follow Christ. Paul may be giving some instruction to preserve order for learning. In that time and culture, men generally were more educated, so this helps us understand why Paul speaks to those with husbands. These women may have had questions, but instead of disrupting the teaching time in the worship gathering, Paul felt it was best for them to first ask their husband later. We may not know all the details behind this command, but what we do know is that it cannot be about women never speaking in church gatherings.

Let me wrap up this section with a quote from Bible scholar guru and personal friend Scot McKnight. Scot writes about these two verses from 1 Corinthians and 1 Timothy, taking into consideration the whole storyline of the Bible and looking at the full context of Paul's treatment of women. He writes:

> Paul's two comments about silence are actually consistent, then, with the story and plot of the Bible. Women, who have always been gifted by God to speak for God and lead God's people, were doing those things in Paul's churches. But women who had not yet learned Bible or theology or had not yet learned to live a Christian life were not to become teachers until they had learned orthodox theology.
>
> What drives 1 Corinthians 14 and 1 Timothy 2 is a principle that much of church tradition has nearly smothered when to comes to women: "learning precedes teaching."

So according to option 1, these verses are not about keeping women silent at all times in the church. Women were encouraged at that time to learn in a respectful way so they could help others learn. To the women back then, this would have made sense.

Option 2: Separate Seating

In Jewish worship at that time and as is still common today in the more conservative branches of Judaism, women and men sit separately. This is done in Islamic mosques today as well. Within Judaism this is just a custom, not directed in the Bible. Some have suggested that this "separate seating" was happening in these early church meetings, and this practice may have led to problems. If women who weren't educated (due to the way women were treated at that time) had questions, they might try asking their husbands, possibly shouting across the room. This would understandably cause distractions for others in the worship gathering. Or if the women were on their own or unmarried and they were confused about the teaching, they might begin talking among themselves, disrupting the worship gathering. If option 2 was the case, it makes sense why Paul would be asking them to stay quiet and wait until later to ask questions.

This is all speculative. We don't know what the situation was in these cities. In the churches Paul was writing to, however, I am sure they did know the situation. They were firsthand aware of what Paul was addressing to them. But it is not super clear to us, and I wish it was, but even the disciple Peter said that in Paul's letters to outside readers, "some things . . . are hard to understand."* This is why there is still some debate about how exactly to understand these verses. What we do know is that Paul could not have been asking women to remain totally silent or to submit to men like servants or people of lesser value. That would invalidate and contradict everything else we see in his writings as well as the trajectory of Scripture as a whole.

---

*   2 Peter 3:16.

There Are Many Other Crazy-Sounding Things about Women in the Bible

In this chapter, I've addressed some of the most publicized verses used to make the claim that the Bible is anti-women. But there are others as well, such as:

- Does a woman have to keep her head covered when church gatherings happen? (1 Corinthians 11:3–16)
- Does a woman need to submit to her husband in everything? (Ephesians 5:24)
- Does a woman need to have a baby in order to be "saved"? (1 Timothy 2:15)

Oh, the many amazingly weird and wonderful questions the Bible raises! But when you look into the backstory to understand the cultural background, there is sense to be made from what sounds so strange to us. You can have confidence that these Bible verses also have legitimate interpretations.

We can conclude with confidence that when we read the crazy-sounding Bible verses that seem to advocate misogynist practices, that's not what is happening. Quite often, we find the Bible teaching the exact opposite of the initial criticism or accusation. Time after time, we find God moving fallen human institutions and practices back toward the trajectory he intended in the beginning. For men and women this means back to the beauty of equality. Jesus brings all people, male and female, into a position of equal value, worth, and significance, breaking down the power divisions and the racial and ethnic divisions as well. Paul's words make this clear, that since Jesus came, "There is neither Jew nor Gentile, neither slave nor free, nor is there male and female, for you are all one in Christ Jesus."*

---

*   Galatians 3:28.

The misogyny and inequality of those times are rejected by Jesus. We are all one, people of equal value and worth. The Old Testament prophet Joel predicted this movement, as we saw Peter the apostle quoting at the birth of the church in Acts 2:17–18. Joel predicted a day when both men and women would be voices for God prophesying (which means they aren't silent!):

> "'In the last days, God says,
>> I will pour out my Spirit on *all* people.
> Your *sons and daughters* will prophesy,
>> your young men will see visions,
>> your old men will dream dreams.
> Even on my servants, *both men and women*,
>> I will pour out my Spirit in those days,
>> and they will prophesy.'"

Something new and unprecedented in human history was happening with the birth of the church. In the fallout of sin in this patriarchal world, God was moving to bring change and restore what had been lost. Dr. Rodney Stark, a sociologist, writes in his book *The Rise of Christianity* that "Christianity was unusually appealing [to women] because within the Christian subculture women enjoyed far higher status than did women in the Greco-Roman world at large." He notes that the early church "attracted an unusual number of high-status women."[4]

Has the church throughout the ages used certain Bible verses against women in wrong, even harmful ways? Sadly, yes. There have been—and still are—some churches and Christians who misuse the text to create misogyny in God's name. But when you study the Scriptures and seek to understand them in their cultural context, it's clear that the Bible is not against women, but an advocate for women. God created women and men to represent him, to make a difference in this world, serving uniquely as men and women, as equals, with whatever gifts God has given them.

Christians Have Been at the Forefront of the Fight for the Dignity of Women Around the World

Among all the major world cultures and major religions, Christian men and women have often been the ones working to empower women and set them free from the cultural institutions that entrap them. For centuries in China, a common cultural practice was to cripple the feet of young girls for life through the horrid practice of "foot binding." This was done to supposedly make them more pleasurable for men later in their lives. Christians were instrumental in ending this practice. In India, widows were required to commit suicide by throwing themselves into the fire of their late husband's funeral pyre (when they burned the husband's body). Efforts of Christian missionaries put an end to this cultural practice.

We still have a long way to go in ending these kinds of cultural practices. There are still many churches where men and women are not valued equally. But if you happen to be driving around and see that fellow in the pickup truck with "Women be silent" and "Read Your Bible" painted on the back, I'd like you to pull up next to him, roll down your window, and shout, "We do read our Bibles! Those verses do not mean what you think they mean. They are not about women being silent! The Bible is an advocate for women!" Then wave and drive away happy. You have shared the good news about women and reminded him that he needs to consider the context before he writes Bible verses on his truck.

Part 3 Summary Points

BOYS' CLUB CHRISTIANITY

- In the beginning, God created a perfect harmony of man and woman—unique but equal. After humans rebelled against God in the garden, patriarchal sin developed with various types of abuse of women, including misogyny and polygamy. This is not what God created; it is what humans put in place.
- The New Testament Bible verses that at first read sound misogynistic and chauvinistic have explanations when you go beyond just reading the isolated verses. Misunderstandings are due to not looking at the specific situations and unique culture of that time period.
- Jesus and the New Testament show the forward trajectory of women being seen as of equal worth, value, and importance in God's sight and serving on mission together with men.

PART 4

Jesus Riding a Dinosaur

Do We Have to Choose Between

Science and the Bible?

CHAPTER 10

Jesus Riding a Dinosaur

Even though we know dinosaurs survived the Flood (on Noah's Ark) we don't know if Jesus ever rode them. . . . But he probably did!

—PAGE FROM A FICTITIOUS SATIRICAL
CHILDREN'S COLORING BOOK

There is a wonderfully creative and humorous shirt sold by a national clothing store where the front of the shirt has a children's coloring book style image of Jesus, and he is riding bareback on what looks like a velociraptor. The shirt ingeniously pokes fun at the logic of a strictly literal word-for-word interpretation of the creation account and the flood from the book of Genesis.

The artwork raises the point that if one holds to a literal twenty-four-hour, six-day creation understanding of Genesis chapter 1, that would mean that on day 6, God created both human beings and dinosaurs. It reads in Genesis that God made "the wild animals . . . the livestock . . . and all the creatures that move along the ground. . . . God created mankind in his own image . . . male and female he created them."* Taken at

---

* Genesis 1:25, 27.

face value, this means dinosaurs would be included in the "all creatures," and dinosaurs and humans were created on the same twenty-four-hour day and existed together.

Naturally this all plays out later when Noah builds the ark. Would dinosaurs have been part of the group of animals, the birds, and "the creatures that move along the ground" that would enter into the ark? Continuing this literal approach at reading the Bible, if dinosaurs were on the ark, it means they survived the flood. So they would likely still have been alive like all the other creatures who were still around at the time of Jesus. Putting this logic together, the shirt depicts that if the dinosaurs were around when Jesus was on earth, then he surely would have had some fun and chosen to ride them.

All Sold Out of Jesus and the Dinosaur

Personally, seeing that image of Jesus riding a dinosaur on that shirt was pretty darn amazing. I tried to get one of the shirts from our local store, but they had sold out of most sizes. I tried searching for it online and learned it was sold out everywhere. I can understand why, as the image of Jesus riding a dinosaur makes a fascinating combination.

If you do an internet search of the words "Jesus" and "dinosaur,"

10.3

you'll find all sorts of creative depictions of Jesus petting a nodosaurus, Jesus lovingly cradling a baby T. rex, and Jesus getting baptized with a brontosaurus in the background. I don't personally know of any Christian who takes their Bible interpretation to this extreme and thinks dinosaurs were alive and around at the time of Jesus. But it makes a brilliant T-shirt and raises some good questions about what the Bible says or doesn't say about creation, evolution, and science.

"If I Can't Believe in Science, Then I Can't Believe in the Bible Anymore."

This discussion goes far beyond fun T-shirts and artists being creative and depicting Jesus with dinosaurs. It's really a discussion about whether we can trust the validity of the Bible when compared to what we know of science in today's world. This is an important issue and a question that prompts some Christians to give up their faith. It's a question that leads others to reject Christianity because they think the Bible can't be taken seriously with what we know of science today.

Stories of college students abandoning their faith can almost sound like a cliché, another statistic, but they are real. I've talked to many students. I once met a college student who was raised in a Christian home and eventually left the faith, now calling himself an atheist. His reason? The conflict he saw between science and the biblical creation account. He had grown up in a church that taught a very specific understanding of Genesis and how to interpret the creation story. His church strongly believed that the Bible teaches the earth is only around 6,000 to 10,000 years old and days were twenty-four-hour time periods. This interpretation is commonly known as "Young Earth Creationism." (We'll have more on this view later.) The young earth viewpoint teaches that human beings and dinosaurs existed at the same time.

This college student had become a microbiology major and began questioning the idea that the earth was 10,000 years old or less based on his studies at the university. He talked to the pastor of his church and to his parents and was lovingly cautioned and informed that if he didn't believe the 6,000- to 10,000-year age of the earth was accurate, he was doubting the Bible. He was told that the words in the Bible clearly indicate the six days were literal twenty-four-hour days, and if you follow the Bible timeline with the various genealogies, this means the earth is 6,000 to 10,000 years old. Because this is so clearly written in the Bible, it means that doubts about the creation account and the age of the earth

155

are doubts about everything else the Bible teaches. If you don't believe in a literal interpretation of Genesis and the young earth view, then why believe Jesus even rose from the dead, since that is in the Bible too?

This dilemma of choice caused this young student great internal anguish. He didn't want to abandon the faith of his youth, but at the same time he was being told that doubting or rejecting a literal reading of Genesis chapter 1, was the same as rejecting Jesus and the resurrection. Sadly, this led to an either/or choice—the Bible versus science. With great angst he chose science.

This is horrifying because it's entirely avoidable.

Thankfully, this student later attended some lectures by a well-respected conservative Old Testament Bible scholar who said that there were other ways of understanding these verses from Genesis. This scholar holds a high view of the Scriptures, seeing them as 100 percent inspired by God and accurate. In the chapters that follow, we'll take a closer look at these interpretations. Seeing there were other ways of viewing Genesis led this student to reevaluate his decision to become an atheist, and joyfully, he came back to faith in Jesus.

Do We Believe in a 6,000-Year-Old Earth, a Talking Snake, and a Rib-Woman Who Ate from a Magical Tree?

If you read through the Bible from beginning to end, you will find all kinds of passages that seem to fly in the face of science. In the Old Testament, you find people living to more than 900 years old. Noah builds an ark to house a massive zoo to escape a global flood. A talking snake, a talking donkey, and so many other strange-sounding things make the Bible sound like a mythical fairy tale—nonsense that defies science and rational thinking.[1]

This doesn't end in the Old Testament, because we read in the New Testament about amazing healings, angels appearing, water turned into wine, a storm calmed by Jesus, and the very focal point of the Christian faith—the story of a man being killed, put in a grave, and raised again to life three days later.* The Bible is filled with many things that make no sense when you compare them to what we know rationally and scientifically. So naturally we see criticism and humorous joking, such as a widely spread meme that Jesus was a zombie or that "a rib-woman was convinced by a talking snake to eat from a magical tree."

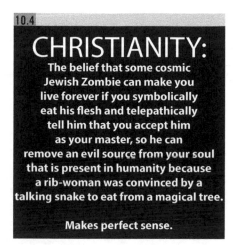

10.4

CHRISTIANITY:
The belief that some cosmic Jewish Zombie can make you live forever if you symbolically eat his flesh and telepathically tell him that you accept him as your master, so he can remove an evil source from your soul that is present in humanity because a rib-woman was convinced by a talking snake to eat from a magical tree.

Makes perfect sense.

We could explore many questions regarding science and the Bible, but for the purpose of this book, we will focus on common critiques and what generally comes to mind when people think of the conflict between science and the Bible. That generally is directed at the Bible's account of the creation of the universe, the earth, and people in the early chapters of Genesis. It's in these chapters where we read about the length of the earth's creation and the rib-woman, the talking snake, and the magical tree. The early chapters of Genesis are the focus of debates about creation versus evolution, which put the Bible to a credibility test. I hope that studying these chapters can help us to gain more trust and confidence in what the Bible has to say.

---

* Matthew 4:23–24; Luke 7:11–16; Matthew 1:20; 28:2–4; John 2:1–12; Mark 4:35–41; John 20:1–18.

CHAPTER 11

In the Beginning We Misunderstood

> The most vital question for the interpreters of any literature (and especially the Bible) to ask is, what did the human authors (and ultimately the divine Author, God the Holy Spirit) intend for his original audience to understand when they read the passage?[1]
>
> —FROM THE BOOK, *IN THE BEGINNING WE MISUNDERSTOOD*

As soon as you open the Bible and read the first two pages, you see some crazy-sounding things. The beginning of the Bible starts out with some verses telling us how God created the universe, the earth, and basically everything that exists in what seems to be six days. The earth was created on day 1, the sun and the moon were created on day 4, and animals and people on day 6. The Bible indicates this is all completed after the six days: "There was evening, and there was morning—the sixth day. Thus the heavens and the earth were completed in all their vast array."*

---

*   Genesis 1:31–2:1.

If you read these verses and take them in the literal sense, you can conclude that the earth is around 6,000 years old. Some believe that since Adam was created on day 6 of the seven days of creation, you should start the timetable there and add up the years that Adam's descendants lived as shown in the various genealogies (records of family lineage) recorded in the Bible.[2] The lists of Adam's descendants take you right up to Abraham and cover around 2,000 years. From Abraham to Jesus being born is another 2,000 years, for a total, from Adam to Jesus, of around 4,000 years. Add on another 2,000 years from Jesus to our time period, and you have the earth created roughly 6,000 years ago. That's how that number for the age of the earth is determined.

You can see why someone looking at the Bible and taking a literal reading of these verses about the days of creation in Genesis chapter 1 has questions. Here are a few of the most common:

- **Length of creation:** Does the Bible say that God created everything— the universe, the heavens, the earth, everything on the earth, including people—in less than a week—in six twenty-four-hour days?
- **Age of the earth:** If the Bible teaches that God created everything in six days, does it mean we have to believe that the earth is only around 6,000 years old?
- **The earth and sun sequence of creation:** How was there light for each day and how was the earth suspended in space if the sun (which the earth orbits around) wasn't created until day 4?
- **Creation versus evolution:** If the Bible teaches God created in the way the words say in Genesis, does that mean what I'm learning about evolution is false? So either evolution or the Bible is correct?
- **Dinosaurs:** If I read the creation sequence as God creating humans and all land creatures on the same twenty-four-hour day, does that mean it is saying that dinosaurs and human beings coexisted? Could Jesus have ridden a dinosaur, like the T-shirt joked about?

In chapters 2 and 3, you read more crazy-sounding verses such as:

- "So the LORD God caused the man to fall into a deep sleep; and while he was sleeping, he took one of the man's ribs and then closed up the place with flesh. Then the LORD God made a woman from the rib he had taken out of the man, and he brought her to the man" (Genesis 2:21–22).
- "Now the serpent was more crafty than any of the wild animals the LORD God had made. He said to the woman, 'Did God really say, "You must not eat from any tree in the garden"?'" (Genesis 3:1).

This is why questions arise about the tree and Eve (who was allegedly made from the rib of a man as told in Genesis 2:21–23) and a talking serpent. These things are repeatedly pointed out and mocked with questions such as:

- Does the Bible say a snake talked?
- Was Eve a "rib-woman" made from the bone of a man?
- Did Eve speak with a talking snake and then eat an apple from a magical tree?

I understand why people poke fun at these verses. I understand why they are not drawn to the Bible or Christianity if this is all they hear about the Bible. It's true that on first reading, these Bible verses sound mythical, like a children's fable. Some people today see the Bible as nonsense. The discoveries of science over the last three centuries seem to disprove this part of the Bible. I understand the criticism. But as we've seen with other Bible criticisms and misunderstandings, they often arise from reading a verse or a few verses. If we don't look at the context, we can easily come to all sorts of conclusions that don't align with what the Bible is actually saying. The Bible is an ancient book written across centuries, and we must use the minds God gave us to examine these claims against the Bible to see if they are true and accurate in the way they are presented.

Genesis Was Written Not to Us but for Us

There is a book with the clever title *In the Beginning We Misunderstood* written by two conservative Bible scholars. They have their doctorates in theology and Bible from a well-known and respected evangelical seminary that is highly committed to the authority of the Scriptures. They tell their stories of how they both were so passionate and focused on studying the text of the Bible and learning the original languages.

They held to the 100 percent full inspiration and authority of the entire Bible and were extremely zealous to correctly understand it. They wanted to be faithful to interpret the words of the inspired Bible as accurately as possible (as we all should be). With the creation account in the book of Genesis, they originally interpreted these verses to indicate that God created everything in six twenty-four-hour days, and that means the earth is relatively young in age, around 6,000 years old.

As the book continues, however, they tell the fascinating story of how they shifted their view about the early chapters of Genesis. They realized they had been too narrowly focused and consumed with intense study of the text, word by word, and they had forgotten something very important. They didn't step back and look at the bigger context. Why were these chapters in the Bible? What is their purpose in the larger story? In their passion to be faithful to the Scriptures, they forgot to ask this basic and important Bible study question. Here is what they learned, in their own words:

> I realized that all my life I had been reading Genesis from the perspective of a modern person. I had read it through the lens of a historically sophisticated, scientifically influenced individual. I assumed Genesis was written to answer the questions of origins that people are asking today.
>
> But I had never asked the most important vital question of all: What did Moses mean when he wrote this text? After all, "my Bible" was Moses' "Bible" first. Was Moses acquainted with Charles Darwin? . . . Was he writing to discredit any modern theory of evolution? Were his readers troubled by calculations of the speed of light and the distance

of the galaxies from earth? Were they puzzling over the significance of DNA? Were they debating a young earth versus an old earth? Would they have had any inkling about a modern scientific worldview?

If you agree that the answer to these questions is obviously no, then the logical question is, what was on their minds? How would they have understood Genesis 1?. . . *What did Genesis mean to the original author and original readers?*[3]

This is really, really, important. We need to stop and look deeply at what they are telling us here. We can faithfully study, read, and intensely examine specific words from Bible verses, but the question "What did Genesis mean to the original author and original readers?" is *the* question. As we've been saying throughout this book, "The Bible was not written to us but for us."

When you and I open the Bible in Genesis, we immediately want to know the answers to our contemporary questions, the ones we raise from our worldview and our cultural experience. We want to know what the Bible says about the age of the earth, the fossil records, dinosaurs, Darwinism, macroevolution versus microevolution, genomes and the DNA sequence of organisms, amino acids, light years, and carbon dating. We open the pages and want to have answers for all the things that consume our current debates between Christianity and science. However, these questions were not the concerns of the original audience that God was communicating to. They weren't the reason or purpose behind what he communicated.

Studying the Bible Doesn't Mean You Mistrust the Bible

All Scripture is 100 percent God-breathed, authoritative, trustworthy, and useful for many, many things.* But just as we do with any part of the Bible, we need to put effort into looking at the original recipients and the original purpose of what is written. This isn't an attempt to lessen

---

*   2 Timothy 3:15–16.

our respect or reverence for the Bible's absolute authority or to doubt the sacred God-inspired Holy Scriptures. Instead, it takes the Bible more seriously, forcing us to dive deeply into it. When we study and ask these questions, we can make better sense of what God wanted his original readers to do and know and what or what not he may be saying for us today to do and know.

As we saw in part 1 of this book, there are different genres of the Bible and different ways we need to approach reading the Bible, depending on what part or genre we are reading. When Jesus said, "I am the bread of life,"* we know he was not literally implying he was a loaf of bread made of grain. When the writer of Psalm 17 wrote to God asking him to "hide me in the shadow of your wings" (v. 8), he didn't mean God has physical wings and looks like a bird. When you read the Bible, you need to ask if it is meant to be a literal understanding of the words. This is not doubting God's Word, it is just being a good student of Scripture so we understand what God was communicating. We want to grasp what God was communicating, what Genesis meant to the original author and the original readers.

Ancient Israelite Bible Study Methods 101

Before we look at questions about a talking snake, dinosaurs, and the age of the earth, we need a history lesson. To understand crazy-sounding Bible passages, we need to look at some Bible context. We need to go back and place ourselves in the world of the ancient Israelites so we "Never read a Bible verse" on its own. We need to ask some questions to help us understand.

1. Who Were the Original Readers of Genesis?
Knowing to whom and why Genesis was written makes a big difference in how we understand it. The primary writer and editor of Genesis is

---

* John 6:35.

believed to be a man named Moses, who was writing to the Israelites. (There may have been some inspired editing and some shaping that occurred later, but Moses is traditionally considered to be the primary author of what we read in Genesis.)[4] You can review the storyline of the Bible in chapter 3 to see where Moses fits in the Bible story. But the real story of to whom and why Genesis was written goes back even further, to a man named Abraham who lived around 2100 BC. Abraham is the person God chose and made a "covenant" with (a promise and agreement), promising him that through his lineage and family all the world would be blessed.[*] Abraham and his immediate descendants didn't know it at the time, but this blessing would ultimately be brought about in Jesus. Jesus would one day come and die for the salvation of all people and all nations—he was born of the lineage of Abraham.

God also promised Abraham that he would receive land for his descendants.[†] This land is what we call "the promised land," and it is where the city of Jerusalem and the Jewish temple would later be built. This is the land where King David lived and where Jesus would later be born, suffer death, and rise from the dead.

As time passed, Abraham and his descendants multiplied and became the people of Israel. In the story, the Israelites went down to Egypt to escape a famine up north. As more centuries passed, they became slaves of the Egyptians. The story has a twist at this point, as God's chosen people were no longer in the land God had promised them. They were slaves living in the land and culture of the Egyptians. Keep in mind this was not just for a few years, but for around *four hundred years*.[‡] Generation after generation of God's chosen people were being immersed in a world controlled by the Egyptians, learning the Egyptian origin stories, their values, and their religious beliefs. There is debate on the exact years, but scholars believe the Israelites were in Egypt for the approximately four hundred years in slavery either in the 1200s BC or the 1400s BC.

---

*   Genesis 12:1–3.
†   Genesis 17:3–8.
‡   Genesis 15:13; Exodus 12:40–41; Acts 7:8.

Keep reading. I know you want to find out about the talking snake
and evolution, but this is so important to know first.

While living as slaves in Egypt, the Israelites would have passed down oral traditions and remnants of stories about Abraham and the promises God made to them. But this was still a long time to live in slavery, hundreds of years immersed in Egypt. Day after day they would wake up to see Egyptian statues of Egyptian gods, living in the Egyptians' world with Egyptian values. The Egyptians didn't worship the God of the Israelites, instead worshiping many different types of gods including the sun, the moon, several animal-like gods, a few goddesses, and even some people. The Egyptians had creation stories to explain how their gods had created everything. This is the world the Israelites lived in—not just for ten years or fifty years or a hundred years—but for four hundred years.

The Israelites' understanding of the world was inevitably affected by their time living in Egypt. Remember, at this time there was no written Bible for them to read. There were no Ten Commandments, no Psalms to read for comfort or to remind them of God and his promises. Day after day they lived in a pluralistic Egyptian world of many different gods and religious practices. We read in the book of Joshua that some of them even served the Egyptian gods.[*] Here is the reason why all of this matters: Genesis was written to the Israelites after they had lived in a land that worshiped many gods to remind them of who the one true God was— not to explain the science and details of creation. Genesis was written to tell the Israelites the story of the covenant he made with their forefather Abraham, not to explain when dinosaurs were around and how to view the fossil records.

After four hundred years of slavery and life in Egypt, God decided it was time to rescue his people, the descendants of Abraham. He chose

---

[*]   Joshua 24:2, 23.

Moses to lead "the chosen people" of Israel into "the promised land." God punished Egypt with a series of ten plagues to knock down the arrogance and confidence of Pharaoh, the Egyptian leader, and force him to release Israel from slavery. The plagues God chose were not random events—they were quite intentional. Each of the ten plagues was a direct assault on one of the gods of the Egyptians. For example, Egyptians worshiped the god Hapi, the Egyptian God of the Nile River, and it was believed that the god Osiris had the Nile River as his bloodstream. God demonstrated his power over the river—and the Egyptian gods—by turning the river water blood red. The Egyptians also worshiped the goddess Heqet, who had the head of a frog. God demonstrated his power over this Egyptian goddess by causing frogs to appear everywhere, showing that the God of Israel is the true God, not Heqet. The Egyptians worshiped the god Ra, the sun god and one of the most revered gods in Egypt. So the God of Israel caused the sun to go dark, showing he is the true God and has power over the mightiest of the Egyptian gods.

After Pharaoh relents and releases the people, Moses leads them into the desert outside of Egypt, where they live for forty years before entering the promised land. Consider that for a moment. You have people who have been immersed in Egyptian culture for more than four hundred years, and they are now out of Egypt for the first time in centuries, living in the desert in tents while they wait for Moses to lead them into the "promised land." The book of Genesis was written to these people during this time.

They had no Bible, so God is telling them who they are. He is giving them their background and teaching them who he is. The people didn't have the full story. They didn't know who had made them or who this God who had rescued them from Egypt was or how to worship him. They had bits and pieces from the oral traditions, but Moses was writing the Bible to the Israelites living at this time. As the ancient Israelites wandered in the desert, they probably had a lot of questions that God wanted to let them know answers to.

Questions Israel Likely Had That Genesis Was Written to Answer

- Are we going to survive here in the desert? Are we safe here?
- Is there really only one God? What about all the Egyptians gods? Are they angry we left Egypt?
- Is this God who rescued us still here, or are we alone?
- What do we have to do to please this one God so we will have crops that won't fail and have food for our families?
- Should we worship the sun? Should we worship the moon like the Egyptians? Or worship like the Canaanites, who are now nearby?
- Is the Egyptian story of how the world was made the true one?

Newly freed from four hundred years of living in the polytheistic world of Egypt, God was about to give them a new story, a new history. God used Moses to write Genesis and four other books that would come to be known as the Law (Genesis, Exodus, Leviticus, Numbers, Deuteronomy). We often separate Genesis from the other books, but it isn't a stand-alone book. Genesis is the first of a five-part miniseries that is the first book in the library of the Bible. This five-part collection is sometimes called the Pentateuch (meaning "five-volume book") or the "Book of the Law." Reading Genesis on its own is like reading Tolkien's *Fellowship of the Ring* but not realizing there are two additional parts to the story (*The Two Towers* and *Return of the King*). This is true of the whole Bible story, from Genesis to Revelation, but the first five books are a complete mini-story on their own. When we look at two or three pages of Genesis, we need to keep in mind that this is but the introduction to a five-book volume Moses was writing. All these things matter if we wish to make sense of Bible passages from the book of Genesis.

In Genesis, God had Moses write what the Israelites needed to know about him to answer their questions about him. It was *not* written to answer many of the questions we have today.

Questions That We Have Today That Genesis Was Not Written to Answer

- How old is the earth? Six thousand years? Six billion years?
- Was it in six literal twenty-four-hour days or six long periods of time that God made everything?
- Does the lack of major transitional forms in the fossil records disprove evolution?
- Could primitive nucleic acids, amino acids, and other building blocks of life have formed and organized themselves into self-replicating, self-sustaining units, laying the foundation for cellular biochemistry?
- Was there really a talking snake?
- Were there dinosaurs on Noah's ark?
- If God created Adam as the first person, did he have a belly button?

These are all interesting, great questions. But these questions wouldn't have made any sense, or even have been asked, by the original audience of Israelites God was communicating to. Today, you and I may want to know the answers to these questions as we read Genesis through a modern lens, but the original audience would not have had these questions. God wanted to teach them other things that were equally important. They weren't the scientific questions of our day. Knowing this matters when reading Genesis, that it wasn't written to us to answer our questions about science and evolution.

2. Why Was Genesis Written and What Did God Want the Original Audience to Know?

With this background, let's turn to some of those crazy-sounding Bible passages in Genesis, remembering that it was written to Israelites who had been living in a polytheistic Egyptian culture for four hundred years and needed to be reminded and taught many things about God they either had forgotten or had never known.

- God wanted the people to know he is the one and only true God, not the Egyptian gods or the other gods of the surrounding people groups.
- God wanted Israel to know that his presence was with them.
- God wanted the people to know who they were—his chosen people—and about the "covenant" he had made with their forefather Abraham. He wanted them to understand that all the world would be blessed through them and that he had promised them a land to live in.
- God wanted the Israelites to know he created the heavens and the earth and all that exists. His story was different from the Egyptian creation story and the other creation stories like the *Enuma Elish* or the *Epic of Gilgamesh*. These stories told about other gods and goddesses creating everything.
- God wanted the Israelites to know he is the one true God and he is personal, compassionate, slow to anger, and abounding in love.* These character qualities were very different from those of the other deities they were familiar with.
- God wanted the Israelites to know how to properly worship him and how to live as a community of people with each other in the promised land.

These are the reasons why God had Moses write what is written in the first five books of the Bible—to teach the Israelites these things. We need to begin our reading not with the questions we may have today, but with the questions they had back at that time. God was communicating to them in a way that made sense to them based on the world in which they lived.

3. How Did the Audience Understand the World around Them?

Once we realize the purpose behind what God was communicating in Genesis, we must also try to understand his audience's worldview or how

---

* Exodus 34:6; Numbers 14:18.

170

they understood the world around them. Many of us wrongly assume that the people of the past thought about the world in the same way, with the same assumptions we have. But that's not true. God was communicating with them in a specific context. Unless we look into that world, we will misunderstand what God was saying. When we open the Bible to any section, we are also opening up the worldview of the original recipients, a way of seeing the world that is very different than our own. God speaks to the people using the worldview they had so they could understand what God wanted them to know.

Thinking with Your Entrails and Living under the Water Dome

For example, at the time Genesis was written, the ancient Israelites didn't know that the brain was the part of the human body that was the source of thinking, learning, and controlling other parts of our body. They believed the control center was the heart, since the heart muscle pumps masses of blood around our bodies.

When you see the word "heart" in Genesis (Genesis 24:45; 34:3), you should know that it is referring to the source of our emotions *and* thinking. Today we would likely refer to this as our brain, not our heart. But they didn't have a word for the brain back then, and they believed the physical heart was the source of thinking. They also believed our emotions and thinking came from our entrails, or our

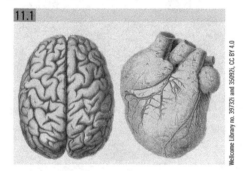

"gut."[5] The people of that time thought the human intellect came from the actual heart and abdominal organs.

So did God lie to them when he didn't correct their improper usage of the "heart," even using it himself? Not at all! God simply chose not to correct them in their incorrect understanding of heart physiology. God didn't provide science lessons on the function of the brain. He spoke to them in the context of what they already believed. God used what they were aware of and the assumptions in their existing worldview to communicate the truths he wanted them to know at that time. He didn't feel it was necessary to correct their "scientific" understanding of how the brain and heart worked. He wanted to make sure they got the point of what he was saying, so to communicate he used what they knew and believed.

The World the Ancient Israelites Knew

This is equally true when we look at how God communicated the creation story to the ancient Israelites. He used the worldview they had and knew. God wasn't seeking to communicate scientific truths as we understand them today. He was communicating truth about who he was in a way they could understand. When the opening verse of the Bible in Genesis 1:1 says, "In the beginning God created the heavens and the

11.2

earth," certain things would come to mind to those hearing the words "heavens" and "earth." We think of "heavens" and think of the solar system, the Milky Way, and the amazing images of space that the Hubble Telescope captured. When we think of "earth," we imagine the whole earth as a sphere orbiting around the sun.

However, Old Testament scholars wisely remind us that unlike what comes to mind when we think of the "heavens" and "earth," the ancient Israelites would have thought of something very different.[6]

If an ancient Israelite saw the image of the earth shown in image 11.2, one we are so familiar with today, they would have had no idea what it was. Remember, this image was first seen when a photograph of earth was taken from space in 1946. We didn't have this view of earth in our minds prior to that time. Three thousand years ago, an Israelite's understanding of the earth and heavens would have been consistent with their specific culture and how that culture saw the world.[7]

When we read Genesis 1:1, it says God created the "heavens and the earth," but the Hebrew word for "heavens" used here can also be translated as "sky," and the word for "earth" can be translated as "land." They weren't thinking of a Hubble telescope photo of space or a picture of the earth's continents from space. They would have immediately thought about the sky and the land they could see. God was telling them he had created *all* the sky and *all* the land they could see. So what was the ancient understanding of the heavens (sky) and earth (land)? The views of the ancient Israelites' were quite similar to those of the Egyptians and other surrounding people groups.

Walk like an Egyptian to Understand the Bible

The ancient Israelites would have been familiar with the creation stories of the ancient Egyptians, Amorites, Sumerians, and other peoples, stories that predated Moses' writing of Genesis. Today we still have records of some of these creation accounts, such as the well-known Mesopotamian *Epic of Gilgamesh* and *Enuma Elish*, stories describing the creation of the earth (the land) and heavens (the sky) by other gods. These ancient peoples also had a story about a flood, similar in some ways to what we find in the book of Genesis chapters 7–8.

First, we need to know that the preexistence of these stories does not mean Moses simply copied and adapted these other stories. God used what the people were familiar with to communicate the true creation story. In telling this story, God was not trying to communicate modern science to an ancient people, he was trying to communicate to the Israelites that he alone is God, the true God who created everything.

Image 11.3 represents one of the Egyptian creation stories. There were several Egyptian creation stories, but the basic storylines are similar, that before creation there was nothing but a dark, watery abyss of chaos. Out of these waters arose one of the Egyptian gods who separated water from land. The offspring of this god were the god Geb, who was the

11.3

Public Domain

A drawing of the separation of sky from earth in Egyptian creation mythology

Earth, and the goddess Nut, who was the Sky. In the diagram, you can see Geb lying down as the earth and Nut holding up the sky. You see the sun god over on the left side riding a boat above the sky. The Egyptians believed there were waters being held up above the sky, and there was a boat floating on these waters. The earth was viewed as a flat land with a dome over it (held up by a god), with water over the sky dome, and a god above this dome of water.

God Didn't Copy the Egyptians; He Told the True Story

When you read these other creation accounts (whether Egyptian or Mesopotamian) you will find some strange similarities to the Genesis account. But this does not mean Israel copied these other stories to create the story we have in the Bible today. It simply shows that people had different oral traditions about two common events—the creation and the flood. Over time, these stories were passed down and adopted into their own cultures, where additions were made concerning the gods involved and how the original creation event happened. What was God's aim in revealing these stories to Moses? God was retelling and correcting these stories to help us understand who was behind everything. God wanted his people Israel, and through them the entire world, to know he is the true Creator—not the Egyptian or Babylonian gods. In retelling these stories, God introduced some important distinctions and differences from the other stories.

The other creation stories portray the gods as violent deities, fighting each other and not caring at all for human beings. This is one of the unique aspects of the Genesis story. It tells of an amazingly wonderful God, who is entirely unlike the Egyptian or Babylonian gods and goddesses.

- Only in Genesis do we meet a single God (not multiple gods) who has a covenantal (committed with promises) and personal relationship with people
- Unlike other narratives, the God in the Genesis creation story doesn't need assistance from other gods to create. He is all powerful and can do it all with just his word.
- The God in the Genesis creation story creates human beings with dignity and beauty, and they are created in his image. None of the other creation stories reveal a god or gods who treat humans with such love and care.
- The God in the creation story entrusted human beings with the task of caring for the creation, rather than creating them as servants to serve the whims of that god.

Put yourself in the place of an ancient Israelite. Are you asking questions about the age of the earth and carbon dating? Are you trying to understand dinosaur fossils or wondering if the ark Noah built could house dinosaurs? Are you asking questions about microevolution versus macroevolution? Of course not. You want to know who the true God is and that he is the one who created everything. God used what the people were aware of at that time to communicate the truth about himself and his work in creating all things.

Looking at the Israelite View of the World
When Genesis Was Written

So when we read Genesis, we want to put ourselves into the Israelites' world and view things the way they did—and it makes a world (view) of a difference! Like most people at that time, the Israelites believed there were three layers to the heavens and earth. We find God speaking to the people using this three-tiered understanding of the world in Exodus 20:4 when he gives the people the commandments, saying, "You shall not make for yourself an image in the form of anything in *heaven above* or on the *earth beneath* or in the *waters below.*"

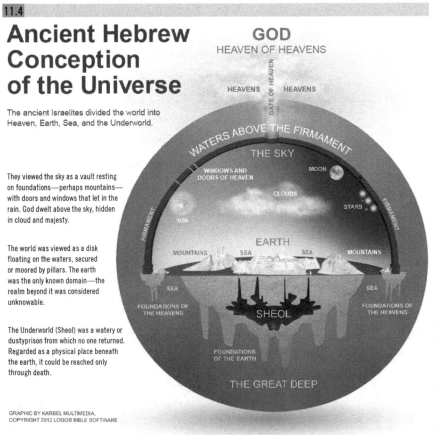

11.4

Ancient Hebrew Conception of the Universe

GOD
HEAVEN OF HEAVENS

HEAVENS   HEAVENS
GATE OF HEAVEN

The ancient Israelites divided the world into Heaven, Earth, Sea, and the Underworld.

WATERS ABOVE THE FIRMAMENT

THE SKY

They viewed the sky as a vault resting on foundations—perhaps mountains—with doors and windows that let in the rain. God dwelt above the sky, hidden in cloud and majesty.

WINDOWS AND DOORS OF HEAVEN
MOON
CLOUDS
STARS
SUN
FIRMAMENT
FIRMAMENT

EARTH

The world was viewed as a disk floating on the waters, secured or moored by pillars. The earth was the only known domain—the realm beyond it was considered unknowable.

MOUNTAINS   SEA   SEA   MOUNTAINS
SEA   SEA

FOUNDATIONS OF THE HEAVENS   FOUNDATIONS OF THE HEAVENS

SHEOL

The Underworld (Sheol) was a watery or dusty prison from which no one returned. Regarded as a physical place beneath the earth, it could be reached only through death.

FOUNDATIONS OF THE EARTH

THE GREAT DEEP

GRAPHIC BY KARBEL MULTIMEDIA, COPYRIGHT 2012 LOGOS BIBLE SOFTWARE

© Faithlife / Logos Bible Software (www.logos.com)

Image 11.4 is a diagram to help you visualize how the ancient Israelites, the Egyptians, and others of that time would have understood this three-tiered view of the world.

Tier 1: The Heavens

When the ancient Israelites looked up, they saw sky. When they heard, "In the beginning God created the heavens," they knew that this referred to God creating what they saw of the sky above them. They also knew that the waters they saw were blue like the sky, so they figured there must be a clear dome in the sky with water held behind it. Genesis 1:6 speaks of the creation of the heavens and says, "Let there be a vault" or "sky," a reference to a "dome" or "expanse"—all possible ways of translating the same Hebrew word into English. This vault separated the water under it from the water above it. The Hebrew word used here is *raqia*, and although it is translated in different ways, it generally refers to something solid and not merely an airy, atmospheric expanse.[8] The English word "vault" is sometimes used because it has this connotation of a chamber or room used for storage. This captures the sense that God is creating a "storage vault"—a solid barrier between waters. When you look at how this word *raqia* was translated in the Septuagint (the Greek translation of the Hebrew Scriptures produced by Jewish scholars in the third century BC) the translators used the Greek word *stereoma*, which also connotes a solid structure. All of this implies that the ancient Israelites believed the earth had a solid dome around it, holding back the water above it.

This made perfect sense, if you stop and think about it. We are taught a scientific understanding of the cycle of water through rain and evaporation, but when it rained, ancient peoples believed the dome/vault that held back the waters above was leaking into our world. Notice Psalm 148:4, where it says, "Praise him, you highest heavens and you waters above the skies." This reflects the ancient understanding that there is water held up by a dome above the visible sky. We should also note that this was written *after* the flood, which tells us that the ancient Israelites did *not* believe all the water above the expanse had been emptied. Some was still present. Or consider Proverbs 8:27–28, where we read, "I was there when he set the heavens in place, when he marked out the horizon on the face of the deep, when he established the clouds above." The Hebrew word for "established" here is *amats,* which is the same word that is used for letting a tree grow firm and hard. This implies that ancient people believed there was a solid dome that had been established above them, keeping them safe from the waters above.

They also believed that God lived above the dome and could even walk on it, and this place above the dome is where they envisioned "heaven" would be. For them, God and his dwelling place in heaven were above the dome. This is why we encounter other verses in the Bible that assume the concept of a solid dome holding up waters in the sky:

- "So God made the vault [*raquia*—a solid dome] and separated the water under the vault from the water above it. And it was so" (Genesis 1:7).
- "Can you join him in spreading out the skies, hard as a mirror of cast bronze?" (Job 37:18).
- "Thick clouds veil him, so he does not see us as he goes about in the vaulted heavens" (Job 22:14). Some translations read, "Thick clouds enwrap Him, so that he does not see, and He walks on the dome of heaven."

This doesn't fit our present-day scientific way of speaking or thinking about the world. We know there isn't an actual dome with waters above the dome, but this understanding was used by God as he communicated truth to the people at that time. He used what they knew and understood to make himself known.

Tier 2: The Earth

As we saw earlier, the Hebrew word in Genesis 1:1 we translate with the English word "earth" can also be translated as "land." The Israelites would have heard this and immediately thought: God created the land,

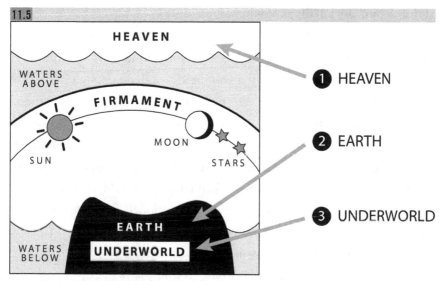

Another simple diagram of the Three-Tier universe that the Israelites would have imagined as how their world functioned. The solid dome (firmament) held up the waters above; the sun, moon, and stars went up and down under that firmament.

the land they could see in front of them. This was what they thought of as "the earth"—not a planet orbiting in space.

Like others of that time, they would have believed the earth was something like a flat disc or an island with water underneath it. Holding up this flat island were "the foundations of the world," which rose up like pillars holding the land firmly in place. This is not our present-day scientifically informed understanding of the earth. We know there are no pillars, nor is our planet resting on anything. But they saw it differently. We see this understanding referenced in several other places in the Bible:

- "For the foundations of the earth are the LORD's; on them he has set the world" (1 Samuel 2:8).
- "He shakes the earth from its place and makes its pillars tremble" (Job 9:6).
- "He set the earth on its foundations; it can never be moved" (Psalm 104:5).

Tier 3: Below the Earth—"Sheol"

The third tier was referred to as sheol and was thought to be the area under the land, an area that held more water. Think about it from their perspective. What happens when you dig down deep enough? What do you find? Water seeps through. You can see why ancient people assumed there was more water present under the ground, why they believed the earth was a land mass above even more water. In the Old Testament we see the word "sheol" used often to refer to the place under the earth where all who died went.[9] It wasn't until later in the Old Testament that the understanding of a future resurrection developed. This idea of a bodily resurrection became even more clear in the New Testament. But the ancient Israelites saw this area under the earth as a third level, a third tier in their understanding of the world around them.

Thinking It Through

It may feel awkward or even confusing to think that God didn't scientifically correct the incorrect views of the earth being flat or the sky as a solid dome with water held above it. Remember, God used what was familiar to the people at that time to communicate so they could understand what he wanted to say to them. God's purpose in writing Genesis was not to give them a twenty-first-century science textbook to counter evolutionary teaching. God's point in having Genesis written was to communicate the truth about himself and what he had done in creating the world to a people who were coming out of Egypt, a place that worshiped many different gods. God wanted the Israelites to know that he was the one true God who had made everything—the universe, the heavens, the earth, and its inhabitants. He wanted them to know there is no other God but the God of Israel.

It's important for us to first understand the world of the people Genesis was written to and to recognize that Genesis was not written to us, but for us. As we do this, many of the perplexing verses that don't make sense to our scientific understanding of the world will make sense. God wasn't communicating science according to our modern standards;

he was communicating truth about who he is and how and why he created all that exists. Knowing this makes the Bible even more amazing as we study it. Even though it is God's Spirit who helps us understand the Bible,* we still need to consider the original readers and their context.

In the next chapter, we'll look at some of the crazy verses that confound our scientific understanding when we read the Bible.

Do you have to believe the earth is 6,000 years old?

There are talking snakes in the fictional books *Jungle Book* and Harry Potter, and there is a talking snake in the Bible. Isn't that snake simply another fictional character?

Comedian Jon Stewart has this famous quote: "Yes, reason has been a part of organized religion ever since two nudists took dietary advice from a talking snake."

Over and over, we see these mocking criticisms of the Bible. Well-known atheist Richard

Dawkins made this statement in his book *The God Delusion:* "You cannot be an intelligent scientific thinker and still hold religious beliefs."[10]

I can understand why many people think Christians can't be intelligent scientific thinkers. Bible verses about a 6,000-year-old earth, a talking snake, and a rib-woman sound like reasons to reject the Bible's credibility. But there is more going on in the Bible beyond what we find in a surface reading of the text. Clever memes and graphics make this all look absurd. So in the next chapter, we'll focus on some of the most common questions dealing with the Bible and science. Does the Bible really teach these?

- The earth was created in six days.
- The earth is 6,000 years old.

---

* 1 Corinthians 2:12; John 16:13–15; Psalms 119:18.

- Eve is a "rib-woman" created from one of Adam's ribs.
- A talking snake lived in a magical fruit tree.
- Evolution disproves the Bible story.
- Jesus rode a dinosaur.

To find answers, we'll first explore where these questions come from.

CHAPTER 12

Making Sense of the Bible-versus-Science Conflict

> The Bible teaches us how to go to heaven, not how the heavens go.
>
> —GALILEO

12.1

Public Domain

Before diving into some of the commonly mocked Bible verses used to attack the Bible's credibility, let's look at an example of how the Bible was once sincerely interpreted, but done incorrectly.

Galileo Galilei lived from 1564–1642 in Italy and was an astronomer, physicist, and engineer. He is sometimes referred to today as the father of modern science for his pioneering work in establishing the scientific method. At the time Galileo lived, the church revered the Bible and wanted to uphold its teachings and their interpretation. Yet like many people at that time, they also believed the earth was stationary and the sun orbited around the earth. This was just common sense. After all, each day the sun appeared on the horizon, rising up and moving across the sky, and then set and disappeared over the other horizon. It looked as if the sun was the object moving around the earth, and not the other way around.

It was more than observation that led them to this conclusion. At that time church leaders believed the Bible taught this as well. Certain Bible verses do seem to teach this, that the earth is unmoving and it is the sun that moves around the earth. We see this in verses such as:

- "The sun *rises* and the sun *sets,* and hurries back to where it *rises*" (Ecclesiastes 1:5).
- "The LORD reigns, he is robed in majesty; the LORD is robed in majesty and armed with strength; indeed, *the world is established, firm and secure*" (Psalm 93:1, emphasis added).
- "Tremble before him, all the earth! The world is firmly established; *it cannot be moved*" (1 Chronicles 16:30).

Galileo was an astronomer involved in scientific research, and he published findings in 1632 that claimed the earth orbited around the sun. People didn't take this notion well, believing his statement contradicted what they believed the Bible said, and Galileo was eventually put on trial for heresy. Another scientist, Nicolaus Copernicus, had formulated the same idea, but he was afraid to make his discovery known widely. On June 22, 1633, the church handed down the following order to Galileo: "We pronounce, judge, and declare, that you, the said Galileo . . . have rendered yourself vehemently suspected by this Holy Office of heresy, that is, of having believed and held the doctrine (which is false and contrary to the Holy and Divine Scriptures) that the sun is the center of the world, and that it does not move from east to west, and that the earth does move, and is not the center of the world." In other words, the church felt Galileo was teaching something contrary to what the Bible taught.

The church leaders put him under house arrest since Galileo refused to change his view and say otherwise.

Looking at these Bible verses today, we understand that God was not speaking or communicating with scientific accuracy in these verses. God was not saying the earth stayed physically motionless and the sun orbited around it. This is an assumption that is being read into the interpretation of this verse, something added beyond what was implied in the original communication. God was simply using common, everyday language to communicate truth about the world—but not making a scientific statement about the orbital patterns of planets. Though they had good intentions, the church imported additional meaning into these verses, going beyond God's intentions. They were seeking to defend the Bible, assuming that the common language God had used necessarily implied a specific way of understanding the relationship between the sun and the earth. They held that not believing that the sun moved around a stationary earth meant not believing the Bible. Over time it became clear scientifically how the earth and the sun related in orbit. We realized that this scientific way of speaking and thinking about the relationship of the sun and earth was different and distinct from how the Bible was speaking of the relationship.

This is just one example of why we need to carefully study a verse to understand what it is saying in context and not importing scientific meaning or drawing scientific conclusions from the Bible when it isn't meant to be read that way. As Galileo said, "The Bible teaches us how to go to heaven, not how the heavens go."

With this in mind, let's consider a few examples of how the Bible is mocked as unscientific and crazy.

Does the Bible Say That God Created the Entire Universe in Less Than a Week?

One of the most mocked and challenged claims of the Bible is that the universe, including the earth, was created in six twenty-four-hour days.

The scientific world today tells us that the universe is much older—billions of years older, in fact.

For this discussion, I want to be clear that in what the Bible says about God, his power and his role as creator, there is no reason to believe God could not create the entire universe in six days if he wanted to. God could create everything in six seconds. Or in 6 million or 6 billion years if he wanted to. The God of the Bible is all-powerful and all-knowing, and he has the power, ability, and freedom to do anything he wants to do.

But the question is not what God can or cannot do. The question is what was God communicating to the ancient Israelites in the book of Genesis? And does what we understand of that communication conflict with what we know today from scientific study of the universe and its origins? Must you choose between what the Bible teaches and what science says? Let's look at some of the verses in the first chapter of Genesis that are used to suggest that we pick a side in this battle.

In the Beginning God Created Everything

The first line in Genesis 1:1 says it all: "In the beginning God created the heavens [the sky] and the earth [the land]." God wants the Israelites who had just come out of Egypt, where there was worship of the sun, moon, and various gods and goddesses to know without any doubt that everything they know and see was created by him, the one true God. This God—the God of Abraham—is the one who created everything.

The Hebrew word we translate as "create" is *bara*, which brings in the concepts of making *and* determining the function of what is being created. It involves giving something a function and purpose. God didn't use the more common Hebrew word to describe the act of creating; he used this word, *bara*, to communicate that he wasn't just making the heavens and earth, he was designing them with purpose and function.

We also need to remember that God was not trying to communicate modern scientific principles. He wasn't providing a textbook on the physics of the solar system, the age of the earth, how the gravitational pull of the sun holds the earth in motion, the subatomic details of the big bang

186

theory, or anything that addresses our typical scientific questions about our origins. He was simply telling the Israelites that all they could see and what they knew had been made by him.

In verse 2 we get this mysterious-sounding description: "Now the earth was formless and empty, darkness was over the surface of the deep." For an ancient Israelite, this language was reminiscent of the stories from other cultures of gods battling and causing chaos and darkness. God was letting them know that he is the true God over it all, ruling over the chaos and bringing beauty, purpose, and order to it all. Verse 2 also has an oft-missed message in it. "And the Spirit of God was hovering over the waters." The word we translate in English as "hovering" is the Hebrew word *rachaph,* which can also be found in Deuteronomy 32:11. It is used in Deuteronomy to refer to an eagle hovering with care over its nest of young birds. Even here, in these first verses, God is saying how he is unlike the other gods. He cares about his people and feeds and protects them like a mother bird hovering over its nest.

Keep in mind the context. The Israelites are living in a desert as Moses is giving them these words, and they are learning that not only is their God the one true God, he cares about them. He cares for what he has created, unlike the other gods. This God loves them and is with them. God then begins a series of repeated actions over the course of seven days. Normally these are thought of as the "six days" of creation, but there are seven days that complete the full act of creating, including the final day of rest.

Six Days? Twenty-Four Hours? Young Earth? Old Earth?

Right after the opening verses, the days of creation begin. What follows are six repeating patterns where God creates different things each day, with an evening and a morning to start and end the process.

The first day, day 1, starts like this: "And God said, 'Let there be light,' and there was light. God saw that the light was good, and he separated the light from the darkness. God called the light 'day,' and

Six Days of Creation

the darkness he called 'night.' And there was evening, and there was morning—the first day."*

If we are trying to read these verses like a science textbook to discover the scientific means by which God created, and we look at what happened on day 1, it immediately raises a number of questions.

- If God created the earth, but the sun wasn't created until day 4, how did the earth stay suspended and not fly off on its own? We now know the earth remains in orbit because of the gravitational pull from the sun.
- If there was light created on day 1, but the sun wasn't created until day 4, how was there light on day 1? How was there light before the sun was created, which we know is what gives the earth its light?
- The Bible indicates there was a "day" and "night" starting on day 1, as though the rotation of the earth around the sun had already started. But the sun was not created until day 4, so how can there be a morning and evening before the sun even exists?

---

*   Genesis 1:3–5.

- The Bible says that God separated the light from the darkness, but light is never comingled with darkness. Darkness is the absence of light, so what does it mean to say they were together and had to be separated?

We also notice that plants were created on day 3. So how did these plants exist without the sun, which was created on day 4? Plants survive and grow through photosynthesis, which is dependent on sunlight. The Bible also says that on day 3 the land produced vegetation: plants bearing seed according to their kinds and trees bearing fruit with seed in it.

So did God accelerate the growth of trees to enable them to produce within a twenty-four-hour time period?

Many questions arise when we try to analyze these verses through the lenses of physics, astronomy, and modern botany. It is difficult to piece together various scenarios to explain how all of this could have happened.

God can do whatever he wants. If, for some reason, he wanted to have the earth suspended in space and held in orbit without the sun, or have light causing day and night from a different source than the sun, he could do any of that. The question is not one of God's ability, but whether we are understanding what he is telling us in these verses. When we try to read these verses like an engineer or a scientist, we miss the point of what God was communicating.

Remember, the Israelites were not asking how photosynthesis works or details about the physics of light and darkness. They weren't wondering how you can have "night" and "day" if these are dependent on the earth's rotation around the sun. They were wondering if the God who had rescued them from slavery was powerful enough over other gods. They were learning that their God didn't battle other gods to make the world. This God speaks and it happens.

By day 2 God has created the mysterious "vault" between the waters above and below to separate water from water. In the last chapter we saw that the Hebrew word *raqia* means some sort of solid dome. The belief at that time was that the earth had a solid dome in the sky holding back the water above it. God wasn't communicating for scientific accuracy. He spoke about water and a solid dome, and everything he said made sense to the people back then based on their understanding of the world. God wanted them to understand that he created it all, has power over all, and that the sun and the moon aren't gods—they are part of his creation. God has no rivals. He is very involved with human beings, who are distinct from the other things he created because humans are created in his image.

If you were to read through the six days of creation—the why and when—with the people God was originally communicating to, you would read it quite differently. No longer would you be asking how it is physically possible for the earth to be created on day 1 but the earth isn't created until day 4. You wouldn't try to figure out where dinosaurs fit into this timeline. You wouldn't debate microevolution versus macroevolution. Remember, we don't have to force answers from Bible verses that weren't written to address the questions we are asking.

So many of the debates within Christianity, as well as the mocking criticism of the Bible, end up being irrelevant when we accept that God wasn't providing details to satisfy questions from our modern scientific worldview. God was communicating vital information to the ancient Israelites. We won't go into detail with all six days of creation in this chapter. Instead, I want to take a step back so we can catch the bigger picture of what God may have been communicating in the creation story.

A Literary-Artistic Structure to the Six Days, Not a Scientific Structure

A surface-level reading of Genesis 1 and the six days often misses the literary-artistic design of the Hebrew text. A closer look reveals a parallel structure in which the first three days of creation parallel the last three days. We catch hints of this framework in Genesis 1:2 when it states, "The earth was formless and empty." This sets up our expectations for what comes next. God is about to take what was formless and, in the first three days, will give it form and function. After he forms it, he fills it. Days 1–3 deal with the formlessness of the earth, giving it shape and function. Days 4–6 deal with the void, filling what is empty. In all of this, the larger point is clear: God is bringing order to the chaos. And he uses the symmetry of the creation narrative to communicate what he has done.

Table 12.1 illustrates this with the first three days describing what God forms, and the second three days showing how he fills what he made on the first three days.

Table 12.1		
	Problem: Creation is "formless and empty" (1:2).	
God's Work	**Forming**	**Filling**
	Day 1: light and darkness	Day 4: the lights of day and night
	Day 2: sky and sea	Day 5: birds and fish
	Day 3: fertile earth	Day 6: land animals, including man
	Result: The work of creation is finished, and God can rest (2:1).	

Notice that God's focus is to communicate that he has purpose and design and is the Creator of all that exists. *He* created and formed and filled—not the Egyptian gods, not the sun or the moon. And the symmetry of forming and filling communicates something profound and powerful. Our technical questions and attempts to dissect the text seem irrelevant, an exercise in missing the point. God is communicating his awesome power and beautiful purpose for everything through the poetic movement and symmetry of the story. We can use all our time asking the Bible our scientific questions about creation, all the while missing the beauty of what God was communicating to the original recipients.

A Day May Be Twenty-Four Hours or It May Be Longer

As you read through the seven days of Genesis 1, it is helpful to understand that the word we translate as "day" in these verses is the Hebrew word *yom*, which can have several different meanings. In the writings of Moses alone (the first five books of the Bible) the word *yom* is used to mean:

- twelve hours in Genesis 1:5 (for half a day he uses the word *yom* too)
- a whole week in Genesis 2:2
- a growing season, probably several months in Genesis 4:3
- an eternity in Genesis 44:32
- a physical lifetime in Genesis 43:9 and Deuteronomy 4:40 and 19:9
- a time period equal to forty days in Deuteronomy 10:10

Moses used the word *yom* to represent twelve hours, twenty-four hours, the creative week, forty days, several months, a lifetime, and eternity. *Yom* can refer to the way we think of a day, as the twenty-four-hour time period it takes for the earth to rotate on its axis. But then in the next chapter (Genesis 2:2), after we go through the seven days, Moses summarizes all seven days together as a "day." Clearly, the word can be used to mean different things, from a twenty-four-hour time period to a much longer period of time.

Even within a twenty-four-hour time period, the word *yom* can simply refer to the daylight hours between dawn and dusk. This is how we see it being used in Genesis 1:16. We find something similar in the English language, where "day" does not always mean a specific twenty-four-hour day. We might say, "back in my grandfather's day . . . ," referring to the time period when he lived, not a specific twenty-four-hour day.

Keeping all of this in mind, the word "day" as it is used in Genesis 1 could very well mean twenty-four-hour days. There is a mix of opinions from trusted scholars on this question. But regardless of how you interpret the word "day," it is clear that memes mocking the alleged discrepancies and contradictions of the six days of creation are missing the point. They aren't listening to what the text is saying. They are reading their own assumptions and questions into the narrative of wonder and awe that showcases God's work in Genesis 1.

Different Viewpoints of the Six Days

There may be more than one option in understanding and interpreting these early chapters of Genesis. In what follows, I will provide a few different interpretations of the six days by credible, trusted Christians. Each way of interpreting these verses has strengths and weaknesses, and due to the scope and aims of this book, I am only addressing a broad summary of these views, knowing you can do further study and look at each one in more detail. Each view has puzzling questions and "what abouts," pros and cons. But each one holds the view that the Bible is 100 percent authoritative, inspired, and true.

The "Young Earth" Interpretation

The first interpretive option we'll consider is often called the "Young Earth" view. This view tends to gets the most attention in the Bible/science debates because it interprets the days of Genesis 1 as twenty-four-hour periods and reads the genealogies of Genesis as complete and accurate accountings of the time from the creation of the universe to the present day. This leads to the conclusion that both the universe and the earth are relatively young in age, created around 6,000–10,000 years ago. This view maintains that human beings and dinosaurs walked the earth at the same time, and interprets Genesis chapters 1 and 2 as straightforward and literal.

Many people, both in the Christian church and outside the church, assume this is the common view of most Christian believers today. As

I hope to show, there are a range of views, all of which take the Bible seriously, but which differ on how to best interpret these passages. While I personally do not hold to the Young Earth view, I believe God can do anything—including the creation of the universe in six days. My concern is not determining *if* God can do it, but seeking to understand what God says in the Scriptures and how best to interpret what it means for us.

One of the weaknesses of the Young Earth view is that it may be asking questions of the text that the text was not written to answer. We saw this happen in the story of Galileo and the church, where church leaders read something into the text that God was not communicating through the text. Genesis is not a modern science textbook or yesterday's newspaper. It does not fit our worldview questions or assumptions.

Why does the Young Earth view conclude that the Bible says the earth is only 6,000–10,000 years old? The answer is fairly straightforward. If you interpret the six days as six twenty-four-hour periods, this begins a clock that allows you to figure the birthday (so to speak) of God's creation on day 6. Biblical genealogies like those in Matthew chapter 1 and Luke chapter 2 provide us with the family line from Jesus all the way back to Abraham and even Adam. And we can find other, more detailed genealogies in Genesis and in 1 Chronicles, sections that read like this: "The sons of Japheth: Gomer, Magog, Madai, Javan, Tubal, Meshek and Tiras. The sons of Gomer: Ashkenaz, Riphath and Togarmah" (Genesis 10:2–5; 1 Chronicles 1:5–7).

Using these genealogies, you can add together the ages to create a timeline from day 6, when Adam was created, until the time of Jesus. When you do this, it adds up to approximately 4,000 years between the creation of Adam and the birth of Jesus. From there, we simply add another 2,000 years to today's date, and you have an approximate age for the earth—6,000 to 10,000 years old.

If you follow a literal, straightforward reading of the Genesis story, the Young Earth perspective seems to make sense. However, as we are showing in this book, good Bible study methods involve more than a plain or literal reading of a verse. For example, it is helpful to know that ancient genealogies were used for more than a strict accounting of years. Genealogies were primarily written for the purpose of establishing the credibility of a family and identifying their tribal roots. The Hebrew word for "son" (*ben*) in these genealogies can equally mean a grandson, great-grandson, or someone even farther down the line, sometimes skipping generations. The word for father (*abba*) can also mean grandfather, great-grandfather, or great-great-grandfather, sometimes skipping generations. When Jesus is called "the Son of David" in the New Testament, this doesn't mean he was actually David's child; it meant he was of the lineage of David, one of his descendants. Looking at the genealogies in Matthew's gospel, we see that Matthew counted the generations in three groups of fourteen. If you try matching the names in his genealogy to the same list in Chronicles, you find they don't match. That's because Matthew is making a different point with his list. Matthew wanted three groups of fourteen because that matches the numerical value of David's name in Hebrew. And Matthew wants David's name to be the fourteenth in the genealogy to highlight his importance. His genealogy was not meant to be used as a strict accounting of years to determine the age of the earth. It was to show that Jesus came from the lineage of David and Abraham, just as the Scriptures predicted. And Matthew reinforced his point with some clever highlighted numbers for emphasis. This is something the original readers would have noticed.

But all of this introduces difficulties when we try to calculate a date of creation by this method. While we should applaud the desire to read the Scriptures accurately, if we attempt to apply our standards of precision or understanding of what a generational relationship should be to the text, we will arrive at inaccurate conclusions.

We cannot look at every aspect of the Young Earth view in this book. I do want to add one final word on this interpretation. I've talked to several people who were from churches that teach the position that if you don't hold this view, you are not taking God's Word seriously. I couldn't disagree more. It is because we take God's Word seriously that we put effort into trying to understand the original context, culture, and to whom and why Genesis was originally written. It would be easier to just read these passages as if there is no difference between the time they were written and today, that God was addressing our need for scientific precision, but that would be poor application of the Bible study methods we have learned. We always need to consider the time it was written, to whom, and why. Deeper Bible study is not an excuse to doubt God's Word. It is simply obeying what the Bible says when it tells each of us to be a worker "who correctly handles the word of truth."[*] This means putting some effort into our study and going beyond a surface reading when needed.

The "Appearance of Age" Interpretation

A second view also holds that the earth is relatively young in age and was created in six literal twenty-four-hour days, but those who hold this view argue that God created the world to look or appear billions of years old. Some hold this view as a way of reconciling a literal interpretation of Genesis and the creation story with scientific studies and theories that suggest the earth is far, far older. A simple way of grasping the logic of this view is to look at the creation of Adam. Since God created Adam as a fully grown adult, it begs the question: why couldn't God create the earth "fully grown" with the appearance of age as well? This position is somewhat speculative, and it lacks any direct support in Scripture. I do not find many people who hold to this view, but it is interesting to ponder. Some criticize this view because it suggests that in creating the universe with the appearance of age, God was acting deceptively, giving what we see an appearance that does not match reality.

The "Gap" Interpretation

A third view argues that there is a gap of billions of years between the events of Genesis 1:1 and Genesis 1:2. In Genesis 1:1 we read, "In the beginning God created the heavens and the earth." Those who hold to

---

[*]   2 Timothy 2:15.

the "gap" view believe this is the start of creation, and there may have been living creatures that were created or evolved over this time. After this long gap of billions of years between verse 1 and verse 2, God initiated a "re-creation" of everything, and this happened relatively recently in a period of six twenty-four-hour days. The gap of billions of years accounts for what we see when we find fossils of dinosaurs, examine ice cores, theorize ice ages, and study geological formations. This interpretation is another way to accept what science teaches about the earth as billions of years old while also holding to a belief that God created something over six twenty-four-hour days *after* that long gap of time. Not too many Christians today hold this viewpoint, but it is an interesting option to ponder.

The "Preparing the Garden and Promised Land" Interpretation

A fourth interpretation is a modified gap interpretation that believes the reference in Genesis 1:1 to "In the beginning" refers to an indefinite long time period that could be millions or billions of years. During this time period God created everything, the heavens, the earth, the sun, the moon, the universe. Then starting with Genesis 1:2, God began the process of taking what was "formless and empty," a phrase which in Hebrew means a desolate and uninhabitable wasteland, and began creating and shaping the garden of Eden and the promised land of Israel his people would later inhabit. The six days of creation are not an attempt to give us a comprehensive, detailed picture of all God did in creating the universe. Instead, they help us understand how God shaped the garden of Eden and the promised land, not the whole earth (as that was already created).[1] This is another fascinating interpretive option to consider.

The "Day-Age" Interpretation

A fifth view is fairly widespread and holds that each "day" of the six days was really a long epoch of time and not a twenty-four-hour day. Since the Hebrew word for day (*yom*) can mean *more* than a twenty-four-hour period of time, this interpretation allows each "day" referred to in the six-day narrative to represent a much longer passage of time, possibly millions or even billions of years. This view holds that the narrative records the sequential order of creation, with each day an age or period in a long process. The objects being discovered today and the scientific theories about the age of the earth would not conflict with the Bible, since the Bible could be simply telling us the order of creation and not the length of time the creation of the world took to complete.

The "God's Temple" Interpretation

The sixth view is an extremely intriguing interpretation that understands God's temple as the heavens and the earth.[2] We see evidence of this understanding in Isaiah 66:1–2. Although God's people were going to rebuild the temple in Jerusalem, God says he cannot have a building to house himself because the earth and heaven are his temple:

> This is what the LORD says:
> "Heaven is my throne,
> and the earth is my footstool.
> Where is the house you will build for me?
> Where will my resting place be?
> Has not my hand made all these things,
> and so they came into being?"

In this interpretive view, the six-day creation story is not intended to give us a detailed account of the entire cosmos, but is rather the story of God creating his temple (heaven, which is his throne, and the earth his footstool). In Genesis chapters 1 and 2, God is describing the process of preparing his temple and putting things in order before taking up residence in the temple on the seventh day and resting.

As strange as this might sound to us reading it today, a story like this would have been quite familiar to the original recipients of Genesis. What's pretty mind-blowing to think about is that an ancient Israelite would have been aware of how deities and kings of that time period often built themselves temple buildings to dwell in. There would even be a six-day process of preparation and inauguration before the king or deity would take residence in the structure on the seventh day. We find this pattern in the Bible, with the account of a seven-day consecration of the tabernacle in Exodus chapters 39–40. There is also the seven-year construction of the temple in Jerusalem under King Solomon in 1 Kings 6:38, which is followed by a seven-day dedication ritual (the Feast of Tabernacles). The Sumerian Gudea Cylinders also recount the construction of a temple ending in a seven-day consecration ceremony.[3]

Matching these temple preparation ceremonies with Genesis 1 and 2 we find several clear parallels. After the six days of preparing the heavens and the earth, God then takes residence and "rests" on the seventh day. But God isn't resting because he is tired from all his work (since God doesn't get tired). It is more like an American president who goes through an inauguration process and at the end takes up residence, or "rests," in the White House. His work and duties are just beginning, and he isn't actually sleeping or resting. He is now in place to run the show. This is one way of viewing what we see when God rests on the seventh day. God doesn't get tired as we think of human tiredness but is now running things after taking up residence in his temple.[4]

It is also fascinating to note many of the similarities between the description of the garden of Eden and the details of the temple built later in Jerusalem (and the roaming tabernacle that preceded it). Both structures have a great deal of imagery taken from or referencing the garden of Eden. This supports the idea that the original garden of Eden is more than just a nice garden. It is an archetypal sanctuary and temple for the presence of God. In God's temple, he set up the garden where he dwelled with Adam and Eve. In fact, many of the responsibilities God gives to Adam are similar to the tasks of a king as well as the priestly responsibilities of those who serve in a temple.

In the temple interpretation of Genesis 1 and 2, the point of the creation story is not to give us explicit details of how God made everything. Rather, the story is God's way of letting the Israelites know that he wasn't just building a universe, he was building a place where he could dwell with his people, much like a temple. God dwelled in his temple garden, the garden of Eden, with his people, Adam and Eve, and now he was going to dwell in a new temple garden with the people of Israel. They would worship God in the temple, just as God had set it up originally in the garden of Eden.

Obviously, the "God's temple" interpretation opens up many options that might explain the mechanics of how God created the world and how that might reconcile with scientific accounts. It does not attempt to give us a scientific explanation. This intriguing view leaves several questions unanswered, as all the views do, but it helps us to better understand the Bible by viewing it through the lens of an ancient Near East worldview.

The "Evolutionary Creation" Interpretation

When most Christians think of "evolution," they assume it automatically refers to a process where life developed without God. Christians may assume that evolution, an alternative to creation, is what atheists believe because they don't believe in God. But this is just one view of evolution, and it assumes that evolution happened by chance, natural selection, and without God's involvement. That's not the only way to view evolution.

A seventh way of interpreting the creation stories in Genesis is that they are 100 percent inspired by God and an authority for Christian life and doctrine, while believing that God may have used the process of evolution in the act of creating. Genesis chapters 1 and 2 are not to be literally interpreted (as we saw with some of the earlier examples), as Scripture is not giving us the scientific details of how God created. It is possible that God used the means of evolution in his creative processes. This is not Darwinian evolution, where life was created through random chance and natural selection. This view sees creation as purposeful and intentional with God directly involved in the process, using evolution to accomplish these purposes.[5]

This concept might be new to some people reading this. This view is often confused with the traditional view of evolution as a random, unguided process without any purpose, clearly at odds with an intentional act of "creation." Because of this, the assumption is that any time you hear the word evolution, you instantly think it is anti-Bible and atheistic evolution. So it means if you are a Christian who takes the Bible as authoritative and inspired, you cannot in any sense believe in evolution. But this is not true for the process called "evolutionary creation." While evolutionary theories that require a process with no divine intervention or guidance are against the Bible's teaching, there is an alternative view that believes God was intimately involved in the creation process while using evolution to do it. In this view, God established and maintains the laws of nature, and these include a purposeful process of evolution. This view sees an Intelligent Designer behind the work of creation, and that designer used the tools of evolution to create this world and its inhabitants.

I once heard someone object to evolutionary creationism by saying, "God didn't create us from a primordial soup!" I've thought about that objection, and I find a similar objection could be made to a literal reading of Genesis where it says God created us from dirt (Genesis 2:7). Does it matter whether we came from hard-packed earth or a muddy soup? What matters is that God is the one who made us. And evolutionary creationism believes God was behind the entire process of creating human beings. This view also holds that God created human beings distinct from other creatures—in his image—so they are different than everything else he created. Only human beings have the "breath of life" given to them, as we read in Genesis 2:7. But in reading and interpreting this verse, we can accept what it teaches us while still asking if the actual scientific process is being explained here. We know from Scripture that God is Spirit, and he doesn't have physical lungs. So when Genesis says that God "breathed into his [Adam's] nostrils the breath of life," we know figurative language is being used. This also suggests that what God has given us in Genesis is not a scientific explanation of the process of creating humanity.

With so many possible ways of interpreting Genesis and the narrative of creation, many "what abouts" come up. One big question is how could God have used the process of evolution when the Bible also says there was no death before Adam.* This is an important question, and there are several ways to respond. One short response would be to acknowledge that the fossil record shows many creatures dying before humans appeared. However, when we read about the curse of Genesis 3 given to Adam and Eve, the curse itself does not say anything about animal life.

When God spoke of the punishment of death for the disobedience of Adam and Eve, God was referring to their death as human beings. Adam and Eve would now experience death because they went against God's guidance and direction. So the death of animals prior to this does not necessarily conflict with the Bible, since we are simply arguing that no human death occurred prior to Adam and Eve, who were the first humans created in God's image. Animal death before the fall is not in conflict with the idea that there was no death before Adam.[6]

Being a Bible-Based Thinking Christian

The goal of this book (and chapter) is to help you understand the variety of options available among Christians, including the evolutionary creationist view that believes God used evolution to create, a view that is still in accord with a high view of Scripture. As you study the early chapters of Genesis, remember that it was not written to explain the scientific process of how God created everything. And when we read it through the eyes of the original recipients, grasping the purpose for which it was written to them allows for many options—including a process of guided evolution—as the means by which he created.

One of my goals in explaining the various views is to help you see that there is no need for conflict between Christianity and science. However, scientific views that remove God or do not allow a place for his existence are clearly in conflict. Many respected scholars and church leaders who

---

* 1 Corinthians 15:21, 45; Romans 5:12; 8:20–22.

hold the Scriptures with high authority are able to reconcile the tension. Even the late evangelist Billy Graham held a similar view when he said,

> Oh, I don't think that there's any conflict at all between science today and the Scriptures. I think that we have misinterpreted the Scriptures many times and we've tried to make the Scriptures say things that they weren't meant to say, and I think we have made a mistake by thinking that the Bible is a scientific book.
>
> The Bible is not a book of science. The Bible is a book of redemption, and of course, I accept the Creation story. I believe that God did create the universe. I believe He created man, and whether it came by an evolutionary process and at a certain point He took this person or this being and made him a living soul or not, does not change the fact that God did create man.[7]

Through this brief review of various positions, I hope to show that if we read Genesis chapters 1–3 and come to different conclusions, it isn't due to a lack of full trust in the Bible. It isn't because some people doubt God and his Word or fail to take it seriously. I once had someone tell me that if I did not interpret Genesis 1–3 in a straightforward literal sense, I was like the serpent casting doubt in Eve's mind, asking, "Did God really say?"* Studying why a book was written and to whom, and learning about the context and cultural world in which it was written is not doubting God's Word. It is taking the Scriptures seriously to make sure we understand what God was saying. It is a commitment to truth, not a lessening of the truth.

We've looked at some different opinions, all held by godly scholars who have full commitment to the authority and inspiration of the Scriptures. Table 12.2 can help you keep track of the different options we looked at, putting the various interpretations in larger categories. You can see that atheistic evolution directly contradicts the scriptural story

---

* Genesis 3:1.

Table 12.2	Atheistic Evolution	Young Earth Creation	Old Earth Creation	Evolutionary Creation
God created earth and all life	No	Yes	Yes	Yes
Earth is billions of years old	Yes	No	Yes	Yes
Evolution describes how life developed	Yes	No	No	Yes

Courtesy of Deborah Haarsma from BioLogos (biologos.org). Deborah used this chart in a presentation I was part of with her, and this is used with her permission.

of creation with God as creator, where the others, including evolutionary creation, don't.

One of the broader points of our look at the early chapters of Genesis and the story of creation is to suggest that there isn't really a clash between science and the Bible. If we look at the original reason and purpose behind why the early chapters were written, we begin to see that God was not addressing most of our scientific objections or questions. Almost every criticism or question that comes up—whether the Bible teaches the earth is 6,000 years old, or how to make sense of the earth being created on day 1 and the sun created on day 4—is a question the Bible was never trying to answer.

Before we close out this chapter, I want to address a few other common objections. Many of the most popular memes floating around the internet are jokes about a "rib-woman" and a "talking snake." So let's take a quick look at how to respond to these.

The "Rib-Woman" Was Not a Rib-Woman

Much mocking of the Bible is about Genesis 2:20–22. In these verses we read that God pulled a "rib" from the body of Adam and created Eve from this rib. "But for Adam no suitable helper was found. So the LORD

God caused the man to fall into a deep sleep; and while he was sleeping, he took one of the man's ribs and then closed up the place with flesh. Then the LORD God made a woman from the rib he had taken out of the man, and he brought her to the man."

That does seem to be a pretty strange process. It appears to suggest that God is taking an actual rib bone from the man to make the woman—and this is where we get the mocking "rib-woman" name in the memes. Image 12.4 is one example.

As you should know by now, we always need to ask what these verses might have meant to the original recipients. We have already looked into the type of genre and purpose behind why Genesis was written, and that indicates there may be more going on here than God taking out an actual bone from Adam's chest. God could certainly do that, as he can do anything. But the real question is not if God can do it, but what the text here is saying. The Hebrew word we translate into the English word "rib" is the word *tsela*. In other passages where *tsela* or its variants are used it usually is translated into the English word "side." In the book of Exodus, also written by Moses, the words *tselo* (a variant) and *tselot* (plural) are used to refer to the equal "sides" of the ark of the covenant. The word is also used for the "sides" of the altar—in both cases meaning the equal and opposite sides of the object.

12.4

SCIENCE KNOWS NOTHING.

LET ME TELL YOU ABOUT HOW A WOMAN WAS MADE FROM THE RIB OF A MAN—WHO WAS MADE FROM DIRT!

Understanding this, it is clear that God was creating Eve here and it is indicating she was half of Adam, an equal half. It is an act imbued with symbolism to communicate that God made Eve to be an equal with Adam—like two parallel sides of the ark of the covenant. Eve is not less than Adam or subordinate to Adam. She is his missing half, a beautiful and equal partner to Adam.

We should read this passage as if through the interpretive lens of the ancient Israelites, considering what they would understand and needed to know at that time. Some trusted scholars see this description as a vision Adam had in which he sees half of himself being symbolically used to form Eve, his equal and partner.

We read that when God created Adam, God made him from the dust and breathed life into him. This verse is not describing a scientific process by which God took dust and transformed it into Adam. When the passage tells us God breathed into Adam, it isn't implying a physical act, since God is a spiritual being who doesn't have lungs. Instead, we find more symbolic meaning. When God tells the Israelites about creating Adam from the dust of the ground, he is saying he is the creator and all human beings are mortal. They will one day return to nothing but dust. This same language is used hundreds of years later in Psalm 103:13–14, "As a father has compassion on his children, so the LORD has compassion on those who fear him; for he knows how we are formed, he remembers that we are dust." It is a poetic reminder to the people of something they already know and understand—that we are all made from dust, not just Adam. This is God's way of communicating truth to the ancient Israelites, with poetry and symbolism, and not an attempt to explain the creation of human beings through a scientific medical lens.

So there was no "rib-woman." Eve was created by God in a way that isn't explained in the scientific detail we might want today. Instead, we are told that Eve was an equal partner to Adam, created in God's image, and that's the point God wants us to understand. So when someone asks you, "Was Eve really created from a rib?" I hope you can help them better understand what God was communicating through this crazy-sounding verse.

How about That Talking Snake?

Let's talk about the talking snake. Over and over again, you'll find this one across social media and around the internet. First, the truth is if

God made the entire universe, and he wanted to make a snake talk, God could do that. It's not strange or unusual because he is God and could intervene with the biological and physical abilities of a snake to somehow make it speak. But is that what the Bible is saying here? Is that why we find a talking snake in these early chapters of Genesis?

The snake is called a "serpent," not a snake, and I mention this because there are some fascinating things happening here when you look deeper. Later in the Bible, in the book of Revelation, we see this serpent identified as Satan, more commonly called the devil.* But here, in Genesis 1, we don't have any specifics about this creature's identity and don't know much about it. The word translated into English as "serpent" is the Hebrew word *nachash*. Hebrew scholars point out that this word is a triple entendre that just doesn't translate well into English.[8] Like some of our English words, *nachash* can be a noun, or a verb, or an adjective. Here in Genesis, the author seems to be having some wordplay with it.

- As a noun, *nachash* means "serpent."
- As a verb, it means "to divine"; the *nachash* means "the diviner."
- As an adjective, it means "shining"; the *nachash* means "the shining one."

Let me get into something broader here about this serpent. The Scriptures indicate that when God created the heavens and the earth, he previously had also created a heavenly council of spirit beings called "the sons of God." We read that they watched him create and even "shouted for joy."† Although we often hear that when Genesis 1:26–27 says, "Let us make humans in our image," the "us" refers to the Trinity, it's likely that the "us" is the heavenly council. They are divine beings that God created like a supernatural family before he created his human family.

---

*   Revelation 12:9.
†   Job 38:7.

You see these sons of God mentioned in Psalm 82, and they comprise what we see called "the heavenly host" or "heavenly council" in Scripture.

The garden of Eden was basically God's temple, where God was, and he was likely with his heavenly council, the sons of God. It would make sense because a king has his council with him. So one of these sons of God from the heavenly council in Eden rebelled against God and in the form of a serpent (*nachash*). Looking at the wordplay of the word "serpent," we can see that a member of the angelic divine council, in the form of shining serpentine figure, rebelled against God and went to Adam and Eve to convince them also to rebel. I know some of this may sound complicated and you may never have heard much about a divine council and sons of God and the serpent possibly being a member of this divine council. I can assure you that these are very credible views you can read about in depth in some great scholarly writings.[9]

So what does this suggest about a talking snake? All we can say for sure is that this serpent was not simply a snake as we think of snakes today. It was more than a mere animal, and was most likely a divine angelic appearance from one of those in the council of God, a being who took on a shiny appearance of serpentine form to oppose God's plan by tempting human beings to disobey God. In the time of ancient Israel, serpents were already considered to be a symbol of evil. Now we have God retelling the story of what happened with Adam, Eve, and the serpent. He is letting them know this was not a simple garden snake that happened to talk one day. There is far more going on here.

When the serpent is punished later in the chapter, its ability to speak is not removed, so we would expect it to continue having that ability. And the passage also speaks of the serpent crawling on its belly and eating dust. This is figurative language, as snakes don't actually eat dust to survive. God is using figures of speech to tell us that the serpent, this divine being from God's council who appeared to Adam and Eve and successfully convinced them to turn away from God, would now be humiliated and disgraced. This being of power was being removed from the position he had once had on God's council.

So was there a talking snake as we so commonly find being mocked in memes and books? No, at least not in the way we typically think of a snake today. Rather, it was a divine angelic being of some sort appearing in serpentine form, a form that was representative of evil in that time period. Exactly what that being looked like, we don't know. The Bible does not tell us, and the language may very well be symbolic or figurative, so it's a mistake to turn this scene into a caricature of *The Jungle Book*. That's far from the meaning of the original text.

We Can Believe in the Bible and Science

Many of the events described in the creation story are criticized for being dismissive of science. But I hope by now you can see there is no reason to choose between science and the Bible because the Bible is not addressing most of the scientific questions we are asking. There are many times when God steps into the regular patterns of natural laws to cause miracles—and these do not act in accordance with scientific theories or understandings of the world. The resurrection of Jesus is the cornerstone of Christian faith, and it is the story of a man who died and was raised back to life after three days. This wasn't just a temporary death of a few minutes or hours or even a day. Three days later, Jesus bodily rose from the dead. And the Bible presents Jesus as someone who could defy all we know of science by walking on water, healing blind people, and instantaneously healing leprosy. You can't explain these miracles away with metaphors or figurative speech. But that's the point. In these places, God was showing us he is God and was using the impossible to show us that.

So often the most common critiques of the crazy-sounding Bible passages from the creation story aren't all that crazy when you look a little deeper to learn what God is actually saying. The next time you see a meme with a talking snake, remember that there is more happening there. The Bible is not *The Jungle Book*. And when you see memes mocking the creation story or the age of the earth, you now know that a literal reading is not the only way to understand those passages. When you see a picture of Jesus riding a dinosaur, well . . . that's just a very clever and interesting drawing on a shirt.

Remember, the Bible is easily mocked, but that's only because we need to learn how (not) to read the Bible. When we pull out verses and fail to put in the time and effort to understand what a verse is trying to say to us, we can come up with some great anti-science Bible memes, but they aren't what the Bible is actually saying in those verses.

Part 4 Summary Points

JESUS RIDING A DINOSAUR

- The early chapters of Genesis were written to the people of Israel after they had been in slavery in Egypt for four hundred years. God wanted to communicate to them who he is, to tell them about the covenant he made with Abraham, their ancestor. God wasn't trying to communicate science and the methods of how exactly he created.
- To read the Bible as a science manual and ask science questions about the age of the earth, the length of days, what specific order everything was created in, and if Eve was made of an actual human "rib" are not what the early chapters of Genesis were written to answer. This is reading Genesis incorrectly and asking questions it was not written to answer and missing the purpose for which it was written.
- There are many valid ways of interpreting the early chapters of Genesis, which even include the possibility that God used evolution to create. There is much mystery we just don't know, details the Scriptures don't give. What we can know is that God created everything.
- The "talking snake" in the garden is not like Kaa in *The Jungle Book* or something from a fable. The creature in the garden wasn't a "snake" but an angelic being who appeared in some form of a serpent-like appearance, a being we later learn was Satan.

PART 5

My God Can Beat Up Your God

DOES CHRISTIANITY CLAIM ALL

OTHER RELIGIONS ARE WRONG?

CHAPTER 13

My God Can Beat Up Your God

Christians have this "my God is the biggest God on
the block who can beat up your God" attitude.
—A NON-CHRISTIAN DESCRIBING REASONS
WHY SHE ISN'T A CHRISTIAN

can still remember a brilliantly sunny day when a disturbing question changed the course of my life. I was a freshman sitting outside the student center at Colorado State University. During the first few days of the school year, there were several tables set up near the student center where various campus groups were giving out materials promoting the different campus clubs. The student organizations ranged from square-dancing clubs to political groups, fraternities and sororities, and religious groups. I casually scanned the religious tables and saw that the majority of the groups were Christian. At that time, I wouldn't have called myself a Christian, nor had I given too much thought to religion in general. I had no family or friends at that time who were Christians, and no one who was trying to convert me to Christianity. Religion was far from my mind. I was consumed with thinking about making new friends and starting out in a new school.

One of the Christian tables had literature and some tiny pamphlets

they were handing out. One that stood out to me that day had something like "Jesus is the only way" on the cover (13.1). It intrigued me enough to pick one up and scan it. It was highlighting a common Bible verse with the words of Jesus, who said, "I am the way and the truth and the life. No one comes to the Father except through me."*

As I read the verse and the rest of the short pamphlet, it was clear to me that they were saying only Jesus was the way to God. This implied that if you had differing beliefs or belonged to another world religion, those beliefs were wrong and would not get you to heaven. They were saying that it was only if you were a Christian and believed in Jesus that you could get to heaven.

Maybe you are a Christian and as you read that Bible verse and the phrase "Jesus is the only way to God," it feels normal to you. You may not think much of it since you are used to hearing it and you believe it. But for someone who is not a Christian (as I wasn't at the time) the claim that Jesus is the only way to God and all other ways are wrong seems bold, intolerant, divisive, and to some degree, even hateful. We live in such a pluralistic and diverse world today, and to many people, the claim made by Jesus that we read in the Bible is just . . . crazy sounding.

I sat down in the courtyard and read more of the little pamphlet. I found even more verses indicating the same thing. This wasn't just one isolated Bible verse claiming this. Here are several others (the italics are my addition for emphasis):

- "For there is *one God and one mediator* between God and mankind, the man Christ Jesus" (1 Timothy 2:5).
- "Salvation is found in *no one else*, for there is no other name under heaven given to mankind by which we must be saved" (Acts 4:12).

---

* John 14:6.

- "Whoever has the Son has life; whoever *does not have the Son of God does not have life*" (1 John 5:12).
- "Enter through the narrow gate. For wide is the gate and broad is the road that leads to destruction, and many enter through it" (Matthew 7:13).
- "*I am the gate*; whoever enters through me will be saved" (John 10:9).

Is Christianity the Religion of Nonthinking Suburban America?

As I read these verses, I had many questions. I looked over at the girl standing behind the table handing out the little pamphlets. She looked like a nice, friendly person, likely raised in the suburbs of Colorado, and I was guessing she had Christian parents and was just pleasantly promoting the Christian faith she had been raised in. But reading those Bible verses brought on a wave of emotions and questions. Here are a few you might have considered as well:

- In our world of more than 7 billion people with so many different world faiths, does the Bible teach that two-thirds of the current world population's beliefs are wrong with their approach to God or the gods they believe in?
- What if that girl behind the table was born and raised in Thailand? Would this same girl be handing out Buddhist pamphlets instead of Christian ones since more than 90 percent of people in Thailand are Buddhist?
- How can Christianity possibly claim to be the only way to God knowing that many other religions exist that even far predate Christianity, which is a more recent faith than older ones like Buddhism and Hinduism?
- If the Bible says that Jesus is the only way, what about all those who never have heard of Jesus around the world and aren't Christians?

My God Is the Biggest God on the Block
and Can Beat Up Your God

I didn't expect to be thinking about Christianity and its claims in relation to other world religions that day. But in the days, weeks, and months that followed, I continued to have nagging questions I couldn't

13.2

There are almost 5,000 gods being worshipped by humanity.

But don't worry, only yours is right.

shake and eventually had to explore further. I knew that Christianity was common in the United States, but I had never considered the Bible's claim that Christianity was the only true religion that could lead you to God. Isn't this why wars had been fought? When religions claimed to be the right religion over all others? Superior to them?

That was several decades ago. Today, this question comes up all the time. With growing awareness of other world faiths and many people leaving (or never having been raised in) the church, this is a question every thinking Christian needs to consider. And beyond that, how do these Bible verses come across to others? I have a friend who isn't a Christian and is more agnostic in her beliefs who recently summarized her experience of Christians—with a touch of human sadness. She told me that most Christians have a "my God is the biggest God on the block who can beat up your God" attitude.

Is that what we want to be communicating to others?

Are these Bible verses about Jesus being the only way to God about winning a schoolyard battle? When you are face-to-face with someone who is an atheist, Buddhist, Hindu, Muslim, or any non-Christian faith, it's difficult to defend these verses. I can see why they sound crazy to them.

Being a Christian Today Is like Being a Yankees Fan in a Red Sox World

I'm originally from New Jersey and grew up going to New York Yankees baseball games. It felt like everyone around me was a Yankees fan, and the assumption was that the Yankees were your team even if you weren't an avid fan. But I vividly remember going on a visit to Boston, whose team is a fierce rival of the Yankees, and I saw for the first time how the Yankees are viewed in Boston. In the sports shops and tourist shops are plenty of T-shirts saying things like, "I'm raising my kid never to hate anyone except Yankee fans," and "I support two teams—Boston and whoever beats the Yankees." There was even a shirt that said, "Jesus hates the Yankees."

It was all quite unsettling. I realized I was in a non-Yankees world. In New York City or New Jersey, you could easily talk about the Yankees. You might have an argument about who should be pitching for a certain game or the batting order, but you were all on the same side—*for* the Yankees. After that visit, I knew that if you were to teleport a Yankees fan wearing a hat and his Yankees jersey into a frenzied beer-filled crowd in Boston, he wouldn't be able to shout, "Yankees are number 1!" and have everyone there agree with him.

Here is my point. If you are a Christian, you've probably been living like a Yankee in New York City. Christians may engage in internal debates and arguments about minor belief differences or styles of worship in churches. But for the most part, we are still together, on the same side. We believe in one God and know that Jesus is the way to God. But today, all of that is changing. Picture yourself (if you are a Christian) being transported into the middle of India visiting a beautiful family of devout and loving Hindus. You sit down at their dinner table, look them in the eyes, and then tell them that the Bible teaches "Jesus is the only way to God." It would not be easy. Yet the Bible teaches us that their beliefs are incorrect. It doesn't matter how you say it, it feels like you are insulting what is sacred and important to them.

The truth is that we don't have to be transported to India to face this, since Christians are surrounded today by people of differing beliefs in our neighborhoods and towns. So how do we make sense of these Bible verses in our pluralistic culture? That's the question we'll be looking at more closely in the next chapter.

CHAPTER 14

Love Is the Way, the
Truth, and the Life

> A man who is convinced of the truth of his religion is
> indeed never tolerant.
>
> —ALBERT EINSTEIN

Many people believe that if you have strongly held religious beliefs, you are intolerant of all other beliefs. That's certainly the sense behind the Albert Einstein quote in the epigraph. And it makes sense. There are many Bible verses that claim that there is only one way to God. Jesus himself said these words: "I am the way and the truth and the life. No one comes to the Father except through me."* This is all not very PC. So how do we handle this verse and others that make similar claims? First, we'll want to "Never Read a Bible Verse" and look at how these verses fit in the broader Bible story. That's the goal of this chapter.

---

*   John 14:6.

In the Beginning, Humans Worshiped One God

The Bible story begins with one God who creates everything (Genesis 1–2). God created human beings, and they lived in harmony with God and each other. There was one single God who existed and was worshiped in the beginning (14.1).

14.1

In the beginning (Genesis 1–2)

harmony with God and each other

It's important to ask why the Bible begins with the idea of one God who created all things. Israel (the original recipients of the book of Genesis) had been living in Egypt for four hundred years, where the cultural norm was to worship all types of gods, including the sun, the Pharaohs, and animal deities. With this creation story, God was telling the Israelites their true origins—that in the beginning there was only one God, not many.

When you examine extrabiblical writings and scholarly research tracing the origin of religion, you find differing opinions. Scholars disagree as to whether archeological records back up the idea that human beings were first monotheistic (believed in one God) or were polytheistic (believed in many gods). However, there are several respected scholars who believe that the earliest human beings were monotheistic and worshiped a single deity. For example, in the classic book *A History of God*, the author states, "There had been a primitive monotheism before men and women had started to worship a number of gods. . . . In the beginning, therefore there was One God. If so, then monotheism was one of the earliest ideas evolved by human beings to explain the mystery and tragedy of life."[1]

This is a view that aligns with the biblical story, which simply teaches that in the beginning there was one God.[*]

---

[*]   Genesis 1:1.

After Humans Broke Harmony with God, They Created and Worshiped Other Gods

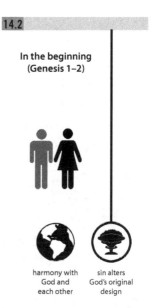

14.2

In the beginning (Genesis 1–2)

harmony with God and each other

sin alters God's original design

The Bible story continues, telling us that after God created human beings, they chose to reject his guidance (14.2). At this point the relationship humans had with the one God was radically changed. Theologians call this the fall, and as we saw in section 1 of the Bible timeline, it's like a nuclear bomb went off in the world, spreading the radioactive waste of human evil that is affecting everything. We live in the fallout of this event.

God Said Someone Was Coming to Restore Humans' Relationship with God

There were consequences to the rebellious actions of human beings that impact us to this day. Not only did we fall away from God, we also experienced the loss of our access to the presence of God. But the good news is that God did not abandon the people he had made. This theme becomes key to understanding why there are crazy-sounding Bible verses telling us that Jesus is the only way to God. In the story of Adam and Eve, we see God telling them that even though they rebelled against him and the relationship and harmony that was there is now impacted, he will not abandon them. He told them that one day he would send someone through their lineage who would deliver a crushing blow to the being (the serpent) who had led them astray, causing this nuclear bomb to go off.* The Bible is somewhat vague about when God says this will happen, but the fulfillment of this promise becomes clearer as the Bible

---

* Genesis 3:15.

story progresses. God promises that someone is coming who will restore what has been lost and reunite God and his rebellious people.

After humans were expelled from the garden of Eden, the people that God created spread across the globe. We see people who continue to reject God or not seek him and end up believing in other gods, and so we see many of the world religions develop over time. I am including only a selection of the major world faiths to highlight this idea, but

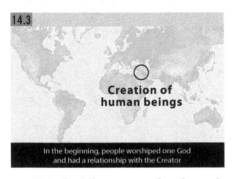

Creation of human beings

In the beginning, people worshiped one God and had a relationship with the Creator

the sequence helps to show the progression from the beginning, when human beings believed in the one God who created them. The map in image 14.3 shows the rough area where the story of Adam and Eve was said to take place.

We don't know exactly where the garden of Eden was in comparison to today's geography. But somewhere in this area is where we find the earliest human beings who began spreading over the earth.

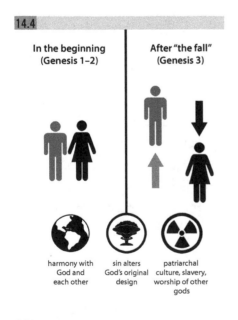

14.4

In the beginning (Genesis 1–2)

After "the fall" (Genesis 3)

harmony with God and each other

sin alters God's original design

patriarchal culture, slavery, worship of other gods

Humans Migrated Across the Planet, Creating and Worshiping Other Gods

After Adam and Eve went against God's guidance and sin entered the world, we see evidence of their distorted thinking (14.4). It happens quickly. There is the first murder, the beginning of a power struggle between men and woman, and we see a world filled with violence. Practices like polygamy and slavery begin. Human beings were not satisfied with knowing the one true God, so they began worshiping other gods they had created in the likeness of the moon or the sun or various animals, and even other human beings. The members of the divine council who rebelled against God were behind these other gods being worshiped.

During this time period, recorded in the early chapters of the Bible in the book of Genesis, we read an account of the tower of Babel (which would be in modern-day

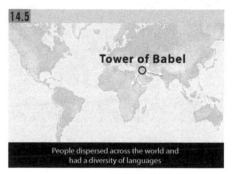

Iraq). In this story we see God responding to human pride and rebellion by causing human beings to speak in different languages. Along with this, we read, "So the LORD scattered them from there over all the earth,"* (See image 14.5.) A fascinating thing we learn in Deuteronomy 32:8–9 is that at this incident, God divided the humans by giving them different languages and caused them spread to them out geographically. The passage says that these geographic regions were divided up by the number of the sons of God, indicating that the new religious worship of gods across the planet may be part of a broader divine rebellion happening behind the scenes.

While there is no settled understanding of the origin of various languages or how so many diverse

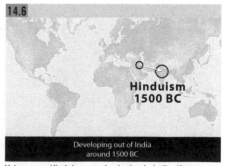

languages developed, we do see a pattern of human beings spreading out across the globe and new "religions" developing as they migrate across the land. Some of these belief systems became major world religions and are still

Yet even as Hinduism was beginning in India, the one true God had not forgotten his promise to Adam and Eve.

---

* Genesis 11:9.

practiced today, such as Hinduism which began in India around 1500 BC (14.6).

In Genesis we read of a man named Abram living in what is now modern-day Iraq. God calls Abram to leave behind his polytheistic culture and promises him that someone will be born into his lineage through

whom "all the peoples on earth will be blessed."* (See image 14.7.)

Here we see God returning to his promise in the garden of Eden, the promise that he would make all things right again between God and human beings. Now this promise ties specifically to Abram and his lineage. The promise itself was still vague, yet it is beginning to be developed as God works through Abram.

Abram (later renamed Abraham) has sons and grandsons and from one of them, a man named Jacob, we see the origin of the twelve tribes of Israel. The twelve tribes were eventually brought into slavery in Egypt and lived there for four hundred years. In Egypt they were exposed to a pluralistic religious system of gods and goddesses, including stories of how the creation of the world had happened. God rescued the Israelites from their slavery, showing them that the Egyptian gods weren't real through the plagues and miracles he did to free them. All of this was to remind them that there is only one God, the one who had called Abraham and had rescued them from Egypt. There is one, true, all-powerful God, not many.

Jesus Was Prophesied about While Hinduism Was Growing and Buddhism Was Birthed

Over time, the religious beliefs of the Jewish people developed into the religion we now call Judaism. God gave the people who left Egypt kings

---

* Genesis 12:3.

and leaders and directions for formal religious practices they could follow for that time period. (See chapters 4–6 on "strange and stranger things.") However, throughout this time we also see the one true God communicating his plans more clearly through prophets. Over and over again God reminds his people there is but one God. In fact, Israel's primary rallying cry began with a reminder that there is only one true God.* This belief came to define their identity as a people.

God continued to reveal to the people of Israel more about the person who would "crush his [the serpent's] head," "bless the whole world," and restore human beings back to God by speaking to the people through their prophets. The concept of a future "messiah" (which means "anointed one") became associated with how all of this would happen. The prophets said some very specific things about this messiah. They predicted he would:

- be born of a virgin (Isaiah 7:14)
- be born in Bethlehem (Micah 5:2)
- take on people's sin and bring healing to people by his death (Isaiah 53:4–5)
- be killed even though he was innocent (Isaiah 53:7)

The people of Israel began compiling their inspired writings into what we today call the Hebrew Bible (or what Christians call the Old Testament). Most of the prophets spoke and wrote during the 1000 BC to 400 BC time period.

So what else was happening during this time? Well, people were spreading out over the planet, and

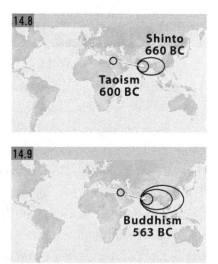

14.8 Shinto 660 BC
Taoism 600 BC

14.9 Buddhism 563 BC

---

* Deuteronomy 6:4–5.

new religions and faiths were developing. Buddhism, Shintoism, and Taoism in the 500s and 600s BC, for example (14.8 and 14.9).

Christianity Isn't a Modern Religion, but Its Roots Predate All Other Faiths

As the centuries continue, we pick up the story with the New Testament. The passages in the New Testament that speak of Jesus as the only way to God don't arise from nothing. They tie in with the consistent monotheism of the Jewish people and the creation in the garden of Eden. Remember, the promise made in the garden of Eden to Adam and Eve was that someone would come who would make things right again, someone who would bless all the nations of the world. That person was Jesus.

The Bible tells us that Jesus was the one born to a virgin in Bethlehem as foretold and written about seven hundred years earlier through the

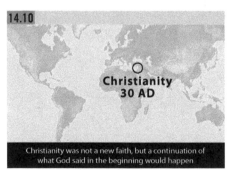

14.10

Christianity
30 AD

Christianity was not a new faith, but a continuation of what God said in the beginning would happen

prophets. Jesus was also the one who took on people's sin (sin is what breaks the relationship between human beings and God) on the cross. Jesus' death was also alluded to in the prophetic writings, speaking about the sacrifice he would make (14.10).

So let's recap how all of this fits together, according to the Bible story. There was one God in the beginning. And from the beginning, this one God said someone would come at a future time and would reveal the way to be forgiven and restored back to relationship with God. When Jesus came, those crazy-sounding Bible verses we read are simply confirming that Jesus was the one God had been talking about since the beginning. The entire Bible makes it clear that there won't be multiple ways of being forgiven or restored back to God. There would be one way, and that one way would be through one person, the man Jesus of Nazareth. According to the biblical story, other world religions are not a reflection of the one true God, and they did not develop from the beginning according to his plan and revelation. They are systems developed by human beings, and they do not accurately point us to the one God. From the beginning, the one God has said that he would send someone so we could be forgiven and restored back to him. I want to emphasize that idea: one way. This is the consistent witness of the entire Bible, and that's why the Bible verses we read state that.

The Message of Jesus as the Other Way Spread Around the Globe

Stop for a moment and think about this. If it is true that God has had a long-term plan lasting thousands of years to save the world from the consequences of human evil, that is great news. The Bible tells us that God provided a way for us to know him and to be forgiven, and that way is Jesus. After Jesus was resurrected from his death on the cross, he ascended to heaven. But before doing that he sent his followers on a mission to tell other people what God had accomplished through him. The church was birthed as small communities of faith empowered by God's Spirit to go tell others that Jesus is the way to know God and that no one comes to trust God except through Jesus—what he teaches and what he has done.

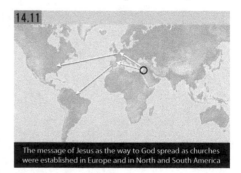

14.11

The message of Jesus as the way to God spread as churches were established in Europe and in North and South America

So the followers of Jesus traveled around the world. They continued the mission of Jesus and started churches (14.11). You'll see on the timeline (14.12) how we have now entered a new time period where the cross marks the intersection of the kingdom of God with God's activity on earth. We are in a time period when God is working through the church, which is on a mission to tell people about Jesus as the way to God. The end of the timeline shows a time in the future when Jesus returns, and all things are restored to how

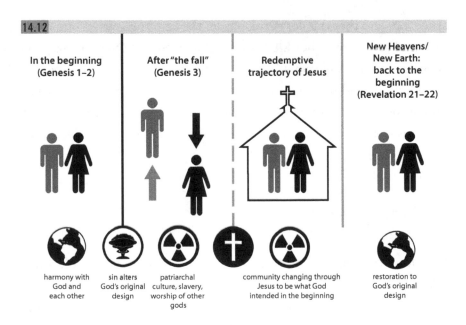

In the beginning (Genesis 1–2)	After "the fall" (Genesis 3)	Redemptive trajectory of Jesus	New Heavens/ New Earth: back to the beginning (Revelation 21–22)
harmony with God and each other	sin alters God's original design / patriarchal culture, slavery, worship of other gods	community changing through Jesus to be what God intended in the beginning	restoration to God's original design

they were in the beginning, with some new things added in as well. There is the restoration of people back to God and the creation of a new heaven and a new earth, all made possible through Jesus and what he has done.

Islam Was Birthed 600 Years after the Church Started

Where does all of this talk of the church fit in with other religious movements? Six hundred years after the church was birthed, a man named Muhammad launches what would become known as Islam (14.13). Islam presented a new and very different story about God, a "God" who is

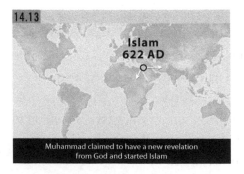

Islam 622 AD

Muhammad claimed to have a new revelation from God and started Islam

very different from the one portrayed in the Bible and revealed in Jesus. In the next chapter we will look at this in more detail, but it is important to note that Islam follows the coming of Jesus by six hundred years, and it presents a very different Jesus than the one we find in the New Testament. Islam was a new story about a different God, one who is not the same as the God found in Genesis through the Old Testament. Today Islam has spread around the world, but we cannot say that the teachings of Islam are the same as those in the Bible. As we will see, they are very, very different.

My goal in this chapter is not to conclusively prove that Jesus is the one true way to know God. My point is simply to show that in our world today there are many different faiths, and they all developed at different times and in different places. One of those faiths is the Christian faith, which developed from Judaism. Christianity has consistently held to the idea, first embraced by the Jewish people, that there is one true God. And it has embraced his message—a promise that someone is coming, and has already come, who will restore people back to relationship with God. Christianity teaches that the world is broken, and this brokenness is our fault. And the only way it can be fixed is through God's work. It's a work that only God can do and there are no other options. The biblical teaching is consistent on this point. This is not about the Bible being intolerant or sounding crazy. It's simply an ancient story stemming back to the creation, a story of one God who sent one Savior, Jesus, to be the way to relate to him and be in relationship with him.

Consider this. If there is one key to my home, a place where I am cared for and loved by my family, it isn't intolerant for me to say there is only one key. There are not many different keys—there is just the one. God made Jesus to be the one key we need to know him, and that has been his consistent position for thousands of years. That's not being intolerant. It is simply letting the world know that if they want to come into God's home, they will need to have the right key—Jesus.

I once shared this map of the development of various world religions with a young Hindu woman (14.14). She knew I was a Christian, and her friend had set up a time for us to meet. She had not been born into a Hindu family,

14.14

Many other sects of faith developed over time, each claiming to know "God" or "gods" or create a deity or deities or believe there is no deity at all (atheist)

but had been drawn to ancient religions. She had assumed that Christianity was a modern religion and had rejected it for that reason.

As we talked, I asked her if she had ever studied the history of different world religions. She had not, so I took out a napkin and drew the global map with the dates indicating when each faith had started. I also drew out the mountain analogy that you'll see in the next chapter. She told me she had never understood the roots of Christianity, that the foretelling of Jesus began at the creation, not 2,000 years ago when the church began.

She asked many questions and soon several of her friends and others in the church were in the conversation as well. Six months later it was a joy to see her put faith in Jesus as the way, the truth and the life, and she was baptized a few months after that. I recently saw her again and she is faithfully involved in a church and following Jesus today.

Image 14.15 is an inverted tree that summarizes much of what we have

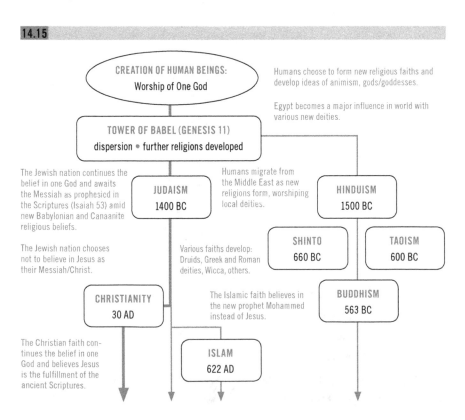

14.15

CREATION OF HUMAN BEINGS:
Worship of One God

Humans choose to form new religious faiths and develop ideas of animism, gods/goddesses.

Egypt becomes a major influence in world with various new deities.

TOWER OF BABEL (GENESIS 11)
dispersion • further religions developed

The Jewish nation continues the belief in one God and awaits the Messiah as prophesied in the Scriptures (Isaiah 53) amid new Babylonian and Canaanite religious beliefs.

JUDAISM
1400 BC

Humans migrate from the Middle East as new religions form, worshiping local deities.

HINDUISM
1500 BC

The Jewish nation chooses not to believe in Jesus as their Messiah/Christ.

Various faiths develop: Druids, Greek and Roman deities, Wicca, others.

SHINTO
660 BC

TAOISM
600 BC

CHRISTIANITY
30 AD

The Islamic faith believes in the new prophet Mohammed instead of Jesus.

BUDDHISM
563 BC

The Christian faith continues the belief in one God and believes Jesus is the fulfillment of the ancient Scriptures.

ISLAM
622 AD

been talking about in this chapter. I use a darker line to show the "trunk" of monotheism that carries the belief in one God forward into Christianity.

In the next chapter we look at how to respond to criticism of the claim that there is one God and one way to God. One of the most common criticisms is the argument that all religions are basically the same. So before we look at those critiques, let's reexamine the key verses that tend to bring offense. Each of these verses indicates that there is one God and only one way to this God.

Key Verses That Indicate There Is One God and Only One Way

John 14:6

John 14:6 is probably the most common verse that comes up in these discussions. Jesus is speaking, and he says, "I am the way and the truth and the life. No one comes to the Father except through me." But this is not an arrogant "I am right and you are wrong!" statement. In context, Jesus is speaking to his followers and comforting them. These were men who were dedicated to following him, and he was letting them know he would soon be leaving them. He was saying how he would be going away, hinting at the crucifixion ahead. Jesus is telling his followers that there is a specific way to follow and believe in him, a way that is different than following and believing in others. Often people will quote verse 6 of this passage without reading the larger passage where Jesus is speaking. Reading the verse in context sets the appropriate tone for this verse. Starting in verse 6 you read, "Jesus answered, 'I am the way and the truth and the life. No one comes to the Father except through me. If you really know me, you will know my Father as well. From now on, you do know him and have seen him.' Philip said, 'Lord, show us the Father and that will be enough for us.' Jesus answered: 'Don't you know me, Philip, even after I have been among you such a long time? Anyone who has seen me has seen the Father.'"*

---

* John 14:6–9.

The heart of Jesus is one of serving others, a heart of humility and not separation or hatred. Jesus isn't out to hammer people who have other beliefs; he is offering comfort and truth. At the same time, Jesus is clear in letting his followers know that following other gods or teachings is not the way to God. At the time Jesus says this, there were dozens of gods and goddesses in Greek and Roman culture. Jesus is making a clear distinction about who he is in relation to other religious views. But it is done in love and out of care that those who follow him know the truth. Theologian and New Testament scholar N. T. Wright writes:

> "Isn't this the height of arrogance to imagine that Jesus or anyone else was the only way? . . . [But] if you dethrone Jesus, you enthrone something, or someone, else instead. The belief that 'all religions are really the same' sounds democratic—though the study of religions quickly shows that it isn't true. What you are really saying if you claim that they're all the same is that none of them are more than distant echoes, distorted images, of reality. You're saying that "reality" God, the divine, is remote and unknowable, and that neither Jesus nor Buddha nor Krishna gives us direct access to it. They all provide *a* way towards the foothills of the mountain, not *the* way to the summit.
>
> It isn't just John's gospel that you lose if you embrace this idea. The whole New Testament—the whole of Christianity—insists that the one true living God, the creator, is the God of Israel; and that the God of Israel has acted decisively, within history, to bring Israel's story to its proper goal, and through that to address, and rescue, the world. . . . The truth, the life through which we know and find the way, is Jesus who washed the disciples' feet and told them to copy his example, the Jesus who was on his way to give his life as the shepherd for the sheep."[2]

Jesus is vastly different from anyone else; he is unlike every other religious leader. Yes, he is making it clear there are no other paths to God. But this is done in love and is consistent with God's purposes from the beginning to restore human beings back to himself through Jesus.

Acts 4:12

Another verse that is often quoted in these discussions is Acts 4:12: "Salvation is found in no one else, for there is no other name under heaven given to mankind by which we must be saved." This statement comes from a speech given by Peter, a follower of Jesus and later a leader in the church. He was speaking to religious leaders, risking his life in uttering these words. He was later jailed for this because the message of Jesus as the only way to knowing God was offensive to the religious Jews at the time. In other words, it was just as crazy sounding back then as it is today. Yet it is still an essential claim of biblical Christianity. Salvation refers to being rescued, and in this case, it is a rescue from death itself through the forgiveness Jesus offers. Salvation implies a holistic healing between God and each other.

Although human beings may seek other ways to God, Peter is firm in his conviction that Jesus is the only way. The early Christians believed it was so important for people to know Jesus they were willing to be jailed for this belief. They didn't want to stop telling people the good news that there is a way to God through Jesus.

1 Timothy 2:5–6

First Timothy 2:5 reads, "For there is one God and one mediator between God and mankind, the man Christ Jesus." This is yet another passage emphasizing that there is one God and one Savior—Jesus. But looking at the full context brings even more love and beauty to this. The full context says, "This is good, and pleases God our Savior, who wants all people to be saved and to come to a knowledge of the truth. For there is one God and one mediator between God and mankind, the man Christ Jesus, who gave himself as a ransom for all people."*

We read here that Jesus was considered a ransom. A ransom is a payment made to rescue someone, as we would pay in a kidnapping. If you are a parent, you know that if your child is taken by someone else, you would

---

* 1 Timothy 2:3–6.

do absolutely anything and pay anything required to get that child back. A loving parent would do anything for their child in need of rescue. And in the biblical storyline, we see that human beings are in need of rescue. So many of us don't realize it, but we aren't in right relationship with God. So this isn't an intolerant or arrogant statement; it speaks about a parent's love for his children and seeking a way to rescue them from harm and death.

Back to the Little Pamphlet

We can feel it sometimes and ignore it. But there is always a gentle tugging at our hearts, knowing that we may believe in a "God," but something is missing as we live our lives without him. That was how I felt as I first read the verses on the back of that little pamphlet on a college campus many years ago. I thought I believed in God, but I also knew something was missing. My being offended by those crazy words of Jesus (about him being the only way) led me to want to learn more, to see for myself if this was really true about Jesus.

As I began to study and learn about God and the origins of various world religions, I sensed truth in Jesus and what he said even though it sounded very intolerant at first. The more I studied what Jesus said and taught, I realized it wasn't intolerant—it was consistent with the rest of the Bible. It was also consistent with the idea that God loves us so much that he sent Jesus to save and ransom us—just like a loving father would. Reading these verses in the context of a bigger storyline changed them from words of intolerance to words of love, from something disturbing to something beautiful. And my life was changed forever as I realized the truth and came to believe in Jesus as the way, the truth, and the life.

CHAPTER 15

Making Sense of the
Intolerant-Sounding Jesus

> I do believe that all paths lead to God. It's a shame
> that we end up having religious wars because so many
> of the messages are the same.
> —MADONNA

Madonna nicely summarizes one of the most common religious beliefs in our culture today. "I do believe that all paths lead to God." If this is true, then the many Bible verses about Jesus being the only way to God are false. And it certainly seems crazy, arrogant, and divisive to make a claim that there is only one way if all paths lead us to God. Are Christians just wrong?

Madonna isn't alone in her sentiment. Oprah Winfrey once said, "One of the mistakes that human beings make is believing that there is only one way to live, and that we don't accept that there are diverse ways of being in the world, that there are millions of ways to be a human being, and many ways, many paths to what you call 'God.' Her path might be something else, and when she gets there, she might call it the light, but her loving and her kindness and her generosity brings her . . . if it brings her to the same point that it brings you, it doesn't matter whether she called it 'God' along the way or not . . . . There couldn't possibly be just one way. . . . There couldn't possibly be."[1]

Gandhi, the respected Indian leader and teacher, said several similar things with a bit more emphasis on how exclusive beliefs end up causing quarrels and fighting. He once said, "Religions are different roads converging to the same point. What does it matter that we take a different road, so long as we reach the same goal? Wherein is the cause for quarreling?"

So Are Oprah and Gandhi Right and the Bible Wrong?

Statements like these are popular today. And there are plenty of memes and graphics online that echo these ideas. They present an alternate view of religion promoting unity and love. It all sounds peaceful and harmonious in contrast to the exclusive and nontolerant Bible verses, verses like these:

- "For there is *one God and one mediator* between God and mankind, the man Christ Jesus" (1 Timothy 2:5).
- "Salvation is found in *no one else*, for there is no other name under heaven given to mankind by which we must be saved" (Acts 4:12).
- "Whoever has the Son has life; whoever *does not have the Son of God does not have life*" (1 John 5:12).
- "Enter through the narrow gate. For wide is the gate and broad is the road that leads to destruction, and many enter through it" (Matthew 7:13).
- "*I am the gate*; whoever enters through me will be saved" (John 10:9).
- "I am the way and the truth and the life. No one comes to the Father except through me" (John 14:6).

Are verses like this a cause of war, hatred, quarreling, and division?

Some of the visuals try to make the point that if God is "love," we shouldn't be seeing so much conflict. This sounds nice, doesn't it? Who doesn't want to see "love" as their religion? But what does that really mean?

One of the common metaphors used to connect various religions under the banner of love is the metaphor that all paths or all roads lead to God. It does sound really nice. We may be on different journeys, but eventually we'll all get to the same place. You may believe one thing, I may believe what Jesus says, but it's all the same thing basically, right? We're all heading the same way, just different paths. Saying there is only one path (like the Bible does) feels wrong and divisive.

I totally understand why we hear quotes by Oprah or others who seem to lovingly care about people and want not to have division or fighting. The idea of all faiths leading to the same God is a very attractive belief. What I have done so many times, in talking to people about this, is to draw what I am about to show you. I love to doodle and sketch, and it's a way to have dialogue to address the "all paths lead to God" concept.

I first draw out a mountain and write "God" at the top (15.2). Then I draw various paths that make their way up the mountain. I label them as different world faiths, such as Christianity, Islam, and Hinduism to illustrate several paths that eventually make it to the top of the mountain (15.3). These different paths may wan-

Do all paths lead to God?

der in a variety of ways, but they all eventually end up at the top where "God" exists. This all sounds wonderful, and I agree that if this picture of God were accurate, it would diminish much of the tension and awkwardness we find in talking about the differences between religions.

239

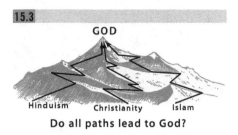

15.3

GOD

Hinduism   Christianity   Islam

Do all paths lead to God?

Because of the importance of this, we should really take a look at each of the paths to see what the various faiths believe. Even looking at some basic beliefs of each world faith helps us to understand what "God" is like at the mountaintop where the paths all meet. We can look at some simple questions to ask each world faith to learn its core beliefs. For example, we can ask:

- **God:** Who is "God"?
- **Jesus:** Who is Jesus? (Even though they may not follow Jesus, knowing how they define him is helpful.)
- **Afterlife:** How does one attain salvation, if that is part of their beliefs? And what happens when you die?

I realize we can't fully define any world faith with just a few questions. These are very simplistic explanations of world beliefs here. But I'm going to show that with even a few core questions, we can see whether each of the paths leads us to the same understanding—the same view of God.

Hinduism

Let's start with Hinduism, asking each of these three questions to learn a few basic Hindu beliefs (15.4).

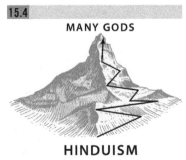

15.4

MANY GODS

HINDUISM

- **God:** Hinduism has thousands of gods, though there is a background force in the universe known as "Brahman" in addition to these gods. For some Hindus, Brahman is thought of as an ultimate force, perhaps a single God behind the other gods. But there is definitely a plurality of gods, and even if there is one ultimate being or force, there are thousands of other gods at the top of that mountain.

- **Jesus:** Jesus was a wise teacher, and he could be one of many gods, but he certainly is not the only way to God. Jesus is viewed as someone who may have achieved a state of self-realization corresponding to one of the goals of Hinduism, dharma.
- **Afterlife:** When a person dies, they are reincarnated to pay off their karmic debt, eventually becoming one with the impersonal Brahman.

At the end of the path of Hinduism, you will find many, many gods. And Jesus may have been a god among thousands of others. Reincarnation is what happens after death until you experience a state of oneness, a loss of your personal identity.

Islam

Let's continue with the Islamic path to see where you'll end up on the mountaintop with these same questions (15.5).

15.5

ONE GOD
Jesus NOT God's Son

ISLAM

- **God:** There is one God, Allah. But Allah is a distinctly different God than the God described by Jewish and Christian beliefs. Islam does believe there is one God, not many, and in this is also different from Hinduism.
- **Jesus:** Jesus is a prophet—but not the Son of God or divine in any sense. Attaining the afterlife does not involve Jesus.
- **Afterlife:** There is a paradise and a place of punishment because salvation is based on weighing the good and bad you have done in life.

On this mountaintop there is one God, but Allah is different than the Hindu gods and very different from the Christian God.

Christianity

Continuing to explore the Christian path (15.6), we find:

15.6

ONE TRIUNE GOD
Jesus God's Son

CHRISTIANITY

- **God:** There is one God who is triune in nature, but One (Father, Son, Holy Spirit).
- **Jesus:** Jesus is the Son of God, and the way to salvation is through what he did on the cross and because of his resurrection from the dead.
- **Afterlife:** Getting to heaven or hell is not based on anything we do, but on whether we have placed our faith in Jesus.

The Paths End Up Not at the Same Mountaintop but at Different Ones

As we begin to ask questions of the various "paths," or religious perspectives, we begin to see a clear pattern emerge—they don't end up at the same place. The "God" of each one is not the same God. There can't be thousands of "gods" on the mountaintop if there

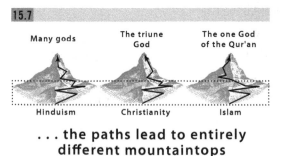

15.7

Many gods | The triune God | The one God of the Qur'an

Hinduism | Christianity | Islam

... the paths lead to entirely different mountaintops

is only one God and no others there. And even if there is only one God, the God of Christian faith is very different from the God of Islam. They are by no means the same God. The ends of the paths are *not* the same. They are contradictory to each other with opposing beliefs.

We can do this with each of the different world faiths, and what you find is they can't all be right. Either one is right and the others wrong, or they are all wrong. Unlike what some might want to believe, these different faiths are not just different paths that end up at the same mountaintop. They are paths on different mountains, leading to different mountaintops (15.7).

In fact, the differences between the world religions are so great at the level of their core beliefs that you would have to water down or ignore the beliefs that define them or believe the God behind them all is intentionally lying to people. God is telling some people he is one type of god and then lying to others and saying something completely different. It's important for us to understand this. To give a specific example, either Jesus took on the sin of people by dying on the cross and physically rising from the dead—or he didn't. If God says Jesus was simply a good teacher, but was not resurrected to one group of people but was for another group, then God is lying to one of those people groups. Or maybe he is lying to both. Either way, who wants to follow a God who lies and misleads people? So either one is right and true and the rest are wrong—or they are all wrong. But you can't have them all be right, or even partially right. And Christianity is not the only religion to say this.

Christianity Is Not the Only World Faith That Claims It Is Right and Others Are Wrong

Christianity often gets a bad rap for being intolerant and believing that Christian beliefs are the only true path to God. But if you look further into most other world faiths, you will find the same thing. Believers of most of the major world religions hold to their specific faith as the right and true way, which directly or indirectly says other faiths are wrong. Even if the belief is that "all paths lead to God," you are suggesting that those who don't hold that belief are wrong.

I was hosting an interfaith panel recently where we had representatives from the major world religions. Each representative stated their beliefs and made it clear that they held their beliefs, Scriptures, and sacred texts to be right and true. Everyone was courteous and polite, but it was obvious after hearing the variety of perspectives that each was extremely different from the others.

Why Do We Often Say All Religions Are Basically the Same?

If everything I've just said is true, and the paths (beliefs and practices) of the major world religions lead us to different mountaintops, why do many people today still say "all religions basically teach the same thing" or "all paths lead to God"? I can't speak for everyone, but after talking to a wide variety of people, I typically find that those who say these things have not looked closely into the different religious belief systems. They have not stopped to consider how different they really are. At a surface level, you might think they are saying similar things, but once you look deeper and study what they really teach and believe, you discover how incredibly different they are—even clashing in their core teachings.

Let's consider the three mountaintops of three different faiths—

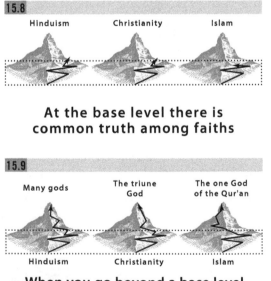

At the base level there is common truth among faiths

When you go beyond a base level see where the paths keep going to . . .

Hinduism, Christianity, and Islam. As I've argued, the different mountaintops, representing the "end" or goal of the path, are quite different. However, at the base level, they may show some similarities. When I teach this, I typically draw out several different mountains and then add a dotted line circling the common areas they share at their base (15.8).

These are the concepts, teachings, and ideas that represent the things the different faiths may have in common. At the base of the mountains, there are some areas of the paths that cross and

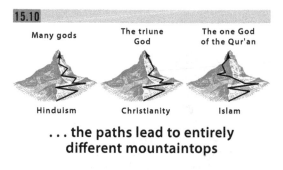

... the paths lead to entirely different mountaintops

intermingle. This represents the similarities among the religions. But here is the important point: the similarities are at the lowest level of the path, not at the end. These differing religious views share some things in common, but they diverge in clear and distinct ways as you move deeper in your belief and practice (15.9). Eventually, you end up in completely distinct places—different mountaintops (15.10).

So, yes, there is truth found within all world faiths. There are even some common teachings they share in their doctrines or holy writings. For instance, most of the major world religions have some version of what is called the "Golden Rule" (15.11). Christians know this from the statement Jesus made:

- **Christianity:** "Do to others as you would have them do to you" (Luke 6:31).

But this idea is not unique to Christianity. You can find similar truths in different world religions. Here are some sayings from sacred texts that predate the New Testament and the birth of Jesus:

- **Confucianism:** "Do not do to others what you do not want them to do to you" (Analects 15:23).
- **Hinduism:** "This is the sum of duty: do not do to others what would cause pain if done to you" (Mahabharata 5:1517).
- **Buddhism:** "Hurt not others in ways that you yourself would find hurtful" (Udana Varga 5:18).

I once visited the United Nations building in New York City, where the famous Norman Rockwell painting *The Golden Rule* is prominently displayed. This painting shows people of different faiths, implying unity around this common teaching.

There are some beautiful truths to be found in other faiths, including some that parallel the teachings of Christianity. These include how to treat your neighbor as yourself, being faithful to your spouse, and speaking the truth and not lying. Christian doctrine does not teach that "only Christianity has all the truth." Christianity acknowledges that the world faiths have many things that are true within their teachings, but acknowledging this does not mean everything each religion teaches is true or that they are all basically the same.

Almost everyone I have ever talked to who believes that all religious paths lead to the same mountaintop or God has never looked at the different world faiths deeper than the surface level. So you do hear some similar teachings about some things at the base level, but going higher up the mountain and really exploring each faith's core tenants shows that they are extremely in contradiction with each other.

The Bible Is Trustworthy and True

Since all paths do not lead to the same mountaintop, we need to examine each one to see which—if any of them—is true. Remember, since they cannot all be true, either one is right and the rest are wrong, or they are all wrong. And while we can acknowledge that some aspects of each have things that are right and good, such as loving your neighbor, when we compare the fundamental beliefs about the world, who God is, and what they think of Jesus, we find they are each very different. Either Jesus rose from the dead as Christianity claims, or he didn't and his body remained in the grave—as all other faiths believe. When it comes to a significant core belief like this, you are either right or you're wrong. There is no room in the middle.

As I mentioned earlier, I was a freshman in college when I began wondering why Christians believe that Jesus is the only way to God and everyone else is wrong. It was a question I had never considered before, but I immediately understood the ramifications. Each faith portrays God differently and teaches something different about how God thinks of us and how we relate to God. Depending on the faith you believe, you will have different things to do to prepare for death and what happens in the next life—if your faith even teaches that there is a next life. The faith you follow determines your values, your worldview, and your direction in life, and even if you do not make a choice to follow one of the major world religions, you are still making a decision.

My questions in college led me to begin studying the Bible and its origins. I began to wonder, Can I have confidence in this collection of documents? Is it a crazy book produced solely by human beings, or is it what Christians claim—a book of God's revelation to the people he has made, inspired and written by God's Spirit *through* people? Over a couple of years of study, the trustworthiness of the Bible became more and more apparent. Yes, I discovered all sorts of very strange and disturbing things in the Bible, and I'm writing this book to help you look at some of them. But in the end, one of the reasons I ended up believing in Christianity was the trustworthiness of the Bible itself. I can tell you wholeheartedly that I would not be a Christian if I felt the Bible was not a trusted library of books inspired by God. It's why so much of my focus as I was first exploring the Christian faith was looking into the Bible's origins and seeing if it could be truly believed as being from God.

Jesus Was Different from Other Religions' Leaders

However, in addition to the trustworthiness of the Bible, I began seeing that Christianity was different from the other world religions. It is not a religion based on what we do; it is a revelation from God, an announcement of what God has done for us. Yes, it sounds crazy to read Bible verses—many of them the teachings of Jesus—that declare Jesus as the only way to God. But it is also clear that Jesus stands out from other religious leaders. He claimed to be God incarnate, fully human like you and me, but also the same one who created everything that exists. No other religious leader has claimed to be the creator of the cosmos. Jesus also is set apart by his death and resurrection. He taught that his death was a means of restoring our broken relationship with God, and he took on our brokenness in a way no other religious leader has ever done.

I once heard a short saying about Jesus, comparing him to the other religious leaders. It stuck in my head and goes something like this: "Founders of other religions claim they are a prophet to help you find God. Jesus came to say, 'I am God come to find you.'"

The Hindu Vedas say, "Truth is one, but the sages speak of it in many different ways."

Buddha said, "My teachings point the way to attainment of the truth."

Muhammad said, "The truth has been revealed to me."

Jesus said, "I am the truth."

This is what sets him apart from other religious leaders and from anyone who has ever been born. As I have been writing these chapters, my prayer has been that Christians reading this would remember the uniqueness of Jesus as the way, the truth, and the life and would live their lives as if this is really true. I have been praying for those of you exploring Christianity and asking good questions, that you will see there is more to Jesus and the Bible beyond those crazy-sounding Bible verses. I truly hope that if you haven't yet, you will begin to dig a little deeper and consider that Jesus really might be the way, the truth, and the life for you. I wish I could sit down with you right now and talk about Jesus and why I so strongly believe that this statement about him is true.

What about People Who Are Faithful to Their Religions but Don't Know about Jesus?

As we close this section, there is one final question that often comes up in conversations with people who are asking these questions about Jesus and other religions. What about people of other faiths who are born into those faiths and never hear about Jesus? Are they saved, despite not knowing Jesus? Are they going to be with God in heaven?

This is a big question, and it's not an easy one to address, but I want to offer a few thoughts as we close this chapter, biblical truths that all Christians can affirm. It may not answer the question in the way you want, but I believe we need to begin with an understanding of God and what we know to be true of him.

1. We Affirm That God Loves People

The more you read the Bible, the more you will come to see that though God brings judgment on people (see the next section), he is truly loving, gracious, slow to anger, and forgiving. The Bible says that God loves the world, meaning he loves the people in the world, not just a generic world system.* He not only loves people but he took action to demonstrate that love by sending Jesus. God's love is the reason Jesus died on a cross and was raised to life again. Through Jesus, God provided a way, *the* way, for us to be restored to relationship with him and forgiven for all the wrong-doings we have ever done or will do, by our faith in Jesus. God does not want anyone to perish, and this is made clear in the Bible.†

2. We Affirm That God Is the Ultimate Loving Judge

God alone will judge people when we die. Death is a reality every person must face, and God promises that when we put faith in Jesus, we are forgiven, given the gift of eternal life, and will be with God for all eternity. For those who don't know Jesus and have never heard of him, we can say that only God knows what happens in the end. We do know he loves people, and the Scriptures indicate that people will be judged by how they responded to the knowledge of God that was available to them. This is a complex and emotional question, and I don't believe we should offer simplistic answers to complicated questions. In the end, while I am convinced that God's desire is for everyone to know him through Jesus, I believe we must trust God and his love for people, knowing that in the end, no one will be judged unfairly.

It can be interesting to consider all the people in the Old Testament who had faith in God but never heard the name Jesus. They didn't have a Bible like we have today, and they didn't know much of what we now know, thanks to the teachings of Jesus. But we believe that if they are saved and restored to relationship with God, it is by the faith they had in

---

* John 3:16.
† 2 Peter 3:9.

their limited knowledge of God. They may have had limited understanding, but they are forgiven and saved through Jesus, even if they didn't know fully who Jesus was.

To be clear, this is different from someone who hears the truth about God and the work and teachings of Jesus and then willingly chooses to reject him. For those who never hear this good news, I am content to trust what I know of God, that God is a God of grace, and the expanse of his mercy and forgiveness goes beyond our comprehension. The Bible is clear that everyone who is saved from sin is ultimately saved through Jesus. Perhaps that will include many of those who never heard his name but responded to what God was communicating to them as they were seeking God's truth.

3. God Wants People to Know Jesus, So He Created Us for Mission

The first two points affirm what we know to be true about God and recognize that there is much we do not know about how God judges individual people. This is especially true when we are speaking of people who never hear about Jesus or what God has revealed through him. There is mystery in knowing how God treats those who died but were faithful to respond to what they did know or sense about God. Here is what we can clearly affirm: there are people all around us today who haven't yet heard of Jesus, and Christians have a responsibility to share what they know.

There are millions of people who don't know that Jesus is the way, the truth, and the life and that no one comes to the Father except through him. This is why you will see Jesus' followers, after his death and resurrection, traveling to new cities and starting new churches. They wanted others to know who Jesus is. In fact, those who were closest to Jesus and knew him best became extremely passionate about telling people of other faiths and beliefs about Jesus. If you read the New Testament book of Acts, you see their zeal for seeing that others learn who Jesus is. As these new believers learned the truth about Jesus, they wanted others to know him as well. They understood that eternity is at stake, and the joy of knowing Jesus in this life is not something we can keep to ourselves.

This doesn't mean being obnoxious or judgmental toward others. But sharing the truth about Jesus is what I hope to do for as long as I live. Why? Because I am so aware of how I have been forgiven by God and how God has shown me grace and mercy I did not deserve, and I want others to know this love. I don't believe all paths lead to God. I am convinced that what Jesus said is true, so I want to spend my life doing whatever is possible to see others come to know Jesus as the way, the truth, the life, and the way to God.

You may not agree with everything in this section, but I hope it has helped you to see why it's not crazy for Christians to believe what the Bible teaches and what Jesus says is true—and why other religions are not true. And why Christians believe that knowing this is one of the most beautiful and important truths we can know.

Part 5 Summary Points

My God Can Beat Up Your God

- The New Testament is clear that the one way of salvation is through Jesus. To know what the Scriptures say and tell others about this one way is not arrogant or exclusive but done simply out of care and love, wanting others to know there is one way. Many things in life have one way to them. It is simply a matter of fact, not arrogance, that there is only one way.

- When you examine world religions, you find they do not all point to the same God or to paths that end in the same place. Their major tenets of belief are different and contradict each other. To say they are all the same makes God a liar, who teaches different truths to different people. Either one is right and the rest wrong or they are all wrong. The claims of Christianity make the most sense and have the backing of historical Scriptures to prove its claims are true.

- Christianity is the one world faith in which people don't have to earn their way to heaven, but it is through the work of Jesus and us putting faith in him that brings salvation.

PART 6

Rated NC-17

The Horror of God's Old Testament Violence

CHAPTER 16

The TV-MA, NC-17 Bible

This is what the LORD Almighty says: . . . . "Now go,
attack the Amalekites and totally destroy all that
belongs to them. Do not spare them; put to death men
and women, children and infants."

—1 SAMUEL 15:2–3

'll be candid as we reach this last section of the book. I didn't want
to write these last chapters. This section deals with some of the most
disturbing Bible passages, the verses that many find most difficult to
understand. I can make sense of the alleged conflict between science
and the Bible. I can understand some of the confusion about the crazy-
sounding verses that speak of shrimp, tattoos, and slavery. And I can see
why people think the Bible teaches misogynist things and is anti-women.
I can understand the history of world faiths and why Jesus is the one way
and the truth. But when I read and consider some of the more violent
Bible verses, verses that speak about the actions of God in killing people,
I too struggle to make sense of them.

In putting together this book, I considered not including the topic of
Old Testament violence, not because it's difficult to find examples, but
because it is so difficult to address. It would have been easier to leave

this section out of this book and focus on another topic. But I hope that by being honest in my own struggle to understand these verses it will provide help for others.

If I were ever to become an atheist or an agnostic, it would likely be because of passages like the ones we will study in this section. It is difficult to read about thousands of deaths and the violence we find in many of the Bible stories. But as I hope to show (and a reason why I am not an atheist), there are reasons why we see violence in the Bible. I hope to dispel some of the caricatures and criticisms of God as a violent, bloodthirsty, genocidal maniac. I hope to show that by applying basic Bible study methods to these troubling passages, we learn there is more happening, much that we may not have been aware of in a surface-level reading. It's easy to make generalizations and level accusations against the God of the Bible when you read a violent passage without the full context of the Bible's storyline. And here is my encouragement. In digging deeper into these verses and studying the violence of the Bible, I have maintained my faith and love in God. In fact, somewhat ironically, it has been in studying these violent passages that I have come to understand even more of God's great love, patience, and compassion.

So that's our goal in this section. We will be looking at some of the most common objections to the Bible based on the violence it contains. My guess is that some of you—even many of you who have read the Bible before—may not be aware of these passages, or you've read over them many times without stopping to think about what they mean.

"I Had No Idea This Was in There!"

There is a fascinating video that originated in Europe and has since been duplicated in the United States. You can easily find it online. Two guys hit the streets with a hardcover book in hand. The title: *The Holy Qur'an*. They open up the book and read several verses from it, including:

- "If you reject my decrees and abhor my laws . . . You will eat the flesh of your sons and the flesh of your daughters."[*]
- "If two men are fighting and the wife of one of them comes to rescue her husband from his assailant, and she reaches out and seizes him by his private parts, you shall cut off her hand. Show her no pity."[†]

Can you guess the reaction of those who heard these violent words being read from this book, what they thought was the Qur'an?

"This sounds ridiculous."

"How can anyone believe in this?"

"That's unbelievable to me."

After getting several reactions like this, the two fellows remove the paper cover jacket from the book. Though the jacket said "Holy Qur'an," the book they had been reading from was actually a different book, a Holy Bible. The verses people had been listening to were being read from the Bible, not the Qur'an.

The responses are fascinating to watch. They vary from a shocked "What the #$?" to a stunned "Seriously?" to "That is really unbelievable. That is sick, that's really sick," and my favorite—perhaps most revealing of all—"Of course I heard Bible stories when I was young, but I really had no idea this was in there."

Most of the people who weren't raised in a Christian home weren't aware of some of the violence contained in the Bible. They thought of it as a book filled with good stories and happy things you could teach children. But even those who were raised in a Christian home or taught the Christian faith seemed to be unaware of the violence. I'm frequently surprised by the number of people who say, "I had no idea this was in there."

---

[*]   Leviticus 26:15, 29.

[†]   Deuteronomy 25:11–12.

Joshua Fought the Battle of Jericho, and He Killed All the Women and Kids

Let's look at a few examples. Some of these are stories we have been teaching children for generations, but we tend to sanitize them and skip the violent parts. Consider the story of Joshua and the battle of Jericho. It comes from the Old Testament book of Joshua, chapter 6, and tells the story of how Joshua and the Israelites marched around the walls of Jericho once every day for six days. On the seventh day, they marched seven times around the walls, the priests blew their horns, the Israelites gave a great shout, and the walls of the city fell down. It's a fun and interesting story and you can easily see why children would like it. You can easily have them reenact the events, walking in circles, pretending to blow a horn, and giving a great shout. In Bible story books you will often find children's cartoon drawings of Joshua and the soldiers marching around outside the city walls with trumpets. There is even a children's song that is popular with kids in church circles. The lyrics of the cheery song go like this:

> Joshua fought the battle of Jericho, Jericho, Jericho.
> Joshua fought the battle of Jericho, and the walls came a-tumbling down.

It's all very true. This is what happened. But there is always more to the story as well. After Joshua and the Israelites entered the city, we read that "they devoted the city to the Lord and destroyed with the sword every living thing in it—men and women, young and old, cattle, sheep and donkeys."*

If we were to adapt that cheery children's song to be a little more realistic, we might change the lyrics to something like this:

> Joshua fought the battle of Jericho, Jericho, Jericho.
> Joshua fought the battle of Jericho, and they killed all the women and kids.

---

*   Joshua 6:21.

Or consider the story of Noah and the flood. We generally portray this story as a fun one for the kids with Noah looking all happy like Santa Claus on a boat with a cheery group of animals. The giraffe is sticking its head up smiling. Often this happy Noah and the ark scene is painted on the walls of Sunday school classrooms. But the reality of the story is a bit more violent and TV-MA or NC-17 rated. An untold, large number of people drowned in that flood— including women, children, and babies. Typically, we don't stop to consider the horror of all those deaths.

When Christians and those who aren't Christians read these stories or hear them without the violent parts removed (as we often do), they are unsurprisingly surprised. Today the internet and social media sites are being flooded with memes and graphics that call out the violent reality behind many of these classic Bible stories. We can no longer skim over the violence.

The first image has a big headline: "Bible Verses you don't hear about in church" (16.1). It goes on to quote the Bible verse Hosea 13:16, which reads, "Samaria shall become desolate; for she hath rebelled against her God: they shall fall by the sword: their infants shall be dashed in pieces, and their women with child shall be ripped up." Another meme (16.2) is titled "The Bloody Bible" and it quotes Isaiah 13:15–16, where it says, "Every one that is found shall be thrust through; and every one that is joined unto them shall fall by the sword. Their children also shall be dashed to pieces before their eyes; their houses shall be spoiled, and their wives ravished."

More and more people today are reading passages like this and asking if the Bible is a dangerous, damaging

16.1

Bible Verses you don't hear about in church

Samaria shall become desolate; for she hath rebelled against her God: they shall fall by the sword: their infants shall be dashed in pieces, and their women with child shall be ripped up

Hosea 13:16 (KJV)

16.2

THE BLOODY BIBLE

Every one that is found shall be thrust through; and every one that is joined unto them shall fall by the sword. Their children also shall be dashed to pieces before their eyes; their houses shall be spoiled, and their wives ravished. (KJV)

Isaiah 13:15-16

book that should be avoided. Someone wanted to point out how often babies and children were killed in the Bible and posted this image of a billboard with the words "'I Hate Babies!'—God" followed by an extensive list of Bible verses (16.3).

There are others that mention every verse in the Bible where someone dies in a battle set in motion by God or where God is directly killing someone or some people group. They added up all the deaths mentioned in these verses for a total of 2,821,364 people killed. The accusation is made that God is "Drunk with Blood"[1] and delights in killing people, which comes from reading Deuteronomy 32:39–42, where God says, "I put to death . . . I have wounded . . . I will make my arrows drunk with blood, while my sword devours flesh." In all of this, God is portrayed as a horrible being who is out to kill, devour, and become "drunk with blood."

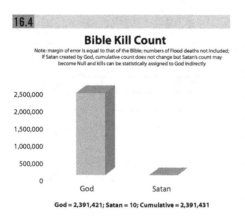

There are even charts that have been made to show how bloody God is by comparing the number of deaths in the Bible attributed to God versus how many are attributed to Satan. The comparison is titled "Bible Kill Count," and while Satan is given ten deaths (all from the book of Job), God has more than 2 million (16.4).

Violence, Murder, Slaughter, Cutting Bodies into Pieces, Cannibalism, and Rape

Many Christian parents screen content for their children and prohibit books that contain violence and graphic descriptions of immoral acts. Yet at the same time, they give Bibles to their children at an early age, hoping they will read them. I sometimes wonder, do they realize that the Bible contains scenes of graphic violence and mentions of cannibalism, including parents eating their babies? Do they know that the Bible has stories about incest, and a scene where a woman is raped and her body is cut up into twelve pieces, and mentions of witchcraft, human sacrifice, and bloody deaths, decapitations, fingers, feet, and hands being cut off, eyes gouged out, impalements, multiple suicides, and thousands of animals being killed?[2] Are they aware of the poetic and erotic descriptions of sexual intimacy, the mentions of harems, gang rape, and sexual organs being cut off and exchanged for a wife?[3] Yes, these are all actually in the Bible.[4] You can find online memes and jokes about this type of content, even a mock

parental advisory warning sticker to put on the Bible because of its graphic, not-for-children contents. Non-Christians know that many Christians have not fully read the book they claim to love and treasure, and they make an understandable and ironic point about Christians who want to keep their children safe from unsuitable content but give them Bibles.

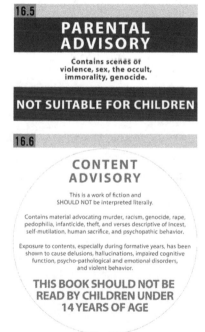

16.5

PARENTAL ADVISORY

Contains scenes of violence, sex, the occult, immorality, genocide.

NOT SUITABLE FOR CHILDREN

16.6

CONTENT ADVISORY

This is a work of fiction and SHOULD NOT be interpreted literally.

Contains material advocating murder, racism, genocide, rape, pedophilia, infanticide, theft, and verses descriptive of incest, self-mutilation, human sacrifice, and psychopathic behavior.

Exposure to contents, especially during formative years, has been shown to cause delusions, hallucinations, impaired cognitive function, psycho-pathological and emotional disorders, and violent behavior.

THIS BOOK SHOULD NOT BE READ BY CHILDREN UNDER 14 YEARS OF AGE

Some parts of the Bible really should have an NC-17 rating. The evil actions of human beings are portrayed throughout the Bible, sometimes in graphic detail, and these activities are condemned by God. But it's very important to remember that just because something evil is mentioned in the Bible does not mean that God approves of the action or that the Bible is positive about that behavior. Many of the violent acts in the Bible are the result of evil human choices and decisions. Using our analogy of the Bible as a library, much of the violence in the Bible library is in the "history books" that record all kinds of events and activities that humans did. God did not inspire the writers of the Bible to "clean up" the story to give us a filtered version of human evil. That actually makes me trust the Bible more, knowing that the difficult parts have not been edited out.

Our focus in this section is not on the violence in the Bible because of the evil acts of human beings but on the violence that is attributed to God's actions. We won't look at every verse, but I hope that by showing a few of these passages, it will provide guidance in how to understand others. We'll look at three broad questions:

- Was God committing genocide when he ordered the killing of people groups?
- What about the babies? Does God really like dashing babies against rocks?
- Why does the Old Testament God seem so different from the New Testament Jesus?

In the next chapter, we'll begin by looking at how others over the years have tried to explain the violence in the Bible. Then, after studying some of the options, I'll explain what I suggest is a balanced view that helps us understand the violence while respecting both the inspiration and trustworthiness of the Bible.

CHAPTER 17

The God of Compassion, Slow to Anger and Forgiving

The God of the Old Testament is arguably the most unpleasant character in all of fiction: jealous and proud of it; a petty, unjust, unforgiving control-freak; a vindictive, bloodthirsty ethnic cleanser; a misogynistic, homophobic, racist, infanticidal, genocidal, filicidal, pestilential, megalomaniacal, sadomasochistic, capriciously malevolent bully.

—RICHARD DAWKINS, *THE GOD DELUSION*

Today, more and more people find themselves nodding in agreement with the very well-known and often repeated quote by atheist Richard Dawkins in which he describes God as jealous, proud, petty, bloodthirsty, homophobic, and genocidal, among other things. I understand why Dawkins wrote this in his book *The God Delusion* and why those who read certain Bible verses agree with him.

But is this accusation true? Is God really all of the things he is accused of being? Unforgiving? Jealous? Infanticidal? A bloodthirsty ethnic cleanser? And if this isn't true, how do we make sense of the Bible

263

verses that show God ordering mass killings? How do we understand the violence that God allegedly commanded and endorsed?

First, let's recognize that these Bible verses aren't new. They have always been in the Bible. This isn't new information. Perhaps we are growing more sensitive to some of the violence today, or people are reading these verses more closely and asking different questions than were asked in the past. Let's start by looking at some of the more extreme ways people try to explain these verses. Then we'll consider what I believe is a more middle-of-the-road approach.

Ways to Explain the Violence in the Bible That *Aren't* Satisfying

There are two ways people try to explain away the violence we find in the Bible that I don't find particularly satisfying. Here is the first approach.

1. The No Apology Approach

God did it. He is God and he can do anything he wants, including killing people. At one extreme, there are those who read these passages and, for the most part, aren't bothered in the least. "God is God and he has the right to do anything he wants. If God chose to kill people or have them killed, it's not our place to question what he did. And they probably even deserved it." I agree with the first part: God is God. And yes, he can do whatever he wants. But it doesn't help us understand *why* God might have utilized violence in a particular situation. This seems to sidestep the tension between God's compassion and his violence, and many feel it doesn't leave us with a satisfying explanation.

I confess that as a Christian I feel a little guilty when I raise these questions. I don't want to doubt God's wisdom. But I also don't believe asking the why behind something is doubting God's wisdom. God wants us to understand him by looking at his actions, and I believe he wants us to know him better by understanding why he does what he does. Asking "Why, God?!" is not a bad thing. In the Bible we see King David growing angry and questioning God after God strikes down a man named Uzzah for trying to do a good thing and keep the ark of the covenant from falling to the ground.* God doesn't rebuke David for feeling the way he did and for asking the question. Wondering "Why?" and trusting that there is a good reason is never seen by God as wrong or sinful.

As important as it is to trust in God and believe that he can do whatever he wants and it is always good, I also believe we need to go deeper than the "God can do whatever he wants" answer. This is especially true when you are talking to non-Christians or others who are asking why God would act so violently.

2. The Bible Is Wrong Approach

God didn't command the violence or do any of it. The Scriptures have the stories in it, but the Israelites and those who wrote the stories were mistaken. This approach is becoming more common today, though it isn't a new way to explain the violence in the Bible and even has roots in the early church. There was a fellow named Marcion, a church leader living around 140 AD in what is now modern-day Turkey. Marcion taught that the God we meet in the Old Testament was not the same God we find in the New Testament. He felt the Old Testament God was violent and was all about killing people, which didn't align with how he understood the God of Jesus in the New Testament.

Marcion's response reminds me of an episode from *The Simpsons*. In this episode, Homer had one of those postcards that changes the image if you angle it a certain way. Angled one way, the card shows an image of a smiling God giving you a thumbs-up. Homer looks at the image and says, "Loving God." Then he angles the image a different way and the God image shifts to a frown and a pointing finger. Homer says, "Vengeful God." He angles the image back and forth, saying, "Loving God . . . Vengeful God."

This is similar to what Marcion was saying when he looked at the God of the Old and New Testaments. The Old Testament God seemed so different from the New Testament God, so much so that Marcion began

---

*   1 Chronicles 13:11.

17.1

Old Testament God   New Testament Jesus

"Kill them" (Num. 25:16)   "Love them"(Matt. 22:39)
"Show them no mercy"   "Forgive them" (Luke 23:34)
(Deut. 7:2)

teaching that the Old Testament was not true. He declared that the Old Testament wasn't inspired, and even removed several sections from the New Testament. He took out anything he felt was inappropriate or too violent, passages about God's judgment or hell, and edited and shaped a new Bible with just the nice things about God (from his own perspective).

We still see forms of Marcion's beliefs today. People may not actually erase or remove parts of the Bible, but we see sections of the Bible being reclassified and treated differently from the more "God-inspired" parts. Some try to suggest that God never ordered the Israelites to attack and kill people. They had it wrong or they didn't understand God correctly, so they recorded things about God that God didn't say or want. If you think about it, this is an easy way to solve the problem of violence in the Old Testament. You just say it's not God who did that, it's the people. The authors of the Bible had it wrong, and God didn't command or do any of the things we read that he did. This way of thinking says that the violent verses aren't telling the truth about God because they were written by people who made mistakes recording what they thought God wanted said.

The big problem with this approach is that it means a whole lot of the Bible is wrong and not God-inspired or true. That's not the way Christians have been reading the Bible for the last two thousand years. It's an entirely different way of looking at the Bible. It means Moses, Joshua, and all the others misunderstood God when they were being directed to attack and battle others. If that's the case, it seems fair to ask: What else did Moses get wrong? And what else did the other writers of the Bible get wrong as they recorded these stories about God? Once you abandon the belief that God oversaw and inspired every single line of the Bible, it brings everything the Bible says into question. We no longer have any way of knowing what God said or didn't say.

If I were to opt for this second approach, I would no longer be able to trust anything in the Bible. Logically, I'd have to reject the entire thing because I don't see how I could simply pick and choose what I felt was in alignment with how I wanted or needed God to be. I believe, in agreement with what the historical church has believed since the time of Jesus, that we must accept God for who he is and that this understanding is preserved for us in the Bible—the entire Bible. We don't get to choose the parts of it we like, and we don't get to shape God into the God we prefer him to be.

One additional major reason to accept the Old Testament stories, including the truth that God ordered the battles and the violence, is because Jesus believed it. Jesus believed the entire Old Testament is God's inspired word. He believed Moses really lived and he accepted the stories about him. Jesus believed what the prophets wrote and never once alluded to any part of the Old Testament not being accurate or true. He never once suggested that the battles or the violence in the Old Testament were not true. In fact, he emphasized the importance of the Old Testament, saying that every word was important. He quoted it often and believed the truth of the Old Testament (see "Postlude: Jesus Loved His Crazy Bible"). Since Jesus believed all that is recorded in the Old Testament, I will believe it as well.

Is the Old Testament God of Wrath Different from the New Testament Jesus of Love?

So was Marcion correct? Is the Old Testament God different than the New Testament Jesus? When you study the New Testament, you quickly find that it isn't void of death or violence. While some will try to argue that the Old Testament God was fond of killing and violence while Jesus was all about love and forgiveness and peace, that just doesn't hold up under scrutiny. We soon learn that talk of violence and judgment didn't end with the Old Testament. There is a change in how God relates to people after Jesus. But the talk about judgment and death doesn't disappear.

In the New Testament there are also times when God intervenes directly and a death occurs. There are the sudden deaths of Ananias and Sapphira, who lied to God, tried to fool the church through hypocrisy, and publicly tested God's holiness. God used their deaths as an example and a warning to the early church not to neglect what they had learned of his holiness. We see Herod struck down by an angel and eaten by worms. And the book of Revelation is filled with talk of judgment and death, as God's judgments are released upon the earth—though not every description is intended to be taken literally.* Much of Revelation is written in symbolic language, so like many passages in the Bible, it takes study and time to understand what it is saying to us today. The point in mentioning it here is to show that God is not passive in the New Testament. He still exercises power and intervenes in ways that at times cause death.

Jesus Spoke about Hell and Judgment More than Anyone Else in the Bible

Finally, let's look at Jesus. As much as we think of Jesus as a man of love and peace, Jesus spoke often of judgment and hell. In fact, Jesus spoke more about hell than anyone else in the Bible. He spoke of eternal fire and punishment as the final state of human beings and angelic beings who rejected God. Jesus warned people who went against God's guidance that they would be in danger of the fire of hell.†

The exact word Jesus used, which we often translate as "hell" in English, was "Gehenna." The people Jesus was speaking to would have known that Gehenna was a valley in south Jerusalem where piles of garbage were burned daily. It was filled with animal carcasses and the dead bodies of those who didn't have families to bury them. Jesus used graphic language in referring to this place, a location the people could picture.

---

*   Acts 5:1–11; 12:18–25; many parts of Revelation contain mass deaths.

†   Matthew 13:50, 18:8.

Jesus described hell as a place where "the worms that eat them do not die, and the fire is not quenched."* Jesus is calling to mind the maggots they would have found living in the dead bodies on the garbage heap. In the earthly Gehenna, the worms would die when they had eaten the flesh off the bodies. Jesus was making a graphic point that the spiritual decomposition of hell never ends—"The worms . . . do not die." This was how he described the consequences of rejecting God.

It's popular to pit Jesus against the God of the Old Testament, and now if you hear that, you know that the person suggesting this has not read all of Jesus' words about the consequences of not obeying God. Jesus even offered this warning to those who would take his words lightly: "I will show you whom you should fear: Fear him who, after your body has been killed, has authority to throw you into hell. Yes, I tell you, fear him."† The writer of Hebrews in the New Testament offers a similar warning, telling us, "It is a dreadful thing to fall into the hands of the living God."‡ A very sobering section of the New Testament speaks about what will happen when Jesus returns, specifically the punishment of being forever separated from God's presence. "This will happen when the Lord Jesus is revealed from heaven in blazing fire with his powerful angels. He will punish those who do not know God and do not obey the gospel of our Lord Jesus. They will be punished with everlasting destruction and shut out from the presence of the Lord and from the glory of his might."§

Even though the New Testament does not have the bloody battles of the Old Testament, we still see evidence of a holy God who hates sin (when we go against God's guidance). Both the Old Testament and the New Testament reveal the same God to us—the creator of all things who became a man in the person of Jesus.

---

*   Mark 9:48.
†   Luke 12:5.
‡   Hebrews 10:31.
§   2 Thessalonians 1:7–9.

God's Pinned Tweet: Exodus 34:6–7

Before we look at some of these violent verses from the Old Testament, I want to pin a tweet for you so it stays before you in all that we are studying. It's one of the most repeated verses in the Bible, where God describes who he is. Exodus 34:6–7 reads, "The LORD, the LORD, the compassionate and gracious God, slow to anger, abounding in love and faithfulness, maintaining love to thousands, and forgiving wickedness, rebellion and sin."

The context of this verse (remember, "Never read a Bible verse") is worth looking at. God had given Moses the Ten Commandments on tablets, and Moses went down from the mountain to present them to the people. While Moses was gone, the people of Israel had grown impatient and began a hedonistic party, even creating a golden calf to worship. God had rescued the people from slavery in Egypt and was bringing them to the land he had promised them, yet the people were quickly deserting him. They were rebelling against God.

When Moses comes down and sees them having this giant party, worshiping and honoring a false god, he smashes the original tablets that outline God's promises and expectations for his relationship with the people. But God gives them a second chance (they get many, many chances), and Moses brings the people the "second copy" of the Ten Commandments. God also wants them to know something important about himself. That's the verse we just read. God wanted the people who had just rejected him to know he is compassionate. He wants them to know he is gracious and merciful. He is slow to anger. He is abounding in steadfast love. And he is faithful to them.

This scene shouts out to us God's forgiving heart and his patience. The people had turned their backs on him. They had worshiped another god—after God had saved them from slavery. Yet he forgives them. There were consequences for their actions, of course, but he did not strike them all down, nor did he turn back from his promises to them. He forgave them.

This message from God is about who he is, and it is repeated throughout the Bible more than any other verse about God. If you were carefully reading the entire Old Testament, you would not find a reactionary God who needs a class in anger management, someone who strikes out randomly, without cause. Instead, you find a God who is patient—again and again—with his people. We'll see a few more examples of this in the next chapter, but this is one of the key messages of the story of the whole Bible. Even in the parts where God is actively behind violence and death, it is not done without first pleading for change, giving warnings, waiting for change, and showing great patience.

There are times when God acts in judgment leading to death. But the people groups that were judged had received warning after warning. God is patient and compassionate and forgiving, but there is a limit to his patience. He is also just and has promised to uphold the cause of justice and punish those who do wrong, defending those who are innocent. God is not slow to love, but he is slow to anger. And as we see throughout the Bible, God does express anger, but it is an outflow of his just love and protection—not a vindictive and selfish anger, the type human beings are prone to display. Love, compassion, patience, and forgiveness are central to who God is. God's immense love for people is why Jesus came and took on their sin. God was providing a way for people to have forgiveness and peace with him.

How Mary Poppins Helps Explain the Violence and Killings

Let's think about the movie *Mary Poppins* for a moment. *Mary Poppins* is a wonderful movie about a caring, magical nanny who helps a dysfunctional family. She is kind and loving and everyone loves her. She is there to help the family.

I once saw a fascinating and creative movie trailer someone had created for *Mary Poppins*. It was nothing like the original movie. Someone had taken short scenes from the film and had edited and arranged them to create a trailer, taking many of the scenes entirely out of context. For instance, they took a scene of a group of nannies being blown away by the wind and then showed Mary looking sternly out through a window at them. In another scene Mary stares at a boy being sucked into a closet and the doors quickly shutting. And there's a scene of a girl being sucked up into a chimney. At the end of the trailer, you see several children running in fear and the words "Scary Mary" appear on the screen followed by the line "Hide your children." Someone who had never seen the real *Mary Poppins* movie would naturally assume it's a horror film. They would think Mary is an evil woman out to get children.

Were all of those scenes in the movie *Mary Poppins*? Yes, they were. And if you've never seen the whole movie and just watched those few scenes, then, of course, she is "Scary Mary." If all you focused on were the scenes of Mary looking mean and sending kids up chimneys, you'd think she was a monstrous and wicked nanny. But if you have seen the entire movie and know Mary from that context, you better understand how the "scary" parts fit into the whole, and you know that the loving and kind Mary is not "Scary Mary."

The same is true for the God of the Bible. We can look at a series of Bible verses that show God issuing commands for war or violence or death, and if that is all we saw, we might assume that God is quite scary. Without knowing the whole story about God, we too create a "Scary God"—a God I would want to hide my children from.

My encouragement to you is to avoid forming your picture of God from bits of stories or Bible verses taken out of context without seeing the whole story. Looking at just the scary bits will lead you to the conclusion that God is "jealous and proud of it; a petty, unjust, unforgiving control-freak; a vindictive, bloodthirsty ethnic cleanser; a misogynistic, homophobic, racist, infanticidal, genocidal, filicidal, pestilential, megalomaniacal, sadomasochistic, capriciously malevolent bully."[1] When you read the entire Bible and see who God is through his interactions with people, you see he is slow to anger, loving, compassionate, forgiving, and patient.

CHAPTER 18

Making Sense of the Texts of Terror

Don't the following Bible verses sound like lines from a horror film or a battle scene?

- "Happy is the one who seizes your infants and dashes them against the rocks" (Psalm 137:9).
- "And when the Lord your God has delivered them over to you and you have defeated them, then you must destroy them totally. Make no treaty with them, and show them no mercy" (Deuteronomy 7:2).
- "They devoted the city to the Lord and destroyed with the sword every living thing in it—men and women, young and old" (Joshua 6:21).
- "I will make my arrows drunk with blood, while my sword devours flesh: the blood of the slain and the captives, the heads of the enemy leaders" (Deuteronomy 32:42).
- "You will eat the flesh of your sons and the flesh of your daughters" (Leviticus 26:29).

As we began exploring in the last chapter, the Bible has many graphic and violent stories with bloody Bible verses. I've heard these called the "texts of terror." In this chapter, we'll look at two examples of these more closely. We'll look at a passage that seems to suggest that God committed genocide, ordering the mass killing of men, women, and children. And then we'll look at another verse that suggests God delights in seeing babies being thrown against rocks. There are many other verses to consider, but by examining these two closely, I think we will learn some broader principles for understanding other violent texts as well.

So let's begin with what is arguably the most mentioned type of the texts of terror and this first question: How do we explain the verses and stories where it looks like God is committing genocide, and mass killing people groups, including women and children?*

There are Bible verses where God is ordering the killing of large population groups, including children and women, and to do it "without mercy." We see many different times when God says, "You must destroy them totally. . . . Show them no mercy," "Do not leave alive anything that breathes," "I will make my arrows drunk with blood."† What are we to make of these verses?

By now, you should know what I'm going to say to you. Never read a Bible verse on its own. We need to first see where these verses fit into the bigger story. So let's make a few observations as we step into that time period and cultural context. We will look at a people group known as the Canaanites, the people God is ordering to be destroyed with what seems like a merciless genocide. There are other people groups in the Old Testament, including the Midianites and Amalekites, that we won't address here, but with each people group you need to look at what was going on at that time and in that place. The circumstances are often similar. Were they in judgment themselves for their activities? Is this a battle where God is moving Israel into the land? There are different reasons for different battles, so you need to examine each one.

---

*   1 Samuel 15:2–3; Joshua 6:20–22.
†   Joshua 11:20; Deuteronomy 7:2; 20:16; 32:42.

Genocide and Mass Killing

When we look at many of these texts of terror, we can make some broad observations.

1. **Most of the violent Bible verses regarding God sending Israel into battles are from a limited time period in biblical history and are not found throughout the entire Old Testament.** There is a common assumption that the "God of the Old Testament" is constantly angry, killing and slaughtering people without mercy. There are some Bible verses that seem to indicate this, such as:

- "You must destroy all the peoples the LORD your God gives over to you. Do not look on them with pity and do not serve their gods, for that will be a snare to you" (Deuteronomy 7:16).
- "They devoted the city to the LORD and destroyed with the sword every living thing in it—men and women, young and old" (Joshua 6:21).

However, when you look at these verses and the other various battles and violent acts that God sanctioned, you will find they primarily come from a specific time period. It is true that there are a lot of battles and deaths throughout the whole Bible, but not all of these are sanctioned or commanded by God. There are times when God intervened to judge a people group for their evils, even his own people Israel. But those times are different than when the Israelites moved into the land and fought the Canaanites. When God sent Israel into battle with various cities in the promised land, his intention was not to destroy but to drive out. He was clearing space for his presence. The land was God's, and he was clearing it for Israel to live there to be with him. There are battles in the Bible and deaths that God is not involved in but are simply human political powers battling on their own. As with anything involving human beings, there are deaths. So the context is important. Most of the violent battles initiated by God occur during one generation when God was moving the people of Israel into the "promised land," and God always gave the people that Israel fought the opportunity to turn to him and avoid battle.

If you recall the Bible storyline (see chapter 3), we see that God made a promise to a man named Abraham that his descendants would inherit a distinct geographic area of land. When Abraham's descendants migrated down to Egypt, that promise was not forgotten. Even as they became slaves of the Egyptians and stayed there four hundred years, the land was still theirs, according to God's promise. After God used Moses to rescue Israel from slavery, they began returning to the land that was originally given to them. This land was not intended just for Israel; it was also set aside for God to dwell there with his people.

However, other people groups, including the Canaanites, were now living in the land that God had designated for Israel. The whole earth belongs to God, so God can give land to anyone. Although different people had moved into the land, it still was the land God had designated for Israel. This land was more than just land; it was the land where God would dwell. It was the land where the city of Jerusalem eventually was established, and in Jerusalem, a temple to worship God was built. Jesus was eventually born in this land and died in this land for the sins of the world.

The geography of the land was also strategic. Israel was a "bridge" between many nations and cultures, a place many people would travel through, which was a key part of God making his message to the world known. Travel through this specific location was strategic for his desire to get the word out to others. This context forms some of the background for why the land was important and why battles were fought over it as the Israelites returned from Egypt. God had dedicated this land for the people Israel, and they were now coming back to the land where they had once lived.

Understand that God was not randomly ordering battles and encouraging violence. He was ordering them for a specific situation during a specific time period, most of it in the span of one generation.

2. These battles were not based on ethnicity, so this is not "genocide."

Another common criticism is that God sanctioned these battles as a form of genocide. Genocide is the deliberate killing of a large group of people, especially people of a particular ethnic group or nation. But it is clear that these killings and battles were not based on ethnicity or race. They were based on occupation of the land. These were people groups who chose not to join with Israel and turn to God, but instead remained in rebellion against God.

As we will see, the Canaanites were given the opportunity to avoid war and violence but chose not to respond to God's opportunity. Later, we even see God allowing his own people, Israel, to be captured and their cities destroyed when they too rebelled against God. So God was not racially biased in his judgment. When they rebelled against him, God included his own people in the same types of judgments he had used them to bring to others. He recruited foreign nations to destroy their cities and take them into captivity.

3. The people who were in the land were extremely wicked in their practices, and God did not want them to influence Israel. We also need to look closely at the people whom God was sending Israel to "utterly destroy." While we cannot stereotype or judge every citizen of the land of Canaan (a people group Israel was sent to battle against), we can look at some of the religious practices their leadership promoted and allowed in that culture.

The Canaanites were involved in some evil worship practices. They had several gods, among whom was one named Molech (18.1). Here's how the worship of this god has been described: "Molech was a Canaanite underworld deity represented as an upright, bull-headed idol with a human body in whose belly a fire was stoked and in whose arms a child was placed to be burnt to death. It was not

18.1

just unwanted children who were sacrificed. Plutarch (a Greek writer and philosopher from the first century) reported that during Phoenician (Canaanite) sacrifices, the whole area before the statue was filled with a loud noise of flutes and drums so that the cries and wailing should not reach the ears of the people."[1]

The people of this land had the horrific practice of sacrificing infants by placing them in the hot metal arms of a statue of their god and hiding with their drums the screams and cries of children being burned to death. It's extremely difficult for us to picture the barbaric horror of this practice, but this was part of Canaanite life and reflected their values. Another worship practice to the gods Baal and Ashtoreth involved sexual rites, including bestiality as well as parents bringing their children to temple priests for use in prostitution. I raise these points so we can begin to understand why God was bringing judgment on the people and the level of depravity and violence in this people group.

God also made it clear that he was not using the Israelites because they were better or more moral or righteous than the Canaanites. "It is not because of your righteousness or your integrity that you are going in to take possession of their land; but on account of the wickedness of these nations."* In other words, this was a judgment by God on these people, and he used Israel to accomplish his judgment. People today criticize God, asking why he doesn't end evil and suffering in the world. In this case, we see him doing that by sending Israel in to end these horrific cultural practices before they can spread to other nations. How ironic that God is criticized for ending the evil by punishing those who engage and advocate for it.

In this part of the larger Bible storyline, God was entering alongside Israel to dwell in this land. God's presence would be with them, so this wasn't just a matter of finding a nice spot of land for his favorite people. The larger purpose was to create a nation where God would dwell with his people, the beginning of a larger project of restoring the community

---

* Deuteronomy 9:5.

lost in the garden of Eden. To do this, he needed to remove those who worshiped other gods and engaged in wicked practices.

Most of these people groups were involved with the worship of false gods. According to some scholars, these false gods weren't just imaginary beings. They were the angelic beings from God's heavenly council known as "sons of God" that we mentioned earlier. These beings often played a role in God's decision making and were used to carry out God's plans. But they rebelled against God and were then assigned by God to geographic areas.* It is believed that possibly several of the sons of God who were in the divine counsel became the various gods that accepted worship from the Canaanites and other people groups.

So there is a whole additional aspect of spiritual, supernatural warfare happening here—concerns that go beyond property and land. These fallen divine beings were also behind some of the conflict between Israel and the Canaanites and give us additional insight into why these battles were important. God didn't want his people, the Israelites, to be influenced and corrupted by false gods whose culture might persuade Israel to participate in the evil practices and worship of these false gods. We see God saying precisely this in offering this warning from Deuteronomy 20:16–18: "However, in the cities of the nations the LORD your God is giving you as an inheritance, do not leave alive anything that breathes. Completely destroy them—the Hittites, Amorites, Canaanites, Perizzites, Hivites and Jebusites—as the LORD your God has commanded you. Otherwise, they will teach you to follow all the detestable things they do in worshiping their gods, and you will sin against the LORD your God."

God understood, far better than the Israelites even, the powerful and corrupting influence of idolatry and evil. And God knew that this evil was like a cancer. If it was not completely removed, it would eventually multiply and spread, taking over the hearts and minds of his chosen people. These battles were ultimately about the protection of Israel from

---

*   Deuteronomy 32:1–43.

corrupt influence so they could one day fulfill his plans to save the entire world. God had plans for Israel to be his witness to the world and for Jesus to be born through them. In other words, the future of the human race was at stake. Any hope for people to eventually be set free from their addiction to evil and their tendency to reject God's guidance lay in preserving Israel for God's future plans.

4. God gave the people warning over hundreds of years. He was patient, waiting generations for them to change. Prior to these battles, God gave warning to the people, asking them to change their minds and turn to him. The decision to judge and punish these people was not an irrational spur of the moment decision by God. We see that God gives people several hundred years to change their ways and turn to him. God tells Abraham that his descendants will be slaves in a foreign country for four hundred years, which is exactly what happened. And he tells Moses the people of Israel will return to the land of Canaan after "four generations." What's fascinating is the reason given for this delay. It is because "the sin of the Amorites has not yet reached its full measure."* What does this mean? It indicates God was patiently waiting for the Amorites (and the other people of the land of Canaan) to turn from their evil practices. God let the people go their own way, choosing the life they wanted for themselves, so there would be no doubt as to the evil in their hearts and minds. He wanted it to be clear that they had rejected him and were not interested in worshiping or following the one true God, their creator. The time of slavery Israel spent living in Egypt was an opportunity for the Canaanite nations to change their minds and place their faith in God. Some did.

We read one story about a prostitute named Rahab who was living in the city of Jericho.[2] She befriended some Israelites and let them know she had heard about the God of the Israelites. She had heard of what God had done in Egypt and how he was with them as a people. She had heard why they were moving into the land. And she made a

---

*   Genesis 15:16.

decision to align with them, to follow the God of the Israelites instead of the false gods of her people. Because she changed her mind and heart, she was spared when Jericho was attacked. And not only was she spared and lived, but she was honored to be part of the lineage of Jesus. One of her later descendants was Jesus, the promised savior of the world. Not only did God forgive and save someone who was a prostitute and worshiped other gods, but because she turned to the one true God, she ended up playing a significant role in his larger plan to save the world. This demonstrates that the knowledge of God and what he was doing with Israel was known by other people. They had the opportunity to respond to God's warning and to be forgiven and saved by turning to him.

At a later time in Israel's history we see God sending a reluctant prophet to warn the city of Nineveh (an ancient city located in what is now Iraq) that judgment from God was coming unless they changed their evil ways. The Ninevites were also known as extremely wicked leaders, described in this way: "Records brag of live dismemberment, often leaving one hand attached so they could shake it before the person died. They made parades of heads, requiring friends of the deceased to carry them on elevated poles. They boasted of their practice of stretching live prisoners with ropes so they could be skinned alive. The human skins were then displayed on city walls and on poles. . . . They commissioned pictures of their post-battle tortures where piles of heads, hands and feet, and heads impaled on poles—eight to a stak—were displayed. They pulled out the tongues and 'private parts' of live victims and burned the young alive."[3]

Because Nineveh was so wicked, God sent a warning that he would bring judgment against the people. In this case, they responded and changed their ways and believed in the God of the Israelites and were saved. The book of Jonah shows the compassion of God by giving people chances to respond.

In another place in the Bible God says, "Do I take any pleasure in the death of the wicked? declares the Sovereign LORD. Rather, am I not pleased when they turn from their ways and live?"* Another section of the Old Testament shows God speaking to his own people Israel before they are judged for their rebellion, and we see God's heart begging them to change. He desperately pleads with them to change and escape his just judgment, saying, "'As surely as I live, declares the Sovereign LORD, I take no pleasure in the death of the wicked, but rather that they turn from their ways and live. Turn! Turn from your evil ways! Why will you die, people of Israel?'" and then he states, "'If someone who is wicked repents, that person's former wickedness will not bring condemnation. . . . None of the sins that person has committed will be remembered.'"†

This fits with the picture we see throughout the Bible of a God who gives warning before judgment, who is slow to anger, forgiving, and who wants people to change and not follow their own evil ways but turn to the true God. He gives them chances and promises that no matter who you are, you can be forgiven and redeemed. This is made even more clear in the New Testament, where it says, "The Lord is not slow in keeping his promise, as some understand slowness. Instead he is patient with you, not wanting anyone to perish, but everyone to come to repentance."‡

5. This wasn't a mass killing; it was a limited strategic strike with a lot of war rhetoric. Most of the visuals and memes that draw attention to these Bible verses emphasize them in a way that suggests God committed mass bloodthirsty slaughter and genocide. Every single life is of great value, so by no means am I suggesting that killing just a few people is an easy thing to dimiss at all. But I want to argue against the idea that this was a mass murder, a ruthless and mindless slaughter.

Remember that these times were very violent. This was a very bloody, violent world, something that is difficult for many of us to imagine today. Battle scenes like those we see in movies like *Braveheart* or the heavy fighting scenes in Lord of the Rings would have been more common in that time and culture. Warfare was normal, in ways we can't imagine.

---

*   Ezekiel 18:23.
†   Ezekiel 33:11–16.
‡   2 Peter 3:9.

What was also common was the war rhetoric that was used. Phrases like "completely destroy" (often the Hebrew words *herem* or *ban*, which are translated into English as "completely destroy") didn't actually mean completely destroy as we think of it today.[4] The goal of such battles was for the cities to be emptied and their identities in that place destroyed. You see God saying, "I am going to drive them out," because this is going to be the land where God would dwell. His tabernacle was there and the temple would eventually be built in the land, in Jerusalem. God was turning this land into "holy land" and needed his own identity associated with the land. He needed the identity of the false gods removed. God is driving out what is contrary to his greater purposes to prepare the land for his presence. If the people refused, they would be killed. But this is not about waging war for war's sake; it was making way for the presence of God and removing what didn't belong in his land.

God didn't want the practices and identities of the Canaanites to negatively influence the Israelites, and this is why God said not to marry them. Later, when Israel ignored God's guidance, this is exactly what happened. Phrases like "utterly destroy," "drive them out," and other language we find in the Bible were common war rhetoric at that time. It was hyperbole, not a literal wiping out of every individual of any age. It spoke of the larger goal of moving people out and emptying the cities, destroying the Canaanite identity rooted in the worship of false gods as well as their religious temples and cities. The goal of these battles was to eliminate the false worship of deities that would take Israel away from the true God and to remove the other people groups from the land, not necessarily kill them all. God's goal was to restore Israel to the land and to take up his place among his people in the land, not simply to kill people.

Today, we aren't used to such rhetoric or we avoid using it in reference to warfare. Instead, we use it for lighter things like sports rivalries and competitions. We might talk of beating another team by saying they "slaughtered them" or they got "wiped out." We aren't all that different from the people of that time in our use of hyperbole to make a point. Back then, the conquest language of the ancient Near East frequently used such hyperbolic rhetoric. So keep that in mind when you read phrases like, "You must destroy them totally," "Do not leave anything alive that breathes," and "Show them no mercy." This was war rhetoric. And while people died, this wasn't a genocidal wiping out of people groups as we might think of it today.

There is a helpful chart I've reproduced in table 18.1 from the book *Did God Really Command Genocide? Coming to Terms with the Justice of God* by Paul Copan and Matthew Flannagan.[5] It clearly shows the repetition of times when there isn't a total wipeout of people—even though that language is used. On the left you see the command, and on the right you see that not all of the people died.

Table 18.1*

"Extermination"	"No Extermination"
Joshua 10:20a: "It came about when Joshua and the sons of Israel had finished slaying them with a very great slaughter until they were destroyed."	Joshua 10:20b "and the survivors who remained of them had entered the fortified cities."
Joshua 10:39: "every person" in Debir was "utterly destroyed."	Joshua 11:21: Later Joshua "utterly destroyed" Anakites in Debir.
Joshua 11:21: The Anakites were "cut off" and "utterly destroyed" in Hebron—as well as from Debir, Anab, and "all the hill country of Judah." There were "no Anakim left in the land of the sons of Israel."	Joshua 15:13–14: Caleb "drove out" the Anakites from Hebron; cf. Judges 1:20, where Caleb "drove out" the Anakites from Hebron.
Judges 1:8: "Then the sons of Judah fought against Jerusalem and captured it and struck it with the edge of the sword and set the city on fire."	Judges 1:21: "But the sons of Benjamin did not drive out the Jebusites who lived in Jerusalem; so the Jebusites have lived with the sons of Benjamin in Jerusalem to this day."
Joshua: 11:23: "So Joshua took the whole land, according to all that the Lord had spoken to Moses, and Joshua gave it for an inheritance to Israel according to their divisions by their tribes. Thus the land had rest from war."	Judges 2:21, 23: "I also will no longer drive out before them any of the nations which Joshua left when he died. . . . So the Lord allowed those nations to remain, not driving them out quickly; and he did not give them into the hand of Joshua."

---

* Scripture quotations are from the New American Standard Bible.

Was this genocide? No. Was it a mindless slaughter? No. It was a series of strategic attacks for God to have the people who had rejected his guidance and his purposes removed from interrupting his plan to save the world. God was preparing to dwell in the land, for the Israelites to host him in his temple, and eventually for Jesus to come and bring salvation to all people.

6. But what about the infants and children and deaths? There is no fully satisfactory answer for this question. I have read dozens of attempts and explanations of how to process the fact that women and children were killed in these battles, and none of them eliminate the sense of sadness and grief I feel when thinking about it. Even if the parents were absolutely wicked and practicing all types of detestable acts of worship and their hearts were set against God, what about their children? Did they deserve death?

There are hints but no clear written explanation of why this happened in the Bible. Yet it seems that God allowed deaths to occur, even of children. Some scholars point out that some of the women and children were not as impacted by these battles, which were typically fought between armies of men. But there were casualties, and it's hard to know why God allowed it to happen, and even commanded some of the battles.

As I mentioned earlier, the evil practices in these cultures were deeply imbedded cultural practices. So some have suggested that these battles were similar to spiritual surgery, a necessary evil to root out the pattern of rejecting God and his guidance. When you remove a cancer, you must take out the whole thing and cannot leave anything behind. We don't know if the children would have grown up to repeat the patterns of their parents, joining in false worship of other gods in that wicked culture. Perhaps, even as horrific as it was, this kept that evil from perpetuating further.

And, as I suggested in the chapter on other religions and people who have not heard the truth about Jesus, we know that God is fair and just and will treat each person according to how they have responded to what they know of him. When a child dies, death is not the end. There is accountability with our life and God, but for young ones before they are fully accountable, they are held to what they know. Some of these children may now be with God, since we know that Jesus covers the sins of all people, from the time of the Old Testament to us today.

Granted, I am speculating here, and there is absolutely no easy answer. Whenever I study this topic, I can understand the logic, but still find it haunting and emotionally difficult to fully understand. What I do know is that based on what we know to be true of God, he deals fairly with everyone. When I struggle with the violence in the Bible, I try to recall the God of the whole Bible—the God who is patient, loving, compassionate, and forgiving. I remember the God who forgave me, who is patient with me, and I trust that although there are mysteries I may not know in this life, I have more than enough truth from Scripture to keep faith and trust he is abounding in love, slow to anger, compassionate, and forgiving. So knowing the whole Bible story and the actions of love that dominate the whole of the Bible puts the violent parts in perspective. I may not understand why violence happened, but I trust the God who does. And it isn't a blind trust whatsoever, it is a deep trust built from a lot of questioning and looking at who God is throughout the Scriptures—not just parts but the whole Bible.

18.2

"HAPPY SHALL THEY BE WHO TAKE YOUR LITTLE ONES AND DASH THEM AGAINST THE ROCK!"
PSALM 137:9

Throwing Babies against Rocks?

Before we end this section, I want to look at a text of terror that is frequently mentioned in memes and online discussions. It is found in Psalm 137:9. How do we explain these verses where we read about killing children and throwing babies against rocks (18.2)?

At first this seems to be a horrific statement by God. But if we look a little more closely, once again, we discover it is not what it seems on the surface. This verse is from the Psalms, and right away, it's important for us to know that Psalms are in the genre of songs and poetry. At the time this psalm was written, the people of Israel were living in captivity in Babylon. Their city of Jerusalem had been destroyed, and they had been taken prisoner and were living far away from their home. It was an extremely sad situation where there was loss of life when the Babylonians captured the city and the people of Jerusalem. The city had been surrounded by the Babylonians, who had sought to starve them out, and there are accounts of this in the Bible. When the Babylonians finally entered the city, they killed many of the people by the sword, spear, or arrow, and a lot of gruesome deaths occurred. In battle, it was common with infants to throw them to their death as they were so small and fragile. Invading armies were not going to care for infants and children, so they regularly killed them. It's horrible and wicked, but that's what would happen in battles back then.

The parents and friends and family members who had survived this horrible invasion by the Babylonians were now prisoners in Babylon. They knew that God had promised they would get to go back to Jerusalem one day, but for now they were in the midst of a desperate situation filled with weeping, grieving, and deep sorrow. The author of this psalm wrote a poem and a song expressing their anguish and grief. And in this specific line, he chose to highlight the horror of what had happened in Jerusalem by remembering the infants who were killed. Think of it as a way of asking for poetic justice. This wasn't intended to be a literal plan to kill babies, nor was it a command by God to go and do this. It was a poetic expression of the horror, grief, and longing for justice the people wanted after such great suffering. Psalms are deep expressions of human emotions, and this poem was giving voice to the pain the people felt, crying for justice and revenge for what had happened to them at the hands of the Babylonians.

Today we have further revelation from God through Jesus—a post-Jesus way of living and thinking, so while we might still feel the same anger, pain, and longing for revenge if we were in those same circumstances, there is an added twist. Jesus' teachings and the rest of the New Testament provide a different way that short-circuits our need for revenge. In Romans we are told, "Do not repay anyone evil for evil. Be careful to do what is right in the eyes of everyone. If it is possible, as far as it depends on you, live at peace with everyone."* How is this possible? Because we have learned to trust God, knowing that he is a just judge, we can leave our longing for revenge and justice in his hands.

This psalm is not about God wanting to "kill babies," as is often indicated in online memes and visuals. It is the deep anguished cry of a broken, mourning person in pain, expressed in poetic song form. It is the cry of a war prisoner who has seen great horror and death, even his or her own children and infants being killed. The author is expressing pain and asking that God render judgment—that what they experienced would be done to those who hurt them. This is another example of a Bible verse that demands a deeper look to bring clarity to what the Bible is really saying.

The Reason We Trust in the God of Compassion and Love

As I mentioned at the beginning of this section, these last few chapters were the most difficult for me to write. I've tried to provide some awareness of context that helps us better understand why some of the violence is in the Bible. We looked at the commonplace use of war rhetoric, and how many of the deaths involved military and religious leaders and not average citizens, but still, these deaths happened. We may never have a fully satisfactory answer to it all, but questions like this should drive us to read and understand the full storyline of the Bible to see how God worked throughout history and why he may have used violent means for limited purposes at times. The broader storyline tells us that he is a God of extreme patience, overwhelming love, and immense

---

* Romans 12:17–18.

compassion—even though we also see him acting at times with violence to ensure his purposes for dwelling with his people and saving the world eventually come to fulfillment. Without knowing the fuller story, verses like the ones we've seen *are* difficult to understand. And that's why we cannot pull them out from the larger story.

Whenever we experience death, either by tragedy or by natural means, it is very painful and difficult. But we have a promise from Jesus that he is always with us, and we can be comforted in our times of grief. This is not a cliché; it is a truth that has brought hope and comfort to millions of people for thousands of years. When my own dad died unexpectedly, it was very difficult for me. It was an accident, and he died much younger than he should have. During that time I had to cling to Jesus and remember that God is a God of compassion and love. I also cling to the promise that one day, death, violence, wars, and evil of any kind will be no more. We see this promise in the book of Revelation where we read, "Look! God's dwelling place is now among the people, and he will dwell with them. They will be his people, and God himself will be with them and be their God. He will wipe every tear from their eyes. There will be no more death or mourning or crying or pain, for the old order of things has passed away."*

Until that day, Jesus wants us to tell as many people as possible about the God who cares and is loving, slow to anger, and compassionate. I want people to truly know this God and to experience his comfort and love. And I want people to know that the Bible is not a crazy book, but a source for knowing and understanding an amazing God who cares deeply for us. As I wrote this book, I prayed for anyone reading this book who might be struggling with the topics we've covered. We have a promise that there will be a day when we won't need a chapter like this to help us understand difficult passages about violence and death, because we will be in God's presence forever. No more violence, pain, tears, sorrow, and suffering. I do look forward to that day.

---

* Revelation 21:3–4.

If You Don't Yet Know the Love and Compassion of God

Earlier in this section I mentioned the story of Rahab, a prostitute who believed and trusted in the God of the Israelites as the one true God. God accepted her faith, and she escaped the destruction of Jericho safely. She trusted God, and he responded. Several centuries later, we read in the New Testament that Jesus was born as a descendant of Rahab. We see that God responds with forgiveness to those who ask and brings them into his plans and purposes to redeem the world from human evil. In the Bible's storyline, God ultimately provided a solution for all of us who stand in need of God's forgiveness and compassion. I am personally thankful for God's slowness to anger, his compassion and forgiveness. The more I read and understand the biblical story, the more I find myself trusting in and growing in my love for the God who truly loves us. Beyond our understanding does he love us, and I do wish everyone could sense how much God really loves them.

The Bible storyline has an ending. It ends with the return of Jesus and a time of judgment. There will be a new creation, a new heaven and a new earth where God will dwell and live with those who have believed the good news of forgiveness through Jesus. This is an invitation to everyone, and I hope that anyone who has not yet put their trust in Jesus will consider this invitation. It is an amazing thing to experience the love and grace of God, and I am so thankful he is patient, compassionate, and loving with us. Please talk to someone at a church near you, or contact me, if you have questions about how to start a relationship with this God of love, grace, mercy, and compassion. My life has been changed and is being changed by knowing this God, and I know yours can be changed as well.

Part 6 Summary Points

RATED NC-17

- Much of the violence in the Bible is not approved or done by God. Human beings on their own did much of the violence recorded in Scripture, and the Bible records what happened.
- God's intention in the conquest of the Canaanites was not to randomly destroy but to clear space for his presence as the people of Israel were returning.
- When God did order violence and death, it was always with extreme patience and plenty of warning to give people the opportunity to repent and turn to him. It was never genocide or ethnic cleansing.
- A lot of ancient boasting war rhetoric was used in reports of Old Testament battles that were not actually unhinged slaughtering of the masses but strategic military strikes mainly targeting the military and the leaders.
- Violence is very difficult to understand, as even one death ordered by God is horrific to grasp. Ultimately we have to trust God and what we know of him as abundantly loving, immensely kind, endlessly compassionate, and exceedingly forgiving. So if violence was used, God knows why even though we may not be able to comprehend the reason.

Jesus Loved His Crazy Bible (And Why Trusting It Isn't That Crazy)

A s we end this book, I hope you have found some things you agreed with, and I'm sure there are some things you may not agree with as well. No matter what you may think now of the various disturbing and crazy-sounding Bible passages, I want you to know one thing. Jesus loved the Bible. When he was on earth, he didn't have the New Testament, since it had not yet been written. But Jesus had the Old Testament and all that is in it. He knew the creation stories about the talking snake and Noah and the flood. He knew those bizarre-sounding verses from Leviticus about not eating shrimp and not getting tattoos and not touching the skin of a dead pig. He knew the verses that allegedly promote slavery and polygamy and sound anti-women. He knew the verses containing all the violence and war and bloody killings. He knew all of this and still loved his Bible. If you look at his life, you see:

- Jesus quoted the Bible when he was tempted (Matthew 4:4–10).
- Jesus read from the Bible when he started his public ministry (Luke 4:14–21).

- Jesus used the Bible in arguments to defend who he was (Matthew 22:43–44, Mark 12:36; 14:27; Luke 20:17; 22:37).
- Jesus frequently quoted Scripture during his teaching (Matthew 19:4–6; 22:37–39).
- Jesus used the Bible to talk about the future and the end times (Matthew 24:15–16).
- Jesus quoted from the Bible when he was dying on the cross (Mark 15:34).
- Jesus taught from the Bible after he was resurrected (Luke 24:25–27).

Jesus had a deep relationship with the Bible, and he saw it as a pointer to him, a story to prepare the world for what he had come to do.

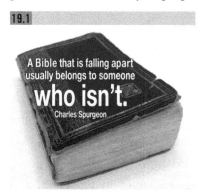

19.1

A Bible that is falling apart usually belongs to someone **who isn't.**
Charles Spurgeon

We see him saying this in John 5:39: "You study the Scriptures diligently because you think that in them you have eternal life. These are the very Scriptures that testify about me."

Jesus also said after he was resurrected, in Luke 24:25–27, "He said to them, 'How foolish you are, and how slow to believe all that the prophets have spoken! Did not the Messiah have to suffer these things and then enter his glory?' And beginning with Moses and all the Prophets, he explained to them what was said in all the Scriptures concerning himself."

The More We Learn from the Bible, the More We Learn about Jesus

This book was just a glimpse into some of the difficult questions people have about the Bible. It won't answer all of your questions about the Bible. But I hope that it brings you one step closer to understanding that when you read a crazy or disturbing Bible verse, there usually is a very reasonable way to make sense of it. When you see a meme about a Bible verse or hear someone quoting a verse, you know there is more to it than what a surface reading of it would indicate. I hope that throughout this book, your confidence in the Bible increased and, even more, that you have begun to see how there is a bigger storyline to the Bible pointing us to Jesus and what he came to do. From Genesis through Revelation, the Bible is pointing us to the life and death and resurrection of Jesus as God's way of restoring what was lost when human beings rejected his guidance. It's a story of God saving us and making it possible for him to live with us again, as we did in the beginning. We need to have confidence in the Bible and to desire to read and learn from it, because the Bible is God's way of helping us to learn about Jesus.

The Bible tells of when Jesus came, died, and rose again, and the hope and life transformation that happens when we put faith in Jesus and believe and trust in him. It's why I cling to my Bible personally and want to read it as much as I possibly can. Reading it not just for information, but for transformation of my mind and heart, to know Jesus and to follow him. I know there are some Christians who know the Bible well but often come across as mean and even arrogant. I can say that they may have head knowledge, but it is not seeping into their hearts. If we really read and study the Bible, God's Spirit will use it to melt our hearts and change us into people who are loving and more like Jesus. It's what I want in my life, because I need God to continually change me and shape me as I read in Scripture more about who he is.

The Bible is a library, and in this book we walked through many Bible study methods and showed the importance of stepping into the world of the original recipients of the books. We looked at genres and showed why it is important to go beyond a surface reading of Bible passages. It's really worth the effort to study and learn. Why? Because it causes us to know God better when we study and read. It also helps Christians better explain their faith . . . and those crazy-sounding Bible passages.

I Pray for Those Who Are Christians to Become Deeper Thinkers

There is an understandable and growing criticism today that most Christians don't know their Bibles and blindly accept what they have been taught without ever studying it themselves. I was talking with a

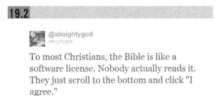

19.2

@almightygod

To most Christians, the Bible is like a software license. Nobody actually reads it. They just scroll to the bottom and click "I agree."

non-Christian, and we were walking down the hallway in a church building. On the wall there was a large piece of artwork that said, "Theologian," suggesting that all Christians should make an effort to study what they claim to believe in the Bible. When this person saw that art piece, he slammed his hand on it as he walked by and said, "This is important!" I asked him what he meant. He said he would be more open to Christianity if Christians were able to have thoughtful discussions about why they believe the things they believe. He was frustrated by his conversations with Christians who didn't seem to know why they were Christians or what they really believed.

I know there are many faithful Christians who pour themselves into the Scriptures daily. But the truth is that most of us who claim to follow Jesus spend more time scanning Instagram or browsing social media sites than we do reading Scripture. There are so many distractions today, and it is easy to put the Bible aside and not read it, because it isn't always easy to read. It does take effort. But that wasn't Jesus' approach. We don't know exactly how much time he spent in the Bible, but he certainly knew it well. That should encourage us to want to know it too. There are so many benefits to our reading how God intended life to be and the guidance he gives in Scripture for how to live it. The Bible speaks to the ups and downs of life, the joys and sorrows. A preacher named Charles Spurgeon, who lived in London in the 1800s, once said, "A Bible that is falling apart usually belongs to someone who isn't."

I don't think Christians have the choice not to be in the Bible regularly in today's world. With the internet and mass media, there are so many discussions and opinions out there about God, theology, and Jesus, which can be great and helpful when they are good ones. But it can also be scary because that means there are a lot of incorrect ones out there as well. The scary part to me is that if we don't know the whole of the Scriptures and the truth that is within it, we can easily get brought into false teaching and thinking about God, salvation, morals, and ethics. I have seen people start believing in Jesus and talking about "my Jesus," but it isn't the Jesus of the whole Bible. I have heard Christian terms used like "gospel" or "salvation," and they aren't actually the true definitions of the terms from the whole Bible. Anyone can take a verse or two or three and form a belief from it about something they want to believe, but that is not how to read the Bible. The more information and opinions there are out there about God, the more deeply we need to grow in our understanding of what is in Scripture so we can screen out what isn't taught in the Bible. We can hear of something that sounds new and may even quote Bible verses to make a case for it, but unless we're using good Bible skills, we could easily be falling for something old that was proven wrong long ago.

If you are a Christian, you will likely encounter criticism of the Bible. For far too long, we have so focused on the nice and positive parts of the Bible that when someone points out to us the not so nice parts, it can catch us off guard. I hope this book has convinced you that the solution to this criticism is to be in the Bible, studying these passages to better understand what God was saying to people at the time they were written. If we study these difficult passages, we will be better prepared when we hear or read them, and this is not only for our own sake, it affects our responsibility to accurately represent Jesus. We need to sharpen our thinking so we are able to help others when they have questions about the Bible. I hope parents, children's and youth leaders, and college leaders will address the topics in this book proactively so when they do come up, students will be prepared and ready with an answer.

May Those Who Are Doubting or Not a
Christian Gain Some Confidence

If you are reading this and doubting your faith, I hope this book has brought you some confidence to know there are ways to respond to the difficult parts of the Bible. I totally understand why you may have doubts, and I hope this book leads you to reconsider the Bible and its teachings as a trusted and inspired book of God, a source of learning for life. Even if you aren't convinced by the reasons I've presented, I hope you are encouraged to continue your journey by learning more.

Please contact me if you have questions or want to tell me stories of your own Bible exploration. I'd love to hear from you. We are in this life but once. May we love and cling to the Spirit-inspired Bible that Jesus so loved, that tells his story and the way to know him, that gives us his teachings and shows us how to grow, to be changed, and to become more like him until the day we are finally with him.

Here's how you can reach me:

Website: www.dankimball.com

 Twitter: @dankimball

 Instagram: dankimball

 Facebook: dankimball

APPENDIX

Resources for Teaching
and Further Study

At www.dankimball.com you'll find a link to the *How (Not) to Read the Bible* resources, which include free downloadable small group discussion guides you can use to deepen your study of the Bible as you read this book. These can also be used if you are teaching through this book or studying it in a class or small group.

You will also find preaching helps, including slides and short videos to use for a preaching or teaching series.

There are some great books I'd encourage you to look at if you are interested in deeper study on the topics covered in this book. Recommended books addressing each of the topics in this book can be found on the website as well.

NOTES

Prelude

1. Erin, @ExXtianErin, Twitter, January 28, 2020.
2. I wrote more about my entry into Christianity in *Adventures in Churchland: Finding Jesus in the Mess of Organized Religion* (Grand Rapids: Zondervan, 2012).

Chapter 1: Yes, There Are Unicorns in the Bible

1. www.evilbible.com.
2. Scene from the television show *The West Wing*, season 2, episode 3, "The Midterms."

Chapter 2: The Bible Was Not Written to Us

1. From the article "Understanding Genesis," https://biologos.org/resources /audio-visual/john-walton-on-understanding-genesis.
2. Originally, the Hebrew Bible contained twenty-four books divided into three parts: the five books of the Torah ("teaching"), the Nevi'im ("prophets"), and the Ketuvim ("writings"). Later some of the more lengthy books were divided into two books and sorted in the way we see it in most Christian Bibles today as sixty-six books. The point is that the Bible is not a single book but a library of sixty-six books in one volume.
3. There are some great resources that go into how the Bible was originally inspired, how it was compiled and copied over time, and why we can have such great confidence that what we have today is so close to what was originally written.
4. From the article "Understanding Genesis," https://biologos.org/resources /audio-visual/john-walton-on-understanding-genesis.
5. This is an adaptation of an illustration that Dr. John Walton uses

explaining how with local traffic reports, they use specific local terms that locals would know hearing them, but nonlocals wouldn't.

Chapter 3: Never Read a Bible Verse

1. See http://www.str.org/articles/never-read-a-bible-verse#.VVKQY9NViko.

2. N. T. Wright's metaphor of the Bible as a five-act play is found in his books *The Last Word* and *Scripture and the Authority of God.* Craig G. Bartholomew and Michael W. Goheen lay out the Bible story as a six-act play in *The Drama of Scripture: Finding Our Place in the Biblical Story* (this is the structure I am using for this book). The Bible Project's study notes (titled "The Story of the Bible") from *How to Read the Bible,* episode 2, "Biblical Story," www.thebibleproject.org, also use a six-act play structure to the Bible and add three movements in it, which I've also used here.

3. Job 38:4–7; Psalm 82:1–5; see Michael Heiser's *The Unseen Realm: Recovering the Supernatural Worldview of the Bible* (Bellingham, WA: Lexham, 2015) for more information on this amazing part of the story.

4. Thanks to John Walton for his insights on the importance of recognizing the loss.

5. Bible scholar Michael Heiser is known for emphasizing that although it is often thought there is only one main rebellion (the fall), we actually see three rebellions that shape the Old Testament story and Israelite worldview:

    Rebellion 1: God's human children, Adam and Eve, rebelling in the garden, along with the divine rebellion of Satan, as told in Genesis 3.

    Rebellion 2: God's supernatural children, the "sons of God," wanting to imitate God by producing their own human children in their own image, as told in Genesis 6:1–4, and this all led to total human rebellion against God, having hearts all bent toward evil. This led to the flood, as told in Genesis 6:5–17.

    Rebellion 3: Humans built a tower—the tower of Babel—to their own glory, and God judged them, disinherited them, and began a new focus for his human family—Abraham and the birth of the people of Israel, as told in Genesis 11–12.

6. The Bible Project, www.thebibleproject.org.

Chapter 4: Strange and Stranger Things in the Old Testament

1. *The West Wing*, season 2, episode 3, "The Midterms."
2. When the television show cited these Bible verses, they added references to death sentences for those who broke these specific commands. But references to stoning and burning for planting crops side by side and wearing garments with mixed fabrics are not in the Bible. The writer of the script likely wanted a more dramatic feel and added that. It's always good to check what someone cites from the Bible.

Chapter 5: The Art of (Not) Cherry-Picking Bible Verses

1. Paul Copan, *Is God a Moral Monster? Making Sense of the Old Testament God* (Grand Rapids: Baker, 2011), 77.
2. Geoffrey Wigoder, Shalom M. Paul, and Benedict T. Viviano, eds., *Almanac of the Bible* (Upper Saddle River, NJ: Prentice-Hall, 1991).
3. John H. Walton, ed., *Genesis,* Zondervan Illustrated Bible Backgrounds Commentary (Grand Rapids: Zondervan, 2009), 246.
4. See part 6, chapters 16–18, for more on violence.

Chapter 6: Making Sense of Shrimp, the Skin of a Dead Pig, and Slavery

1. Tim Keller, "Old Testament Law and the Charge of Inconsistency," https://www.redeemer.com/redeemer-report/article/old_testament _law_and_the_charge_of_inconsistency.
2. Be healthy, because we know bacon and certain meats contain a lot of fat, but there is no command from these verses that we cannot eat them today.

Chapter 7: The Boys' Club Bible

1. I tell about this experience in *Adventures in Churchland: Finding Jesus in the Mess of Organized Religion* (Grand Rapids: Zondervan, 2012).
2. I later learned that elders in a church are the ones who help watch over the church and help spiritually guide and protect it. A description in the Bible is in Titus 1 and 1 Timothy 3.

Chapter 8: Can't Keep a Good Woman Down

1. We'll look further into how to interpret the early chapters of Genesis in part 4: "Jesus Riding a Dinosaur: Do We Have to Choose between Science and the Bible?"

2. Scot Mcknight, *The Blue Parakeet: Rethinking How You Read the Bible,* 2nd Edition (Grand Rapids: Zondervan, 2018), 225.

3. *Menahot* 43b.

4. Abraham Cohen, *Every Man's Talmud* (New York: Schocken, 1949), 160–61. Thanks for these quotes to Rich Nathan, *Who Is My Enemy?* (Grand Rapids: Zondervan, 2002).

5. Alvin Schmidt, *How Christianity Changed the World.* Originally published under the title *Under the Influence: How Christianity Transformed Civilization* (Grand Rapids: Zondervan, 2001), 98–99.

6. Ibid., 101.

7. Herbert Danby, trans., *The Mishnah* (London: Oxford University Press, 1933), 'Abot 1:5.

8. Craig S. Keener, *IVP Bible Background Commentary: New Testament* (Downers Grove, IL: InterVarsity, 1993).

9. Keener, *IVP Bible Background Commentary,* commentary on Luke 8:1–3.

10. Depending on what church or denomination you may be from or are familiar with, there are different ways churches structure leadership. I have pastor friends who take the Bible seriously and differ on how to implement the roles of men and women in church leadership. These Bible verses still need explaining, which we will look at in the next chapter.

Chapter 9: Making Sense of Inequality in the Bible

1. See part 1, chapter 3.

2. E. Randolph Richards and Brandon J. O'Brien, *Paul Behaving Badly: Was the Apostle Paul a Racist, Chauvinist Jerk?* (Downers Grove, IL: InterVarsity, 2016), 113.

3. Ibid.

4. Rodney Stark, *The Rise of Christianity* (San Francisco: Harper Collins, 1997), 109.

Chapter 10: Jesus Riding a Dinosaur

1. Adam lived 930 years (Genesis 5:5). Enosh lived 905 years (Genesis 5:11). Kenan lived 910 years (Genesis 5:14). Methuselah lived 969 years (Genesis 5:27).

Chapter 11: In the Beginning We Misunderstood

1. Johnny Miller and John Sodem, *In the Beginning We Misunderstood: Interpreting Genesis 1 in Its Original Context* (Grand Rapids: Kregel, 2012), 35.
2. The 6,000-year age of the earth theory is based on taking the first five days of creation (from earth's creation to Adam), following the genealogies from Adam to Abraham in Genesis 5 and 11, then adding in the time from Abraham to today. Matthew 2:1–16 and 1 Chronicles 1–3 are used.
3. Miller and Sodem, *In the Beginning We Misunderstood*, 21.
4. Bill T. Arnold and Bryan E. Beyer, *Encountering the Old Testament* (Grand Rapids: Baker Academic), 43–49. We see Jesus referring to Moses as the author of the Pentateuch (Matthew 19:7; Mark 7:10; 12:26; John 1:17; 5:46; 7:23).
5. John Walton, *The Lost World of Genesis One: Ancient Cosmology and the Origins Debate* (Downers Grove, IL; InterVarsity, 2009),18.
6. We see scholars such as John Walton, *The Lost World of Genesis One*; Michael Heiser, https://drmsh.com/cool-motion-animation-video-of-ancient-israelite-cosmology; and Tim Mackie, The Bible Project, https://bibleproject.com/blog/genesis-ancient-cosmic-geography, describing the worldview the ancient Israelites would have had.
7. The illustration viewing the earth from outer space was used in a lecture Dr. John Walton gave at Vintage Faith Church in Santa Cruz, CA, in 2012.
8. Tim Mackie, "Interpreting the Bible's Creation Narrative," http://www.timmackie.com/science-and-faith.
9. Michael Heiser, *I Dare You Not to Bore Me with the Bible* (Bellingham, WA: Lexham, 2014), 3–5.
10. Richard Dawkins, *The God Delusion* (New York: Houghton Mifflin, 2006).

Chapter 12: Making Sense of the Bible-versus-Science Conflict

1. This view is written about in John Sailhaimer, *Genesis Unbound: A Provocative New Look at the Creation Account* (Portland, OR: Dawson Media, 2011).
2. This view is written about by John Walton, *Lost World of Genesis One: Ancient Cosmology and the Origins Debate* (Downers Grove, IL: IVP Academic, 2010).
3. Gudea Cylinder B, XVII:18–19.

4. Walton, *Lost World of Genesis One*, 87–92.

5. Francis Collins is an American physician-geneticist who discovered the genes associated with a number of diseases and led the Human Genome Project. He started the Biologos Foundation, which is a great source for looking at why many Christian scientists believe God used evolution to create. You can find it at www.biologos.org.

6. This is a good question to be asking but is not something that prohibits the evolutionary creationism view to contradict Scripture. All of these different views raise questions. That is actually some of the fun of Bible study as we explore different viewpoints and discover there is validity to ones we may not have ever explored before.

7. David Frost, *Billy Graham: Candid Conversations with a Public Man* (Colorado Springs: David C. Cook, 2014), 81–82.

8. Michael Heiser, *The Unseen Realm: Recovering the Supernatural Worldview of the Bible* (Bellingham, WA: Lexham, 2015), 87–91.

9. For example, Heiser, *The Unseen Realm*.

Chapter 14: Love Is the Way, the Truth, and the Life

1. Karen Armstrong, *A History of God* (New York: Ballantine, 1993), 3–4.

2. N. T. Wright, *John for Everyone: Part 2* (Louisville: Westminster John Knox, 2004), 57–58.

Chapter 15: Making Sense of the Intolerant-Sounding Jesus

1. "Oprah—One Way Only?" YouTube, https://www.youtube.com /watch?v=cOxmd3cpxgY.

Chapter 16: The TV-MA, NC-17 Bible

1. Steve Wells, *Drunk with Blood: God's Killings in the Bible* (Lahore, Pakistan: SAB, 2003).

2. 2 Kings 6:29; Genesis 19:32–35; Judges 19:25–29; 1 Samuel 28:3–25; Genesis 22:2; Judges 11:30–39; Deuteronomy 12:31; Josiah 10:26; Mark 6:24–28; 2 Kings 10:1–17; Judges 1:6–7; 2 Kings 25:7; Esther7:9–10; Joshua 10:26; 1 Samuel 31:4–5; 1 Kings 8:63.

3. Song of Songs 7:8–9; 4:16; 8:10; Ezekiel 23:9–21; 1 Kings 11:3; Judges 19:25; 1 Samuel 18:27.

4. Extreme violence, Judges 19–21 and 2 Kings 10; cannibalism, 2 Kings 6:26–29 and Lamentations 4:10; incest, Genesis 19:32–35; rape,

Judges 19 and 2 Samuel 13:1–14; witchcraft, 2 Chronicles 33:6 and
1 Samuel 28; human and child sacrifice, Genesis 22:2, Judges 11:30–39,
and 2 Kings 16:3; poetic description of foreplay and lovemaking, Song of
Songs; graphic sexual descriptions using animal anatomy, Ezekiel 23:20;
parts of sexual organs being exchanged for a wife, 1 Samuel 18:27.

Chapter 17: The God of Compassion, Slow to Anger and Forgiving

1. Richard Dawkins, *The God Delusion* (Boston: Houghton Mifflin
   Harcourt, 2006), 51.

Chapter 18: Making Sense of the Texts of Terror

1. Clay Jones, "We Don't Hate Sin So We Don't Understand What
   Happened to the Canaanites," *Philosophia Christ* 11, no. 1 (2009): 01.
2. The story of Rahab is told in Joshua 2.
3. James Bruckner, *Jonah, Nahum, Habakkuk, Zephaniah,* The NIV
   Application Commentary (Grand Rapids: Zondervan, 2004).
4. Paul Copan, "Yahweh Wars and the Canaanites: Divinely Mandated
   Genocide or Corporate Capital Punishment?" (Evangelical Philosophical
   Society).
5. Paul Copan and Matthew Flannagan, *Did God Really Command Genocide?
   Coming to Terms with the Justice of God* (Grand Rapids: Baker, 2014).

ReGENERATION
PROJECT

About the ReGeneration Project

If you are interested in joining with others who believe in the central importance of theology, apologetics, and the Bible to minister to new generations, please go to the ReGeneration Project website for more info.

We are a ministry of Western Seminary that is passionate about seeing younger generations become thinking Christians who love Jesus, Scripture, theology, and the church and desperately desire others to know Jesus too.

www.regenerationproject.org